The Social Organization of Strikes

Warwick Studies in Industrial Relations

General Editors: G. S. Bain and H. A. Clegg

Also in this series

Labour Shortage and Economic Analysis
Barry Thomas and David Deaton
Shop Stewards in Action
Eric Batstone, Ian Boraston, and Stephen Frenkel
British Employment Statistics
N. K. Buxton and D. I. MacKay
Trade Unionism under Collective Bargaining
Hugh Armstrong Clegg
Union Growth and the Business Cycle
George Sayers Bain and Farouk Elsheikh
Social Values and Industrial Relations
Richard Hyman and Ian Brough
Industrial Relations in Fleet Street
Keith Sisson
Industrial Relations and the Limits of Law
Brian Weekes, Michael Mellish,
Linda Dickens, John Lloyd
*Social Stratification and Trade Unionism**
George Sayers Bain, David Coates, Valerie Ellis
*Workplace and Union**
Ian Boraston, Hugh Clegg, Malcolm Rimmer
*Piecework Bargaining**
William Brown
*Dispute Procedure in Action**
Richard Hyman
*The Docks after Devlin**
Michael Mellish
*Race and Industrial Conflict**
Malcolm Rimmer

*PUBLISHED BY HEINEMANN EDUCATIONAL BOOKS

The Social Organization of Strikes

Eric Batstone

Ian Boraston

Stephen Frenkel

BASIL BLACKWELL · OXFORD

British Library Cataloguing in Publication Data

Batstone, Eric
    The social organization of strikes. — (Warwick studies in industrial relations).
    1. Strikes and lockouts
    I. Title II. Boraston, Ian III. Frenkel, Stephen IV. Series
    301.6'34   HD5306

    ISBN   0-631-18320-5
    ISBN   0-631-18330-2 Pbk

Typeset by
Malvern Typesetting Services Ltd
Printed in Great Britain by
Billing and Son Ltd,
London, Guildford and Worcester.

Contents

Contents

II. The Strike That Never Was

Contents

List of Tables

Glossary of Terms and Abbreviations

Unions

ACTSS	Association of Clerical, Technical, and Supervisory Staffs
APEX	Association of Professional, Executive and Supervisory, and Computer Staffs
AUEW	Amalgamated Union of Engineering Workers
CSEU	Confederation of Shipbuilding and Engineering Unions
DATA	Draughtsmen and Allied Technicians Association. Now called TASS—Technical and Supervisory Section of the AUEW
EEPTU	Electrical, Electronic, Telecommunication, and Plumbing Union
NSMM	National Society of Metal Mechanics
TGWU	Transport and General Workers' Union
UCATT	Union of Construction, Allied Trades, and Technicians

Stewards and Members

Convener	Senior steward, or lay union representative in the domestic organization. Elected annually either by the members or stewards of the relevant union
Griever	A member who makes frequent resort to stewards because of largely individual problems. Accounts for a disproportionate number of

	grievances, many of which are rejected by leader stewards in particular. A few grievers are also opinion-leaders
Joker	A member who through joking and practical jokes maintains the morale of members. Highly respected and often also an opinion-leader
Leaders	Stewards who espouse union principles and define their role as acting as a representative rather than a delegate of their members. Also nascent leader: a steward who is attempting to achieve such a role but can do so only with the support of members of the Q-E
Opinion-leaders	Members, including stewards, who act as informal leaders in relation to their fellows; that is, they have a disproportionate amount of influence over their fellows
Populists	Stewards who less fully accept union principles and who in practice accept a delegate role in relation to their members
Q-E/Quasi-elite	A group of experienced stewards who have close contacts with conveners on general issues and who act effectively as an informal cabinet
Steward	Elected lay union representative within a domestic organization but with formal credentials of steward provided by his own union. On the staff, the normal term is representative

Work Organization

C & P/custom and practice	Rules whose primary legitimacy derives from their long standing. Such rules may have developed by error, oversight, or informal negotiation, often outside that permitted by formal agreements and procedures
Craftsmen	Mainly those who have undergone a period of apprenticeship to qualify for their present jobs. In addition, the term includes skilled workers whose wages are linked to craftsmen's rates of

	pay. These together form an important group within the shop-floor domestic organization
Indirects	These workers are not directly involved in production tasks. They include groups such as storemen, internal drivers, and labourers. The term is used in this book exclusive of maintenance craftsmen
Manufacturing staff	These staff workers are intimately involved in the production process and with the shop-floor. They tend not to work in the conventional office situation. In our use of the term are included planners, progress chasers, and fire-men and security personnel
MDW	Measured Daywork in which the pay of the employee is fixed on the understanding that he will maintain a specified level of performance, but the pay does not fluctuate in the short term with his actual performance
Non-manufac-turing staff	Other staff workers in a more conventional clerical or secretarial situation
Production workers	Those workers directly involved in the pro-duction process
Section	A team of workers on the shop-floor, often electing their own shop steward. The section often operates controls over overtime, lay-off rotas, and labour allocation. In piecework areas, bonus is paid on a section basis

Editors' Foreword

The University of Warwick is the major centre in the United Kingdom for the study of industrial relations. Its first undergraduates were admitted in 1965. The teaching of industrial relations began a year later in the School of Industrial and Business Studies, and it now has one of the country's largest graduate research programmes in this subject. Warwick became a national centre for research into industrial relations in 1970 when the Social Science Research Council, a government-funded body, located its Industrial Relations Research Unit at the University. The Unit has a full-time staff of about twenty and undertakes research into a wide range of topics in industrial relations.

The series of Warwick Studies in Industrial Relations was launchèd in 1972 as the main vehicle for the publication of the results of the Unit's projects. It is also intended to disseminate the research carried out by staff teaching industrial relations in the University. The first six titles in the series were published by Heinemann Educational Books of London, and subsequent titles have been published by Basil Blackwell of Oxford.

In this book Eric Batstone with the assistance of his colleagues investigates the social processes involved in the build-up to strike action. Their material is drawn from a continuous on-the-spot investigation of industrial relations in a major engineering plant over a period of four months, which has already led to their study entitled *Shop Stewards in Action*. During this time they were able to observe strikes and situations in which strikes were narrowly averted. They were therefore able to trace the patterns of power among workers within which movements towards strikes were promoted or restrained, and to analyse the vocabularies with which strikes were advocated or opposed. These tasks are performed in the first part of the book. The second part examines in detail the build-up to a plant-wide strike over an attempt by the company to change the system of payment. The central aim of the authors is to show *how* strikes occur, a question which must be of major interest to anyone who wishes to understand industrial conflict or shop-floor organization and behaviour.

George Bain
Hugh Clegg

Preface

This book is a 'spin-off' from our study of shop stewards in an engineering plant. The reader who wishes to gain most from this book should therefore read our previous volume, *Shop Stewards in Action*, although we have written our present work so that this is not vital. However, fuller details of the plant and our conceptual and methodological approaches are given only in *Shop Stewards in Action*.

The debts we owe for this volume are as great as in our previous work. First and foremost, we owe tremendous debts to those in the company on which the book is based. This goes far beyond mere access to the plant. They endured our presence and frequent naïveté with great fortitude; more than that, they actively helped us, explaining events and introducing us to a wide range of activities within the plant. They taught us much, and we owe an enormous amount to them. Unfortunately our commitments in terms of confidentiality and anonymity prevent us from naming the many stewards, workers, and managers who did so much for this book.

In addition to the help in the field, our academic colleagues both past and present played an important role. The existence of the IRRU was vital; it provided us with the opportunity to take the time, run the risks, and clear up the confusions inevitable with intensive observational work. More than that, within the Unit there existed a fund of deep knowledge of industrial relations. We have found considerable help — both in supporting some ideas, and modifying our more manifest absurdities — from them all, and in particular from George Bain, Hugh Clegg, William Brown, and Richard Hyman. Many lengthy discussions were held with past and present colleagues both at the Unit and elsewhere.

The design, execution, and writing up of a piece of research involve massive administrative and secretarial work. Here again the staff of the Unit were invaluable — all the secretaries in the Unit have been involved, and in particular Annemarie Flanders and Wendy Hudlass, who have endured our poor organization, atrocious handwriting, and a number of redrafts with an extra-ordinarily high level of tolerance.

Finally, research of any kind — and particularly intensive observation — becomes, indeed has to become, a major priority in the lives of researchers. Our wives, Toni, Joan, and Sheena, have endured weird hours of work, and hours of debate over what rapidly became known (partly in accordance with the norms of confidentiality) as 'the unmentionable', with not merely tolerance but also understanding. Toni Batstone was also useful in her comments on the work in the later stages of its writing. Despite the active support and help of those mentioned and many others, errors and absurdities undoubtedly still exist in the work — it would be amazing if they did not. They are my fault.

Eric Batstone

1
Introduction

In this book we consider the mobilization of strike action. Strikes do not just happen. As a form of collective activity they require the development of a degree of unity among those involved. Such organization is not only important once a strike has begun; it is equally necessary in creating a stoppage of work. Particular individuals or groups are likely first to introduce the idea of a strike and then to persuade their fellows of the validity of this course of action. The mobilization of strike action, then, is a social process involving systems of influence and power.

The study of the mobilization of strikes cannot be seen as providing a complete theory of strikes. But it does begin to highlight certain aspects of industrial conflict which have received scant attention in the literature. For, with a few notable exceptions, most theories of strikes have concentrated upon the distribution of strikes between countries, industries, plants, or work groups. We have no wish to suggest that these theories have no value, but in their concern with strike-*proneness* they tacitly admit their partial nature. They are concerned with the conditions under which strikes are *likely* to occur rather than with whether they will *actually* occur. They therefore pay little attention to the question of how strikes develop from these conditions.

The importance of this question, however, is suggested by many of the existing theories of strikes which emphasize the role of organizational and institutional factors. At one level, for example, Ross and Hartman (1960) and, from a rather different perspective, Wright Mills (1948) stress how the degree to which workers or unions are politically and socially integrated affects the level of strikes. Similarly, institutions of collective bargaining are often seen as important, while the nature of union organization (e.g. Lester, 1958) and of worker organization at the place of work (e.g.

1

Kuhn, 1961; Sayles, 1958) are also thought to affect strike patterns. However, such an organizational emphasis is essentially static. Few writers have attempted to look at the day-to-day processes of interaction and negotiation which constitute organization and mean that strike frequency may vary within any one establishment.

Changes in strike levels have generally been 'explained' less in terms of the dynamics of organizational behaviour than by large-scale trends in industrial and capitalist development (most impressively, see Shorter and Tilly, 1974). Such theories are particularly important since they stress the inherent delicacy of institutional arrangements. However, they operate at a very high level of generality and focus upon proneness to strike, rather than on how it is that the delicate balance between industrial 'peace' and open conflict is shifted.

While there may be structural factors and trends conducive to particular levels of strike activity, the occurrence of strike action depends upon the actors involved in the situation. Not only do trends in society exist in part because of the endeavours of actors, but also, as Karsh argues:

> The causes [of strikes], if there can be any fixed list of 'causes', cannot be treated apart from the individuals and groups who do the striking . . . Since a strike is first and foremost a form of human behaviour acted by individuals who are immediate participants in groups, their causes are social as much as, if not more than, economic or historical. Persons caught in a strike situation carry burdens and play roles which no graphic representation can adequately represent. (1958:2)

Such a view is recognized by a number of writers who have stressed the relatively independent role of consciousness which means that strikes may occur in what would appear to be unfavourable circumstances. 'Explosions of consciousness' have been put forward as an explanation of such major strike phenomena as May 1968 in France and 1960–61 in Belgium.

However, such arguments suffer from the same weaknesses as notions of subjective deprivation, in that they ignore the collective nature of strike action. So, for example, studies have shown that the large strikes in Belgium and France developed in areas where militant union organization existed and had been active immediately before the strikes (Chaumont, 1962; Dubois *et al.*, 1971). Similarly, a study of a 'spontaneous' strike in South Africa pointed out that 'the spread of spontaneous action . . . will almost certainly depend upon and be influenced by pre-existing, informal

2

communication networks' (Institute for Industrial Education, 1974:92).

In other words, as a number of detailed analyses of strike action have shown, processes of strike mobilization have to be considered. At a general level, Hiller (1969) has outlined the methods and strategies involved, while studies such as those of Paterson and Willett (1951) and Gouldner (1955) have shown how important leadership is, and how it changes during the course of strikes.

The role of leadership is recognized more generally in discussions of strikes. For example, the role of 'agitators' is frequently referred to, while the importance of stewards 'educating' their members similarly implies a leadership role. The 'agitator' theory of strikes is of course far too simple, for it ignores the constraints upon leadership and the organizational conditions necessary if anyone is to play a leadership role (Hyman, 1972:56-8). These aspects can, however, be illuminated by detailed case studies. For example, Karsh shows in detail how a union organizer was able to recruit influential workers in a small plant and thereby invoke a strike over union recognition and wage demands (1958). In a quite remarkable study, Kapferer discusses not only the impact of larger structural factors upon the African workplace he studied but also the changing systems of influence within the plant and how these facilitated strike action (1972). One crucial role of the leader is often, in Wright Mills's classic phrase, 'the management of discontent' (1948:9). In moving towards a strike, 'inhibitions must be relaxed. This is accomplished by accepting or creating interpretations of the situation which encourage action: supplying justifications for striking and minimizing the hazards of the undertaking. Justifications are provided by rehearsing grievances and claiming merits' (Hiller, 1969:49).

Two related elements appear, therefore, to be of crucial importance in strike action: first, patterns of influence among the workers concerned, and, second, a range of vocabularies or systems of argument which can be employed in relation to collective action. Such vocabularies may be quite consciously manipulated by those with influence. As Mann argues, leaders view workers' consciousness '*tactically*, as convincing management that they are desperately holding back the workers from excessive violence. Once management has given in to their specific bargaining demands they will see no further point to the agitation' (1973:49).

An emphasis upon the mobilization of strike action serves to suggest that the act of striking is problematical. It is necessary to investigate not merely situations in which strikes actually do occur, but also those where this possibility does not become reality. For, in the same way that leaders mobilize their influence and exploit vocabularies in pursuit of work stoppages, they may equally employ them to prevent strike action. Again, such a possibility is widely recognized, particularly in arguments that union officials attempt to limit the range of demands and use of the strike weapon.

There are a number of factors which have to be taken into account in any satisfactory and total explanation of strikes. First, it is essential to recognize that strikes, as an expression of industrial conflict, reflect the subordination of workers within industry and, indeed, society more generally. Second, the institutions of collective bargaining, forms of social and political integration more generally, and management and trade union organization all have some relevance to the probability of strike action. However, the extent to which strikes do actually occur will be most immediately determined by processes of negotiation among workers themselves. For this reason an understanding of the distribution of power among workers and the sorts of vocabularies employed is crucial to an analysis of strikes. In themselves these factors cannot explain the whole phenomenon of strikes. They constitute an important but relatively un-studied aspect. In this book, therefore, we focus upon the mobilization of strike action.

The Background of the Study

This book stems from the research we undertook into shop steward organization which has been discussed in our previous volume, *Shop Stewards in Action*. During our fieldwork we observed a number of stoppages and collected a good deal of data on strikes in the plant more generally. In a relatively strike-prone plant it was, of course, very likely that we should observe numerous cases of collective action. Moreover, stoppages of work were important as critical situations which might serve to provide insights into the nature of what we termed domestic organization. In our analysis we paid a good deal of attention to strikes and situations where strike action appeared probable. In one respect, therefore, this volume can be seen as looking in rather more depth at a number of events crucial to an understanding of the distribution of power and influence in our domestic organization.

As we analysed our data, a second point became increasingly important. In many respects our fieldwork provided us with a unique opportunity to study strikes. Discussion of such collective action is common but, as we have noted, detailed sociological accounts of strikes are rare. In part this appears to reflect the hesitancy with which academics climb out of their ivory towers, and the problems of gaining access to situations where strikes are likely to develop. But in part it reflects the difficulties of understanding how strikes occur, without a good deal of knowledge of the situation and the opportunity to collect reliable data on the processes of strike mobilization. Our primary research aim, our presence in the plant, and our knowledge of the organizations therefore provided us with considerable advantages. Moreover, since more general theoretical approaches and more specific 'explanations' of strikes are increasingly oriented towards the dynamic aspects of organizational behaviour, our primary research also provided the beginnings of a framework within which to analyse strikes. This book derived from an attempt to make use of these opportunities. It originated as one chapter for our first volume, but, like Topsy, 'just grow'd'. Our aims are twofold: first, to attempt to improve understanding of the social organization of strikes and, second and relatedly, to test more fully some of the propositions which we made in our first volume.

For those who have not read the previous volume it will be useful to describe briefly the nature of the workplace studied. The company is a trans-national involved in vehicle manufacture. At the plant studied they employ about 4,500 manual workers in the machining of parts, assembly of vehicles, and the various supportive tasks involving craft workers and other indirects. The great majority of production workers are paid on a group or section piecework basis, while the others receive an hourly rate. Earnings are relatively high for the area, itself one of the highest-paying in the country.

A pre-entry closed shop operates so that union membership is 100 per cent. The AUEW and the TGWU, with plant memberships roughly equal in size, together account for about 90 per cent of the total membership, and the NSMM for about 8 per cent, while the remainder belong to a variety of unions including the EEPTU, the two sheet-metal workers' unions which existed at the time of the research (1973), and UCATT (see the Glossary for the meaning of these and other abbreviations). Except in craft areas, sections are made up of members of a variety of unions. The shop steward

5

organization consists of over 150 stewards, including three full-time conveners recognized by the company. The Joint Shop Stewards' Committee (JSSC) meets at least weekly, while departmental steward committees meet with similar frequency in the machine shops and assembly shop, and rather more rarely among the craft and related groups. Through the organization of work by sections in particular, stewards and members are involved in a wide range of managerial decisions, and certain areas are under their unilateral control.

Our research included as well a staff domestic organization and we shall also make some reference to this body. It consists of about 600 clerical, secretarial, and related staff, including junior purchasing personnel, security workers, and groups such as progress chasers. A large minority are women, who make up a very small proportion of the shop-floor organization. The staff can be broadly divided into manufacturing and non-manufacturing groups, the former being much more closely involved in the actual production process and including such groups as the progress chasers. Staff are paid salaries on the basis of a managerially determined job-evaluation system which divides the staff into a multitude of groups. For the bulk of the staff there is automatic annual progression to the mid-point of their various salary scales, and from then on increments depend upon 'merit'.

While a closed shop formally exists, the clauses in the Industrial Relations Act designed to preserve 'individual liberty' slightly reduced union membership below the 100 per cent level. Two unions, ACTSS and APEX, are represented, each having about half of the membership. There are twenty-six stewards, including two conveners. A Joint Shop Stewards' Committee exists but meets less regularly than its equivalent on the shop-floor, and no area steward committees exist. Compared with the shop-floor, the union plays a relatively small role in the work situation of its members.

It is useful to provide here a brief summary of our approach and main findings, first, because the theoretical basis of this volume derives quite directly from *Shop Stewards in Action* and, second, because certain terms which we employ in later chapters require some explanation. Our basic approach to the study of 'domestic organization' — union organization within the plant — involved an emphasis upon the 'negotiation of order': organizations are not simply created but have to be continually reaffirmed (or changed) by the actions of participants. Such negotiation involves networks of relationships through which arguments can be promoted and sanctions imposed upon others. Underlying these networks are important dimensions of power: it is necessary not only to look at who raises issues, but also why particular issues are raised rather than others and why conflicts fail to exist on many issues. These questions, in our view, indicate the importance of the 'mobilization of bias' involved in ideologies and institutions which serves to bolster the power of some rather than others and to facilitate the identification and pursuit of some kinds of issues as against others.

In our empirical work we began by distinguishing two main types of steward. The first, the leader steward, was committed to union principles and adopted a representative rather than a delegate role in relation to his members: leaders demonstrated these character- istics in their day-to-day behaviour and in their general attitudes. A large minority of shop-floor stewards were leaders, while few staff stewards were. Those who were leaders tended to achieve higher earnings for their members, limited overtime, and imposed greater day-to-day constraints upon management but at the same time resorted less to strikes or formal procedure than did stewards of the other main type, namely populists. These adopted a delegate role in relation to their members, and demonstrated a lower commitment to union principles.

The bulk of our previous volume addressed itself to two inter- related questions: why there were differences in the degree of leadership on the shop-floor and among the staff, and why individual stewards were leaders or populists. Our explanation concentrated on several aspects. First, on the shop-floor a strong leader-steward network existed which fostered the idea of steward leadership and provided information and recipes of action which facilitated the adoption of such a role. This steward network focused upon the conveners and a key group of leader stewards — the quasi-elite (Q-E) — who acted as an informal cabinet to the conveners. The conveners and Q-E also had a major influence upon events within the various steward committees. On the staff side the steward network was less strong while the conveners and Q-E were also less dominant.

Second, leader stewards were more able to influence their members. While populist stewards tended not to be opinion-leaders (influential members of their sections), leader stewards generally were, and also had close contacts with other opinion-leaders. Leadership on the shop-floor was also facilitated by more basic aspects of power. Shop-floor members more readily espoused the norms of steward leadership, although active steward negotiation was still required in the face of conflicts between these norms and the immediate, expressed demands of members. More generally, however, ambivalence was found to exist in the attitudes of both shop-floor and staff workers, and accordingly social imagery was itself an inadequate explanation for the broad differences in steward leadership between the staff and the shop-floor. The third element in our explanation of steward leadership, therefore, concerned the mobilization of bias involved in the institutions of the workplace. The organization of work and bargaining on the shop-floor, particularly in production areas, fostered the adoption of collective attitudes and behaviour. On the staff side, particularly in non-manufacturing areas, the opposite was the case. These points are discussed more fully in Chapter 3 of this volume.

Fourth, leadership tended to exist where stewards had strong bargaining relationships with managers which permitted the exchange of information in 'informal chats' and the manipulation or evasion of agreements. Such relationships reflected the more common pattern of inter-managerial relations in crisis-prone areas of the plant. Fifth, shop-floor conveners' relationships with their full-time officials were such that the latter acted as a leadership resource rather than assuming the leadership role themselves, as tended to be the case on the staff side.

To summarize, we observed quite marked differences in the extent to which stewards led their members and the sorts of goals which they attempted to pursue. We explained these differences in two interrelated ways: by the mobilization of bias in the institutions and dominant ideologies of the organizations, and by the more general patterns of relationships and influence within the plant. Our analysis of the organizational conditions for strike action develops these themes a little further, while subsequent chapters employ our basic approach and concepts in outlining the mobilization of strike action.

The Book Outlined

Chapter 2 first considers the nature of strike statistics, and in particular the social processes within the plant which lead to the definition of particular acts as strikes. There are often problems in deciding whether some form of collective sanction exists, and whether it is a strike or some other type of sanction. In Chapter 3 we look at the general background conditions for strike action. In particular, we attempt to explain why the strike level is so very different between the staff and the shop-floor organizations, and why the strike pattern has varied on the shop-floor.

Chapter 4 develops more fully one aspect of the organization of strikes. It looks at the rationales put forward in support of, and in opposition to, strike action. These rationales are contrasted with officially recorded 'causes' of strikes, for they show that workers place a great deal of blame upon management for strike action. The various rationales put forward in strike situations are, however, only one side of the picture. We need also to ask who puts forward these rationales and with what success. This is done in Chapter 5 where we look at who initiates ideas of strike action and the groups which they are able to mobilize. Chapter 6 then attempts to draw together the two previous chapters to look at the actual processes involved in moving towards a strike.

The chapters so far discussed go to make up Part I of the book, which is largely concerned with strikes which happen to be both unofficial and unconstitutional. Part II is devoted to a detailed study of the movement towards a strike stemming from the annual negotiations, in which the company was unwilling to offer the legal maximum wage increase without the workers accepting measured daywork.

Part I
Strikes: Conditions and Mobilization

2
The Social Processes of Strike Definition

In this chapter we consider the way in which particular actions are defined as strikes, and events which are apparently similar to the observer are not defined in this way. For strike statistics are not an accurate reflection of stoppages of work, as numerous authors have pointed out (e.g. Turner, 1969; Eldridge, 1968:15ff.). But such criticisms have in the past been primarily concerned with the coverage and criteria of official strike statistics. We, however, are concerned with strike definition within the plant itself. This process is important not merely in terms of general statistics but also because it helps to illuminate the power processes involved in what would conventionally be defined as strike action. Consequently, it illuminates the role of management in the creation of strike statistics.

In looking at the role of management in defining strikes, we begin to see the part which it plays more generally in stoppages of work, and this is also noted in other sections of this volume. For strikes, as a form of conflict, involve two parties. However, the role of management will not be specifically discussed for two reasons. First, we are concerned with the mobilization process as far as workers are concerned, and, second, our data are not of a kind which allow us to understand in detail the managerial role in the creation of work stoppages. When we talk about strike initiatives in later chapters, therefore, we are concerned solely with such 'initiatives' among workers, even though they may often be managerially fostered.

Stoppages and Strikes in the Plant

How do stoppages become classified as strikes within the plant? This question can be usefully approached by looking at the problems of definition which those actually involved encountered. In some cases which we observed, particularly as far as overtime bans and go-slows were concerned, arguments between management and conveners occurred as to whether or not particular sections were imposing restrictions (such arguments could be of great significance in determining whether those laid off were paid). It was not unusual for more junior management to claim that a section had imposed a restriction, but for this to be contradicted upon investigation by the conveners and more senior management. For example, in one lay-off senior management stated there would be no lay-off pay since, on information provided by more junior managers, stewards were imposing sanctions. The conveners and senior managers finally agreed that in fact sanctions existed on only one section.

Contradictions between formal and informal social definitions of collective action in the plant were relatively common. For collective action to be formally defined as such, it would seem that a definite democratic decision had to be made by workers, and management informed of this fact. If this was not done, then it was often very difficult for management to claim — at least to workers generally — that a sanction was being applied. On one occasion, for example, a mass meeting, on the advice of the conveners, rejected an overtime ban and instead very few people made themselves available for overtime. On a number of occasions, conveners proposed that an overtime ban be dropped and instead individual section members should all have prior engagements — 'You're all going fishing' or 'You've all got to go to church on Sunday.'

A similar problem for management occurs with go-slows. It is very often the case that during piecework negotiations, when sections are not working on an immediate incentive basis, output falls. This may be seen as part of the general negotiating game with work study; but at the same time it can be a costless (to the workers) means of imposing pressure upon management to reach a favourable agreement. Management are only too fully aware of such problems, and indeed complaints about restrictions of output were an important factor in their proposals to change the payment system. Similarly, members of the Q-E often attempt to prevent sections limiting output (although they also try to prevent sections increasing output dramatically during and immediately after negotiations). On one occasion, for example, a Q-E member, passing a section involved in as yet unsuccessful piecework negotiations, noted: 'They're really putting management through hell — they're really dragging the job out.' The point is that these limitations cannot normally be publicly defined by management as restrictions or as duress. There is no public statement of the restriction, while the fall in output could be legitimated by workers either in terms of technical problems or else in terms of the fact that under a piecework system management cannot complain about the actual level of effort and output (since this is a matter to be decided by workers themselves).

It was precisely because junior management, more immediately involved in the realities of shop-floor activity than in the formal niceties of agreements, were unaware of the distinction between reality and the formal requirements of proof, that disagreements over the existence of restrictions occurred.

In the same way, what are in reality stoppages of work may not become classified as strikes because of foremen. It will be useful to take two examples of this:

The Tags Issue. A group of men complained that inspectors were refusing to check certain components in terms of safety, thereby increasing danger to them. The men stopped work, and the steward told the foreman that the men would not help the inspectors if they failed to put safety tags on. The foreman accepted this, did not suspend the men or define it as a strike, and an agreement was reached quickly. The men resumed work.

The Pairs Issue. A group of men refused to do a job unless they were allowed to work in pairs, and hence stopped work. The foreman complained to the steward, who supported the men and said the foreman's request was 'not on' because it was contrary to shop rules. The foreman complained that this was not a very co-operative attitude, but accepted the steward's argument. Again, the men were not disciplined nor was the situation defined as a stoppage.

In both these cases stoppages of work occurred but they were not defined as such, and no disciplinary action was taken. Moreover, in these cases the stoppage was a collective one — that is, it involved more than one person. In contrast, we can look at a number of situations where such action was either defined as a stoppage, or where management suspended the offenders and this led to what was defined as a stoppage. This tends to occur when the immediate problem is part of a more general issue, and suspensions constitute one of the most common causes of strikes on the staff side. For example:

The Regrading Issue. A group of staff had lodged a regrading claim on the basis of additional and new responsibilities; this claim had been through procedure and a lengthy delay had occurred over the selection of an arbitrator, to the disgruntlement of the members. At the same time, more new work had been given them and the workers involved had refused to do it. After several meetings, the company gave an ultimatum that unless they were prepared 'to work in accordance with the Company's wishes, your name will be removed from the payroll'. The staff concerned went home and hence were on strike. They returned the next day when swift arbitration was promised.

The New Work Issue. In support of a wage claim, a section decided to refuse to do any new work. Management instructed a member of the section to do a job; he claimed it was new work, management disagreed, and suspended the man. The section went out on strike in support of him; after some time, a return to work was agreed, but within a matter of hours exactly the same course of events occurred again, and so the strike was resumed.

A comparison between these examples and the previous two is of interest on a number of counts. First, they all involve workers, individually or collectively, refusing to undertake particular tasks and thus causing a stoppage of work. But in the first two cases management are prepared to negotiate in an attempt to overcome the cause of the stoppage, whereas in the last two cases management choose to adopt a much harder line; and certainly, in the last case cited, this was part of a larger strategy on the part of management, not centrally linked to the immediate problem in hand. Management, then, play a major role in the existence and duration of strikes.

Other writers have noted the strategic nature of strike definition. Kuhn cites the case of a foreman who failed to report a two-hour stoppage on the grounds that 'it was a nuisance, it created a problem, but as long as I get enough production, I'll take a nuisance' (1961:198). As a result, Kuhn argues, even where statistics on walk-outs are recorded, they are unreliable 'since different members of management define a work stoppage variously according to the bargain situation in which they may find themselves' (1961:157-8), or, as Ingham puts it, 'the hasty definition of a work stoppage may often prove a barrier to negotiations and a resumption of work' (1974:27).

Another point about the examples is of interest — both of the first cases cited occurred in the assembly shop, whereas neither of the latter did. While it is dangerous to exaggerate the differences, we would suggest that there is a greater tendency for management in assembly, compared with other areas of the plant, not to define a stoppage as a strike. In assembly informal arrangements between men and management tend to be more common (Batstone *et al.*, 1977:Chap. 10); management are especially dependent upon the co-operation of workers in order to achieve output. It is not surprising, therefore, that they attempt to overcome stoppages — which on the assembly line can of course lead to the immediate stoppage of work for many men — rather than adopt a more autocratic approach. Consequently, a stoppage may be defined, in the words of Turner *et al.*, as 'a pause for discussion' rather than an actual stoppage (1967:53). Similarly, management's attitude varied towards lunch-time meetings of workers running over into working hours. In some areas there were unwritten agreements that the men would make up the lost production. But even in these areas, when a high degree of conflict existed, foremen might make the men lose pay for the period concerned. It would appear that in some firms this might be defined as a stoppage. Certainly a meeting during working hours was so defined by management in our plant on one occasion.

Management's use of suspension is also worthy of consideration. In the regrading issue outlined above, it was never clear to us how management defined the situation; it had been their threat of suspension which led to the workers walking out, but it was generally defined by workers, stewards, and at least some managers as a strike. In the other case, suspension was formally something relating solely to an individual, but management were well aware that the individual concerned had the backing of his fellow workers. The suspension of the individual worker can therefore be seen in any of three ways; it can be seen as management formalizing the fact that the worker had effectively gone on strike; it may be seen as something broadly similar to a lockout; or it may be seen as an action designed to test the strength of feeling of other members, and possibly to foster, if necessary, an all-out strike.

These points can again be seen most clearly in the case of the staff. The Regrading Issue is not atypical; indeed at least half of the staff strikes we know about occurred in this way. We shall take one further example:

The Suspension Issue. In support of their claim, a group of workers went out on strike. Other workers were instructed to handle work, formerly done by the group but now done by an outside agency. When they refused, they were suspended. This occurred several times, and finally the whole staff agreed to strike, and did so.

Here we have a number of collective suspensions which are related to refusals to carry out management orders and which therefore involve stoppages of work. It is difficult to decide, on the basis of conventional definitions, whether these situations should be seen as suspensions, a form of lockout, or strikes, or a combination of these.

This difficulty is in many cases inevitable. It is not unusual for social processes to be sufficiently complex for any simple definition or categorization to be less than totally satisfactory. But in the case of our plant one feature does exist which serves to define the strike clearly. This is the managerial action of 'taking men off the clock' or, in other words, ceasing to pay them. It is almost invariably the case that if men leave the plant they are 'taken off the clock' but sit-downs or 'downers', which are quite common, may not lead to this managerial action. Again, we can take a number of examples:

The Safety Issue. A stoppage of work occurred when a couple of workers pointed out to their steward that a piece of machinery they were working was unsafe. The steward told them to stop work, informed the foreman of this, and gained his agreement to have the machine made safe before any resumption of work. Again, despite the fact that this stopped the work of several hundred men for about an hour, the men were not taken off the clock.

The Fan Issue. A group of men ceased work because an extractor fan broke down and this meant that they had to work in very bad fumes. Management attempted to get them to continue work but, on failing to do so, agreed to repair the fan as quickly as possible. The men went home — management therefore took them off the clock and hence the stoppage was classified as a strike.

The Pay Issue. A steward had been negotiating with management over the level of pay his men were to receive for that week; he failed to achieve what he saw as an acceptable figure, and therefore requested permission for an immediate section meeting. This was refused, so he merely went back to his men and told them to leave their jobs and meet outside. They did so and the work of many others was interrupted for fifteen minutes; they were taken off the clock for this time and the event was classified as a strike.

The Meetings Issue. As on many other occasions, a section meeting was held which interrupted production. But this was not classified as a strike. The main reason was that management had agreed to the meeting. They gave a time limit for the meeting, but even when this was overrun the stoppage of work was not classified as a strike.

We have quoted these four cases because they indicate two important points about the social definition of a strike. The first is that strikes are defined as such primarily by the managerial act of taking the men involved off the clock; this is virtually automatic if the men leave the plant. Hence if we compare the Safety and Fan Issues the only difference is that in the latter the men left the plant and were accordingly taken off the clock. Several stewards were discussing the Fan Issue and one pointed out, with the agreement of the others: 'The steward made a blunder — when they stopped work, management took them off the clock. They should have stayed [at work], but instead they went home. If they'd stayed, they would have been paid, because management were in the wrong.' The stewards went on to quote a number of other examples which supported this argument.

This leads to the second and more important point. Management often have the power to define a situation as a strike or not. We have seen that often a stoppage is not defined as a strike because management, in the interests of co-operation, production, and their assessment by their superiors, choose not to define it as such (cf. Eldridge, 1968:13; Ingham, 1974:27-8). Their concern is less how to define the situation in these terms than how to overcome it. But more importantly, as a comparison of the Safety and Meetings Issues with the Fan and Pay Issues shows, they do not define stoppages as strikes if the workers do not leave the plant and if, at the time or afterwards, the men's case is seen as legitimate by management.

Below we shall attempt to redefine a strike. But, before we do so, this discussion suggests a number of other interesting and significant conclusions. Stoppages of work at the initiative of workers are far more common than the strike statistics suggest, not merely because minor strikes are ignored, nor merely because doubts may be registered about the reporting of strikes either to the Department of Employment or to higher management. There is another reason: strikes which are seen as legitimate by management are often not defined as such. Our experience would suggest that such attribution of legitimacy by management is particularly common in relation to stoppages over such issues as safety and working conditions. If this is generally so, then the official strike statistics will also tend to underestimate significantly the number of stoppages over such issues; in other words, the traditional importance of money questions as the cause of strikes may be considerably exaggerated.

We have seen that the process of defining an act as a strike is a social process. It involves, first, particular acts or statements of intent on the part of workers, and it requires, secondly, the managerial actions of taking men off the clock and defining the grievance of the workers as illegitimate. Particular *de facto* collective actions cannot be publicly defined by management as duress or sanctions because they do not involve total stoppages of work and because no clear statement of the collective intention of imposing sanctions has been made by workers. Moreover, it is often difficult to distinguish between strikes, overtime bans, and other restrictions, and lock-outs and suspensions. Finally, for an act to be defined as a strike, the relevant senior management have to be informed of the fact and more junior management may be loath to do so.

For an act to be defined as a strike involves a social process on the part of both workers and management. It is not surprising to find differences in the strike records of unions and employers. For example, Kuhn found that, in one case, management records over a seven-year period showed 75 per cent more strikes than did union records (1961:158). What is perhaps more surprising is that, over a two-year period in our plant, management and union records show little disparity — the former give a figure of forty-five strikes, while references to forty-six strikes are to be found in JSSC minutes. More generally, the very act of keeping detailed records appears somewhat unusual, possibly reflecting a concern on the part of management with a 'strike problem', if only as an excuse for unsatisfactory performance. Certainly it is of interest that in the plant we studied detailed records were kept from only a few years before our fieldwork. This was because management became concerned with the production loss through strikes and were hoping to discover the reasons for such 'problems'.

These factors within the plant are important in a consideration of both company and official statistics. But so far we have been concerned simply with the number of stoppages. Official and company statistics also typically cover other aspects and it is to a consideration of these that we turn in the next section.

20

The Conventional Dimensions of Strikes

In this section we consider certain dimensions of strikes. We first look at the statistics of workers involved and, associated with this, the number of days lost through strikes. We then look at one of the major sources of concern over strikes, namely the unofficial and unconstitutional nature of many of them. The aim throughout this section is not merely to discuss these dimensions in general terms but also to outline the important considerations for the discussion of our own empirical data. We turn first, then, to the question of the number of workers involved in strikes.

The Number of Workers Involved

Strikes vary in their size and it would, from certain perspectives, be ridiculous to treat, say, a nation-wide strike and a stoppage by a few workers as essentially similar. The organization involved in the two strikes and their economic and social impact is very different. However, when we look at official statistics, this interesting and possibly important dimension begins to become confused. For, in presenting general figures, individual strikes are added together, and hence we do not know how many workers were involved in strikes. We do not know, for example, whether a figure of, say, 100,000 workers involved in strikes refers to 100,000 different workers or the same 10,000 workers going on strike on ten different occasions. While the economic implications may be broadly similar, such a confusion can be problematical if we are concerned with questions concerning the readiness of workers to undertake collective action. This difficulty is further compounded by the inclusion of those 'indirectly' involved in strike statistics. The inclusion of workers from the plant indirectly affected in statistics of the number involved in strikes can lead to possible misleading conclusions; for example, the Department of Employment reports (February 1976:116) that the number of working days lost per 1,000 employees is greater in large plants. But in a large plant many of those indirectly affected are in the plant and hence included in the statistics. On the other hand, few of those affected by strikes in small plants may be employed in the plant where the strike occurs; consequently they are excluded from the statistics. The Department of Employment finding is therefore, at least in part, a definitional artefact.

The amount of effort which goes into finding alternative sources of supplies or alternative work in strikes clearly may vary, and accordingly so will the numbers indirectly involved in the stoppage. In periods when managers are keen to maintain production, such endeavour is likely to be greater than when they are not. Similarly, laying off other workers may be part of a larger management strategy designed to impose pressure upon strikers from their fellow workers. The number of workers directly and indirectly involved in a stoppage is not technically or automatically determined but is subject to influence by the strikers, other workers, and management.

However, more basic questions can be asked concerning the usefulness of statistics relating to the number of workers involved in strikes. While such figures have certain uses, they tell us only a limited amount concerning the nature of strikes. We have already noted that they do not tell us how many people have undertaken strike action in any year. More than that, they fail to provide us with any understanding of the organization of strikes, that is, the level at which they occur. We do not know from the official statistics how many strikes were of individual work groups, or departments, or of individual trade unions. When a thousand workers go out on strike they may be members of a particular occupational or skill classification within one or a number of plants, a department, or a whole plant or multi-plant company. Or the organizational level may be one trade union. Clearly, at an aggregate level the collection of data in a form which recognized such variations would be difficult. There could be complex combinations; data collection would involve a great deal of dependence upon those involved in the dispute for identifying its organizational shape; and it would have to take account of widely differing patterns of union and plant organization. Nevertheless, from a sociological viewpoint the question of the organizational level of strike action is an important one. In the remainder of this book, therefore, we shall be less concerned with the number of workers involved in stoppages than with the organizational level of strike action.

Working Days Lost

The number of working days lost is frequently used as the basis for approximations of the economic costs of strikes, and some authors have based their explanations of strikes primarily upon this statistic (Ross and Hartman, 1960). Its great weakness for such purposes, in addition to those discussed above, is that it is impossible, using this figure alone, to tell what combination of strike frequency and duration is involved (e.g. Lester, 1958). Given our interest in how strikes develop, statistics on working days lost are of limited use.

However, we noted that a second usage of this figure is as an indicator of the cost of strikes. This aspect is not of direct concern to us in this volume. But it is perhaps useful to point out that 'working days lost' not only involves a considerable bias of phraseology (since it assumes days really are lost and it implies this is unnecessary) but may also considerably exaggerate or under-estimate the costs of strikes both to companies and workers (Turner, 1969; Hyman, 1972:35; Eldridge, 1968:83; Gennard and Lasko, 1974; Durcan and McCarthy, 1974).

Unofficial and Unconstitutional Strikes

Numerous criticisms have been made of the general usefulness of classifying strikes as 'unofficial' or 'unconstitutional', in terms of the failure to recognize that 'constitutionality' reflects more general inequalities (Hyman, 1972:37-8; Cole, 1939:86-7; Goldthorpe, 1974) and the nature of union government (Eldridge and Cameron, 1968:68ff.). We are here concerned, however, less with these more general questions than with whether these aspects of strikes serve to illuminate the strike process (in our study the great majority of strikes were both unofficial and unconstitutional). Management would inform full-time officials of the larger strikes, seeking their co-operation in achieving a return to work. But the officials never took action unless the conveners requested it. Several officials told us that they 'filed' such management communications 'in the waste paper basket' (cf. H. A. Clegg, 1954:133).

Given our concerns, we would make a number of criticisms of the use of the unofficial and unconstitutional dimensions of strikes. Within our shop-floor organization, for example, a complex pattern of recipes of action and definitions exists. Workers are involved in a developing situation which is, from their perspective, primarily parochial. They perform particular limited tasks in association with others whom they know, and they have a number of persons whom they know as individuals who represent, for them, management and the union. The niceties of agreements and union constitutions are much less real or meaningful to them than, say, the fact that a machine is dangerous, one of their colleagues has been victimized, or a member of management is 'taking them for a ride'.

Their 'horizons of consciousness' (Berger *et al.*, 1974) rarely include as central features documents which many of them will never have seen. Add to this the fact that the rules laid down in such documents may often be quite contradictory to or different from the 'recipes of action' and 'pragmatic rules' (Bailey, 1969:76) which have developed over time through interactions with management, and it is not surprising that they should be so rarely followed. Industry and industrial relations are both essentially practical activities. Where the value of particular methods has not been proven, and even more where they appear to be positively disadvantageous, it would be absurd to use them.

In the shop-floor organization we studied, certain problems where written procedures and union constitutions seemed of little use were handled by other means. In particular, stewards were concerned with the adverse effects upon other workers of strikes by small groups. As a consequence, they have developed their own procedural rules. A JSSC rule exists that the conveners must address workers before they walk out. In some departments the chairman of the departmental stewards' committee is provided with a similar right. More recently, attempts have been made to set up a stewards' Disputes Committee which would assess the justice of proposed strikes and either advise against any strike or seek plant-wide support for it. As we shall see in later chapters, these rules are generally followed. For, in workers' and stewards' minds, they have far more legitimacy and fit more consistently with their images of workplace experience than those which surround a procedure which is long-winded and which management specifically declare will not permit certain types of compromise between annual agreements.

Another problem exists in the use of 'formal' procedure. Much of the work experience of shop-floor workers is surrounded by a network of *ad hoc* verbal agreements and custom and practice. Many of these, which are vital to the day-to-day operation of the plant, are legitimate only within particular sections. Disputes over certain practices (for example, that men can sit around once a specified amount of work has been completed) cannot therefore be taken through procedure since the agreement at issue would be considered illegitimate by more senior management, or full-time officials, or both. The interpretation of the 'agreement' might cease to become the issue and the parties to it might well be subject to criticism. All that procedure would do would be to disrupt a particular *modus vivendi*. In addition, the expertise for the interpretation of the agreement at issue lies not with more senior personnel but those who moulded it, possibly over many years, on the shop-floor itself.

Formal procedure is often seen, therefore, as a less effective method than strike action. The shop stewards' own procedure for strikes is often preferred. However, even this is not always followed. On occasion groups feel strongly about an issue and believe that other stewards and the conveners would be opposed to strike action (in other words, these are 'unofficial-unofficial' strikes). They therefore do not raise the matter with them. Sometimes, on perishable issues, or on questions which arise suddenly, there is not time to find a convener. On other issues stewards find it difficult to gain meetings with managers to negotiate. As one steward explained to a convener when asked whether he had 'failed to agree' with a particular level of management, 'You can't catch the buggers to fail to agree with them.'

Descriptions of strikes, then, as 'unofficial' and 'unconstitutional' are of limited usefulness, and we do not employ them in the remainder of this book. Both are very crude and rigid terms which do not satisfactorily illuminate the real social contexts or social processes of strike action. In a later chapter, however, we consider the role of other members of the shop-floor organization in the strikes or proposed strikes of particular sectional groups.

In this chapter we have been concerned with the conceptual and empirical problems involved in defining a strike and its various dimensions. We have noted that strikes merge into other forms of collective action and that not all worker stoppages are defined as strikes. There is an important social process of strike definition within the plant itself as well as in the administrative bodies charged with compiling strike statistics.

We have also argued that the dimensions of strikes generally employed, while of use for some purposes, can provide us with few insights into the social organization of strikes. Indeed the only statistic of a conventional kind we employ relates to the number of strikes.

The number of days lost through strikes has little use in our book, and we have suggested that it is important to look at more specifically organizational dimensions of strikes. In later chapters we therefore focus on the organizational level at which strikes occur and on who, within the organization, becomes involved in the consideration of strike action.

Throughout our discussion we have stressed that strikes are merely one expression of conflict. Moreover, if we are to understand strikes we have also to understand non-strikes. We are therefore as interested in proposed strikes which do not actually occur as in those which do. However, in our next chapter on the historical trend of strikes we lack the data necessary to discuss 'near-strikes'. We are also dependent upon strike statistics which have been created by the stewards and management themselves. These weaknesses are inevitable in practical terms, but we think that the resultant figures are of use and interest if treated with caution.

3
The Context of Strike Action: Power and Organization

In this chapter we consider some of the general conditions which facilitate strike action. The literature suggests that many factors are relevant and we shall not consider them all here. For example, we shall not discuss the impact of unemployment and the general state of the economy; nor shall we consider directly the impact of economic rewards, the nature of jobs, or work attitudes, for we found that these did not satisfactorily explain the pattern of recorded strikes in the plant. We confine ourselves to a discussion of technology and work-group organization, and the institutional and organizational conditions of strike action.

Technology, Work Organization, and Power

The technical organization of work is often said to influence strike activity in two ways. First, it provides workers with varying degrees of power since technology determines the disruptive ability of groups. Second, much organization theory has stressed the influence of technology upon the more general organization of a plant in terms of management structure, workers' unity, and a variety of institutions. However, the term 'technology' tends to be confusing. It may refer either to the pieces of machinery within a plant or to a broader set of factors which include technical knowledge and social organization as well as the physical equipment employed. (With the latter usage the idea of the impact of technology on social organization is tautological, although it may permit recognition of the range of choice of technical method (Child, 1973) and the negotiation which accompanies the decision to organize work in one way rather than another.) The technology of the workplace in terms of machinery clearly gives varying degrees of power to different work groups. For example, a small group on the assembly line can easily stop the whole track because the production of others is directly and immediately related to their work. On the other hand, sweepers have little direct relationship to production. They are rarely crucial to the production process and hence their power might be expected to be a good deal less.

We consider four aspects of power which relate to the organization of work (see Hickson *et al.*, 1973). The first source of power relates to the extent to which a group of workers have scarce skills so that they cannot easily be replaced (see, for example, H. A. Clegg, 1970:31). Second, we consider the power which derives from occupying a crucial position in the production process (Sayles, 1958:4); and, third, we discuss the immediacy with which a group can disrupt the company (Sayles, 1958:61-2; H. A. Clegg, 1970:32). Finally, we look at the ability of a group to create or cope with uncertainty in the production process (Crozier, 1964). While these may be important aspects of power, we argue that they by no means provide a total picture and that they do not relate simply to technology. We look at each of the sources of power in turn.

A low degree of substitutability means that if a group employs scarce skills it will be difficult to replace its members, who accordingly have a high degree of power. But a low degree of substitutability may have little to do with either skill level or the state of the labour market. For equally important in the context of strikes is whether workers will accept 'substitutes', commonly known as blacklegs, no matter what skill level is involved. Workers' own values and organization are crucial factors in this aspect of power, even when unskilled tasks are performed.

On the shop-floor in our plant, management have rarely, if ever, attempted to 'man up' strikers' jobs. The workers on the shop-floor — unlike the staff — would consider it to be against trade union principles (see also Johnston, 1975:57-8). Consequently, the most unskilled job has a very low degree of substitutability even when there is a large pool of labour apparently available either inside or outside the plant. But there are exceptions; in the case of one group of workers who had continually gone out on strike, laying many others off, workers did finally threaten to man their jobs up. The power of the strikers thereby disappeared immediately and they agreed to work normally. In other cases workers have permitted management to take over such jobs as essential maintenance. Generally on our shop-floor this would be forbidden, although workers and management did once co-operate to ensure the continuation of production when the foremen went out on strike. In contrast, when work-study officers went on strike and instituted a symbolic sit-in, the workers decided to co-operate with the strikers. Hence, the shop-floor increased the substitutability of the foremen and connived at extending the power of the work-study officers. In sum, the degree of substitutability of a work group is very dependent upon the behaviour of other workers.

If a group occupies a crucial position in the production process then it can affect the work of many other groups; it may therefore have a good deal of power. But, on the other hand, such an important position may make a group weak if it means that many other groups can disrupt it. In our plant this was a problem for the assembly workers. The machine-shop groups, internal transport drivers, stores, and so on could all stop the work of the assembly workers precisely because they were central to the production process. Moreover, because some groups are important in the production process, it is possible for management to stir them to strike action to avoid having to pay those laid off when breakdowns occur, markets slump, or supplies run short. Power deriving from an important position in the production process may be turned against the group itself.

Strike action, worker organization, and management action can all affect the importance of a group within the production process. For example, the pervasiveness of a group can be increased by the use of pickets and sit-ins, and by extending the size of the group which undertakes strike action. In our plant, shop-floor workers have on occasion used the tactic of picketing. In a recent dispute they extended their picketing to have a wider impact upon the company's operations. They blockaded the gates to prevent even management from gaining access, they employed flying pickets at places where the company stored vehicles, and they sent delegations to groups such as the dockers to prevent the handling of vehicles for export.

The sit-in has also been used in the plant. For our present purposes the importance of this strategy is again the obstruction of the work of others. Sit-ins in managerial areas may not only obstruct management but also provide useful information. One of the most interesting examples of this strategy was used by a group of technical workers in the plant. In their normal jobs they had little ability to disrupt production. They therefore instituted a sit-in in particular areas of the plant. They 'sat' on stop-start buttons on key pieces of machinery to prevent their operation and picketed important routes through some of the shops. Since the shop-floor agreed to recognize these largely symbolic gestures, the technical workers achieved a higher level of disruption than they would have otherwise. They had become more pervasive.

The third means of increasing the impact of a group on production is by achieving sympathetic strike action by other groups. This is relatively common. Many strikes in our plant develop from disputes involving only one or two workers. These seek support from other members of the larger work group or section. Hence, many work-group disputes find expression in section-level disputes. On occasion whole departments or the whole shop-floor have gone out on strike in support of one or two sections.

During our period of observation there were moves among the shop stewards on the shop-floor to play an active role in influencing pervasiveness in all strikes. It was proposed that a Disputes Committee be set up which would discuss proposed stoppages. If the action was deemed legitimate, then all workers would strike in support. Some were proposing that, where strikes were not deemed legitimate, then strikers' jobs would be manned up.

Many of the criticisms we have made of a simple approach to the importance of a group in the production process apply equally to the idea of immediacy, or the speed with which other groups can be stopped. Immediacy can be increased by the adoption of particular forms of strike action and by the skilful timing of strikes. For example, when management want production badly and there is a major breakdown, maintenance workers have a great deal of power. When, however, equipment is running normally then the power of this group is less great.

Workers can increase the immediacy with which strikes affect the company. In the machine shops, for example, most work is of a large-batch nature. Sizeable stocks exist, so that production could continue for some time. Strike action is thus more effective if workers gradually reduce their output and thereby reduce the level of stocks. This may happen as an issue develops. For example, during major piecework negotiations a section may limit its output while work study looks at the job. Then, if no agreement is reached over the new piecework price, overtime bans, work-to-rules, and working without enthusiasm imposed by the section may further serve to deplete stocks. If workers then strike their position will be stronger because stocks are nonexistent.

Leader stewards in the machine shops keep a close check, therefore, on stocks which may increase for a wide variety of reasons. For example, if the assembly shop is laid off, many machine-shop sections continue to work largely for stocks. This may lead to the achievement of required output for many months to come. Consequently, the power of these machine-shop sections in the near future is dramatically reduced because they cannot swiftly halt the assembly lines.

In the same way, management can affect immediacy. The relevance of their general policy on stocks is obvious. But, in addition, they may purposely build up stocks when they expect a strike. This occurred when management expected a plant-wide strike (see Part II). For several months they expanded production beyond immediate requirements and stockpiled completed vehicles at various locations outside the plant so that, if the strike were to occur, it would still be possible to meet orders.

Management can influence the immediacy and impact of disruption in other ways, depending upon how badly production is required. In some cases they will accelerate the impact of any strike action by laying off other workers. They may do this in the face of declining sales or as a means of turning other workers against the strikers. On other occasions, however, management may take a great deal of effort to minimize the impact of a dispute. For example, the combination of vehicles made may be changed to avoid the use of components in short supply due to strike action. In other cases in our plant management have continued production with parts missing, or by using 'slave' components.

Our final source of power concerns coping with uncertainty. For example, maintenance workers may achieve a good deal of power because they cope with the crises involved in the breakdown of machinery. Underlying the notion of uncertainty is the view that rules are the real source of power (S. Clegg, 1975:47-8). If rules are not conformed to, then the degree of uncertainty increases. By conforming to rules any one group reduces the level of uncertainty for others. Strikes or other forms of collective action inevitably involve breaking rules of organizational behaviour so that they

31

increase uncertainty. On the other hand, uncertainty may also be reduced by following 'informal' practices which break official rules. The fitting of components in assembly by 'tricks of the trade' is one example of this. Another is knowing the idiosyncrasies of particular machines so that breakdown is avoided. Agreeing to break 'formal' rules concerning work methods may be an important counter in bargaining. In negotiations in our plant, stewards frequently stress the co-operation which the men have given to management. This means that the breach of certain 'formal' rules has permitted management to underman or move men from task to task in order to ensure continuity of production. Managers are often ready to pay extra allowances either in recognition of such co-operation or in order to ensure that its removal is not used as a sanction.

In this section we have been concerned with power in terms of the technical ability to disrupt production. What we have tried to show is the manner in which the social organization and changing goals of both management and workers have a major impact upon what can be seen as the purely technical aspects of power. The power of work groups changes dramatically as may also the unit of group action. We go on to consider more fully the way in which management and worker organization affect power in terms of the obstruction of the other's goals.

Worker and Management Organization

In this section we go on to look at worker organization and solidarity more fully and in doing so discuss various aspects of strikes and industrial relations in the plant.

The Institutional Centrality of the Union

Between 1960 and 1973 the staff workers in the plant have engaged in strike action on only fifteen occasions. In the same period, over two hundred strikes on the shop-floor are recorded in JSSC minutes. Moreover, manufacturing staff account for about three-quarters of the staff stoppages even though they are only a third of the staff organization. Our explanation of these differences rests upon the institutional centrality of the union: where work is collectively organized there is a mobilization of bias in favour of strikes and other forms of collective sanctions. On the staff side, the relatively weak institutional supports for the collective expression of grievances may lead to more individual expression of dissatisfaction. For example, this may be one factor in the higher turnover among the staff: five or six times the rate on the shop-floor.

On the shop-floor the union plays a much more central role than among the staff. Recruitment for the shop-floor occurs only through the unions, while union membership among the staff is expected only on joining the company. In the same way, the shop-floor organization has negotiated a complex set of rules concerning job mobility, promotion (except to foreman), and transfers, while no such rules exist on the staff side.

In the day-to-day act of work, however, there are also very considerable differences. The section system on the shop-floor fosters collectivism. In piecework areas, workers are paid on a group basis and the sections operate a range of controls over work. Section-operated rotas exist for overtime, shifts, mobility, and lay-off. In addition, workers operate their own rules concerning the sick and often provide their own welfare benefits. Members of sections not merely often work in teams, they also typically determine exactly how they will work.

This system has been developed and maintained in large part because of the efforts of the workers themselves. But, in addition, management in their day-to-day behaviour generally accept and thereby reaffirm the collective nature of shop-floor work. Hence, they rarely approach individual workers, and most proposed changes in work involve prior consultation, if not negotiation, with the stewards. Consequently, bargaining occurs over a very wide range of issues and has a clear impact upon the worker both in terms of the nature of his work and the financial rewards accruing to him.

On the staff side the situation is very different. Neither steward constituencies nor workers in the non-manufacturing sections have collective job controls, while in the manufacturing areas such powers are largely limited to overtime rotas. The range of negotiation and consultation with management is small, and merit pay and regradings mainly occur at the initiative of managers. The work situation, particularly for non-manufacturing staff, is dominated by management. Supervision ratios are higher than on the shop-floor and the bulk of contacts of the non-manufacturing staff are with members of management. This is rather less true of manufacturing staff who have greater contact with colleagues and the shop-floor, more freedom, and a less subordinate relationship with management. Nevertheless, management foster individual rather than collective relations with staff members in all areas.

While the extent of collective experience and organization should not be exaggerated, it is clear that it is greater in manufacturing than in non-manufacturing areas. This would appear to be a factor in the greater strike-proneness of the former. It also helps to explain the contrast between the shop-floor and the staff. However, again it cannot be a total explanation, for the variations in the degree of union centrality do not correlate neatly with strike-proneness on the shop-floor. Another relevant factor is the nature of collective organization.

The Nature of Collective Organization

Even when the collective unit and the union are central to work experience, it is difficult to predict the pattern of strikes. Where collectivism is weak, strikes are likely to be rare. But where it is strong strikes may be more or less common. Grievances may be resolved in other ways, depending upon the resources available to the collectivity and the distribution of power and influence within the collectivity. We can usefully focus our discussion of these questions on the historical pattern of strikes on the shop-floor in our plant.

TABLE 3.1

THE SHOP-FLOOR STRIKE PATTERN, 1953–1973

	Average Recorded Strikes per Year	Ratio of Work-Group and Section Strikes/Strikes by Larger Groups
1953–6	2.75	1.2
1957–9	10.00	3.28
1960–65 [a]	10.17	2.81
1968–73	24.16	5.67

SOURCE: Union files.
NOTE: a.Data not available for 1966 and 1967.

Table 3.1 shows the strike pattern since 1953, divided into periods sharing common strike characteristics. Strikes have increased in frequency and, in periods when this has occurred most rapidly, many more stoppages have been accounted for by small sectional groups. Small strikes are now far more important than they were in 1953-6. An explanation of the changing frequency and level of strikes has to recognize that stoppages within the plant are part of the more general social processes within the workplace, for there is a complex interaction of issues and organization.

Before 1953 strikes were very rare in the plant, and to a large degree this is true of 1953-6. Wages were higher than the average for the area, and in addition the plant was defined as one section sharing a common piecework bonus. The result of this was that power was highly centralized within the JSSC; the incentive for smaller groups to undertake strike action was therefore relatively low and the ease with which they could do so was limited. However, there were strains within this apparently united and centralized pattern of organization and these led to a multiplication of sections in 1956. For some time, assembly stewards had sought their own piecework system but this had been rejected both by other stewards and by management. In 1956 two important changes occurred: a new model was introduced during a period of recession for the company and there was a change in top management. The new managers, keen to develop more direct incentives, agreed to a multiplication of sections but at the same time felt unable to pay substantially higher wages despite the new model. The result was that strikes increased, the assembly-shop increase being more than double that for the plant as a whole. Centralized control had been reduced with the multiplication of sections and had led to more strikes.

The trend to decentralization was partially reduced in 1960. The plant was taken over by a new company which replaced plant bargaining by a company-wide system of collective bargaining. The stewards and workers in our plant and in others belonging to the company were strongly opposed to this. A Combine Committee was formed, and concerted attempts to ensure plant influence over company negotiations ensued. As a result, the JSSC and the conveners once more became rather more central figures in the plant. Sectional action became rather less important and strikes increased only marginally over the level of the late fifties.

The introduction of a new model in 1965 — a period of healthy demand for the company — allied with a return to more decentralized bargaining led to a significant increase in strikes, particularly at section and work-group level. In order to meet demand, management agreed to high piecework prices, particularly for assembly workers who increased their bonus by an average of 40 per cent in a matter of months. Successful sectional bargaining by some groups led to greater disaffection among others who increasingly resorted to strike action. The ease and success of bargaining for some sections and the resultant fostering of sectional action by others meant that the extent to which the domestic organization was united and power centralized was lower than at any other period in the last two decades. The factionalization of the domestic organization and the reduced centralization of decisions led to more strikes by small groups.

The factors associated with the pattern of strikes in the plant are therefore many and complex. The impact of market forces and management initiatives is clear. But these do not inevitably lead to particular patterns of action by the domestic organization. However, with the partial exception of the early sixties, these external forces as well as factors within the domestic organization have led to a steady decline in its central control. The multiplication of sections has made the maintenance of unity more difficult and has led to a pattern of earnings which is seen as unjust, particularly by certain groups. These two elements have, in the recent period, reacted upon each other in such a way as to develop something like a vicious circle. Strikes are about the management of discontent, both in its organizational and substantive aspects; less unity has meant a higher level of sectional strike action.

Our historical account requires certain cautions to be attached. First, we are using records of strikes which are probably incomplete and unsatisfactory in the terms outlined in the previous chapter. Second, any historical analysis generally has to treat the dynamics of organization in a more superficial manner than would ideally be the case (a fuller account of the history of the plant is to be found in Appendix B of our previous volume). However, the remaining chapters of the book look at the nature of organization on the basis of detailed observation. But we can usefully consider here some aspects of the role of management in the strike pattern: these constitute the subject of the next section.

Management Organization and Bargaining Relationships

In the discussion of power and technology, the influence of management organization over workers was clear. Underlying the technical arguments concerning work-group power are assumptions that management goals are in some way obstructed by immediate disruptions to production. As a general statement this is likely to be valid. But power of this kind is exercised at particular times and in particular situations. Management may not want pro-

duction at a *particular* time. They may be seeking an excuse for interruptions to production, and to avoid or alleviate the costs
normally associated with such interruptions. Second, management
is not necessarily a single, united entity. Different managers have
differing sets of priorities and sanctions exerted by workers are
likely to have varying degrees of impact upon different managers.
We have, therefore, to specify which managers work groups have
power over and, in looking at the general impact of workers, we
have to understand the balance of power within management.

These themes have been discussed in some detail in our previous
volume. There we suggested that priorities varied among managers
so that, where stoppages appeared imminent, different managers
would have differing susceptibilities. Assuming they wanted and
were otherwise able to achieve production, production managers
would be likely to ignore budgetary constraints or 'formal'
agreements in order to ensure a continuation of output. Factory
accounting might demand that a strike be withstood because of the
financial implications of conceding workers' demands. Labour
managers might object to concessions because they were contrary
to agreements. In the main, therefore, production managers were
more ready to concede to worker pressure than other managers.
Furthermore, since they were such an important group within the
company (for they were central to company activity and coped with
frequent crises) they were often able to make concessions even in
the face of opposition from other managers. The power of
production managers was not, however, assured. Other managers
sought to impose controls upon them, while the balance of power
within management varied according to the problems confronting
the company. Where production was badly wanted, production
managers had more influence than when supplies, sales, or cash
problems were the dominant priorities. The identification of
priorities, and thereby the relative power of different managers,
constituted an important element of management politics.

The power of work groups varies with the manager towards
whom sanctions are directed, with that manager's immediate
priorities, and with the current balance of power within the
managerial political system. Furthermore, on occasion workers
may be able to form coalitions with certain managers against
others. We observed numerous cases of this on the shop-floor but
only rarely on the staff side. For example, on one occasion a
production manager made an agreement with a steward which got
round the intransigence of the work-study department. In another

case when a similar 'deal' was made, the manager concerned was reprimanded by the managing director when the matter came to his notice a few weeks later.

From the perspective of workers, a number of points follow in terms of the efficacy of strikes or threats of strikes. It is important that workers are aware of the best time to threaten sanctions and at whom they can most effectively direct particular types of sanctions. These, it may be noted in passing, need not merely involve disrupting production. They may also include highlighting professional misconduct and playing upon personal knowledge, links, or failures. Other forms of pressure relate to 'indiscretions': in another plant one steward claimed considerable success in negotiations after he had caught the manager in a compromising position with his secretary. Bluff may also be important.

The timing and direction of action are, of course, widely recognized in relation to other forms of conflict and competition — for example, in war and football. But the formulation of effective strategies involves some knowledge of 'the enemy' or 'competition', and in rapidly changing circumstances it demands up-to-date knowledge. In our plant the shop-floor steward network was important in this respect. The leader stewards, particularly the conveners and Q-E, had a wide range of management contacts and frequent 'informal chats' with managers. Hence they were able continually to up-date their theories of management politics and accordingly plan how, when, and to whom they would present demands and associated threats of sanctions.

Such pressures are part of strong bargaining relationships. These are based upon a degree of trust and mutual respect between manager and steward. But at the same time such relationships can only exist if there is recognition of the importance of power in industrial relations. In a strong bargaining relationship, steward and manager are able to assess the balance of power and impose pressures upon each other in subtle ways. In addition, trust permits deals to accommodate the demands of the other. As a consequence, leader stewards have a higher success rate and fewer strikes. They are able to identify issues through their range of contacts with other stewards and management and are more able to resolve these issues without resorting to member action.

The delicate forms of pressure and compromise which exist with strong bargaining relationships mean that if a group is powerful and is represented by a leader steward it may seldom need to strike. Consequently there is a very real difference between the ability and readiness to engage in effective strike action on the one hand and actually striking on the other. Furthermore, as a consequence of successfully imposing subtle pressures, powerful groups may have less to complain about (Sayles, 1958:34-5). On the other hand, of course, success may lead groups to increase their demands.

While strong bargaining relationships improve understanding of the balance of power, the 'learning' argument — that workers gradually develop an accurate assessment of their power and consequently reduce their strike rates (Sayles, 1958:35) — does not follow. We have suggested that workers' power depends upon their own social organization, the organization of management, and the present priorities of different managers, as well as the more general organization of work. Many of these factors may change and such change may be very rapid. In addition, there may be a turnover of personnel. Hence, not only is it often difficult for a group to assess its 'real' power, but explanations for past failure can be made in terms of poor timing, bad strategy, or treacherous behaviour on the part of other workers. The 'learning' argument also assumes that strike action is based on some form of economic rationality. This may not be so. In our plant we often observed workers taking strike action not because of financial considerations but because they believed that they had to demonstrate, if only briefly, their opposition to certain managerial actions. Opposition was often in terms of principles; for example, when a worker was suspended unfairly a section went out on strike. Moreover, to the extent that stoppages are often of a 'demonstration' nature they are meant less as the beginning of a power struggle and much more as an indication of serious concern on their part (Hyman, 1972:23-4; Turner *et al.*, 1967).

Another objection to the 'learning' view is that workers and managers seldom make use of all their power potential in strike situations. Strikes are typically a limited form of warfare. Exactly how much power they employ will depend upon the seriousness of the issue and their estimated chances of success. Such decisions may of course change during the course of a dispute. Generally speaking, for example, workers do not destroy machines or indulge in physical violence, and they frequently permit safety crews to remain at work. In one near-strike we observed, the seriousness with which the stewards viewed the issue was reflected in their refusal to permit any such safety crews to remain in the plant. Similarly, management's actions are limited: in a recent case where it appeared that a company employed 'strong-arm tactics' against strikers it was not only 'left-wing' workers who deplored their actions.

One reason for such restraint on the part of both sides is that a strike is only a temporary cessation of work. Damage to machinery could hurt workers when the strike was over. A high level of aggression during a strike can similarly sour bargaining relationships which are crucial for day-to-day industrial relations. We have heard of a number of cases where workers have later refused to have dealings with particular managers because of their behaviour during a strike. In other words, if the 'rules of the game' of striking are broken there is a danger that the other side will adopt a similar strategy both during the strike and afterwards (Batstone, 1974:89; Lane and Roberts, 1971:16; Hiller, 1969). On occasion, of course, one side or the other may aim to do precisely this in the hope that it will then be able to develop new rules which are more to its liking.

The final difficulty with the 'learning' argument is that a group's power may well change as a direct result of strike action. Power may increase or decrease through its use. For example, management may lose important customers because of a strike and hence become more concerned with maintaining a contented workforce. Through strike action, workers may experience not only substantive success in relation to a particular issue but also the 'excitement' of collective action. Defeat may destroy the ability of workers to act collectively or it may convince them of the need to present stronger challenges to management in the future. From a simplistic viewpoint it might be said that certain groups in our shop-floor organization 'never learn', for they continue to strike over the same issue even though they fail to meet with any success. In another case, a powerful group of the staff had continually challenged management. Reorganization of the plant provided management with the excuse to reduce the size of this group and split it into a number of sections. Thereby its power was reduced or made more difficult to mobilize.

In this section we have considered the nature of management and their consequent susceptibility to various pressures. The threat of a stoppage may be sufficiently effective for workers not to need to engage in strike action. However, there is a range of sanctions available to workers between the two extremes of threats in the process of negotiation and strike action.

Alternatives to Strike Action

In our plant, strike action often developed from situations in which other sanctions had been employed. More generally, overtime bans, refusals to undertake new work, and the application of limited effort, and, on occasions, collective sabotage were employed, in addition to more individualistic means such as absenteeism, 'skiving', and going home while still clocked in.

There appeared to be a pattern in the use of most collective forms of action (other than sabotage) particularly where there were leader stewards, although often it was difficult to identify when sanctions were being imposed. In some areas of the plant, for example many parts of the assembly shop, management were very dependent upon the co-operation of workers in order to continue production in the face of shortages of certain components. Not surprisingly, leader stewards often hinted that such co-operation would be less readily forthcoming if management refused to concede certain of their demands. On occasion they did refuse as much co-operation as they would normally give. Such action had a number of advantages from the stewards', and to a lesser degree the workers', perspectives. First, it meant that there were few costs involved on the part of workers. Second, such collective action sometimes involved the withdrawal of what has been termed 'utilitarian sabotage' (Taylor and Walton, 1971) which could be extremely effective as a form of pressure upon management. Third, since such co-operation was sometimes contrary to agreements, or custom and practice, the sanction imposed by its withdrawal would be defined as conformity with the rules. Fourth, since many aspects of this day-to-day co-operation were negotiated continually between stewards and foremen or other members of management, it was an easily available sanction. Fifth, the members were often unaware of the details of these negotiations and hence the stewards could more easily impose these sanctions on their own initiative, since they did not require an *active* compliance on the part of the membership.

The limitation or withdrawal of co-operation could be particularly effective in relation to more junior management, and therefore it tended to be used over issues negotiated with them which could not easily be raised at higher levels of the management hierarchy. Hence, common subjects were the make-up of bonus and also claims for small groups of men, which were valid in terms of 'natural justice' or 'decency' rather than public, 'formal' rules and agreements. Action of this kind tended to be limited to issues which were not seen to be of immediate importance or which were of insufficient significance for members to be prepared to undertake more costly forms of action.

Other forms of collective action also grew easily and naturally out of the work situation. These included the limitation of effort, particularly in piecework areas. Again, such action generally involved some form of collective organization and was typically initiated and managed either by stewards or opinion-leaders. Moreover, the limitation of effort imposed costs upon the workers themselves in the short-term because of loss of piecework earnings. This form of action was particularly common during new piecework negotiations and, indeed, was often an important element of these negotiations. In bargaining over what could and could not be done, and what was a reasonable level of effort, workers naturally wished to ensure that they did not make an agreement which committed them to high levels of effort for relatively little return. The 'stretching' of jobs, including carefully working the job as it was formally laid down and excluding any 'short cuts', was therefore seen as an important means both of 'proving' their arguments and of imposing pressure upon management through consequent blockages in the production process. One example of such behaviour has been discussed in some detail in our previous volume (Chapter 6); there we showed how the steward and a member of the Q-E controlled the behaviour of members of one section during a trial of a new piecework system.

Limitation of effort is, then, often a carefully managed form of collective action which has direct relevance to the issues over which it occurs. Its strengths are its limited form and the fact that it can be undertaken over relatively long periods. Strikes develop on occasion from the limitation of effort when the company ultimately fails to provide an acceptable offer.

Overtime bans are another form of action typically employed on issues of somewhat limited importance or as a means of imposing long-term pressure upon management in the process of negotiations. Nevertheless, on some sections a good deal of effort can be required in order to persuade some members to engage in an overtime ban, since overtime earnings may be an important element in total earnings. Unlike the other two forms of collective action just discussed, the overtime ban generally involves a clear statement of intent by the workers concerned to management, and can therefore be defined by the latter as duress. However, leader stewards, in particular, sometimes overcome this problem simply by operating an 'informal' ban. No statement of a collective sanction is made, but all workers happen to have prior engagements when management request overtime. As will be seen in Part II, this strategy was employed as a prelude to a planned strike over the annual negotiations. In this case it had a number of attractions: it limited the number of vehicles management could complete and remove from the establishment; by being selective it could prevent lay-offs of groups which might have occurred with a total overtime ban, and, finally, since the restriction of overtime was not formally declared to be a ban, the company could not claim that the workers were imposing duress, and use this as an excuse for failing to negotiate.

The final form of collective action which we can briefly consider is the refusal to undertake certain jobs. This may be due to a number of reasons. The job may itself be an issue of contention: we have discussed such a case earlier: the refusal of a machinist to stack work. Or a ban on new work may be a means of imposing pressure upon the company over other issues. So, for example, a group of indirect workers refused to handle any new work, as a means of encouraging management to provide them with a piecework system. Again, this refusal to do new work was a means of imposing long-term pressure upon management, since the workers concerned knew that it was quite impracticable for a piecework scheme to be introduced overnight. However, in both of these cases the effect of these limited forms of action was to hand the initiative to management, for they could decide how to treat this refusal to obey their instructions. Hence, management suspended the worker who refused to stack work and a member of the indirect group who refused to undertake new work. Their colleagues then had little choice but to take strike action, and later, to withdraw both sanctions.

There is, then, a considerable range of forms of collective action. In the main, and especially where there are leader stewards, they are used with some skill. In particular, these forms of action tend to be employed either over matters which are not so major that they appear to justify strike action or where their resolution will take some time, such as major piecework negotiations. The sanctions clearly are not used on perishable issues nor on what become defined as major matters of principle. However, if only because these long-term pressures fail or because management react in some way (for example, by suspending workers), it is not unusual for overtime bans, limitations of effort or co-operation, or refusals to undertake new work to lead to strike action. Over half of the strikes we observed were preceded by these more limited forms of collective action.

In this chapter we have considered the background conditions which facilitate strike mobilization. While the technology of the workplace may provide work groups with varying degrees of power, we have emphasized the way in which worker organization may independently facilitate strike mobilization and cut across managerially-defined work organization and technology. The actual pattern of work organization in part reflects past actions by workers as well as by management. In our plant the consequence was that on the shop-floor the institutions of the workplace fostered a collective perspective. This was far less true among the staff. Given this mobilization of bias on the shop-floor, the strike pattern was strongly influenced by the degree of unity and leadership within the domestic organization, although these in turn are influenced by the more general situation in the plant. One important aspect of leadership is that it frequently results in strong bargaining relationships with management. These relationships provide greater opportunities for reaching some accommodation between conflicting demands and for the subtle imposition of pressure.

Finally, we noted other forms of collective pressure which, again, tend to be used more skilfully by leader stewards. We have attempted to outline some of the conditions which facilitate strike mobilization and to indicate alternative means of imposing pressure upon management. Having outlined these considerations, we are in a position to look in detail at the mobilization process itself. We have tried to indicate that workers' power is in no sense automatic. Not only does it depend upon current events in the plant and within management, but also upon the social organization of workers. Individually, workers rarely have any significant power. This is equally true of the workers' leader, whether he be national official, shop steward, or opinion-leader. In order to exert power over management, workers or their leaders have to persuade other workers to withdraw their labour, or at least not to 'blackleg'. Power derives, therefore, from the combination of each individual worker disrupting his part of the work task and possibly others', under the aegis of collective organization. Without the ability to create and maintain such a collective identity the power of individual workers is extremely limited.

4
Vocabularies and Strikes

In the previous chapters we have stressed the organizational preconditions for strike action. The next three chapters look at the actual processes of strike mobilization in more detail. The present chapter concentrates upon the vocabularies employed in moving towards strike action. Throughout our discussion we have been at pains to emphasize that issues and problems do not occur automatically. Someone has to identify an event or a situation as a problem. In a strike situation, someone generally has to go further than this and declare that something is not merely a problem but also one which deserves some form of collective sanction.

Official statistics on the 'causes' of strikes are of limited value. First, official data collectors necessarily play a role in attributing reasons to strikes. But they are provided with an account of a strike by others. It would seem that such accounts are generally given by management. The latter are unlikely to demonstrate in their reports the full complexity of the issue in dispute even if they are aware of it. It is not management who undertakes the strike action. Workers are the ones who do this and it is quite likely that they have a different picture of the 'causes' of a strike.

Second, any uni-causal explanation of strikes will necessarily provide only a partial understanding. A dispute, for example, may be sparked off by disciplinary action on the part of management. But this may arise directly out of an issue concerning working arrangements or the systems of payment. The disciplinary action is merely part of the strategic game being played by both sides. This was a quite common situation in our plant. The general situation or context of strike action is important, and therefore strikes are invariably multi-causal.

To summarize, if we are interested in the reason for strikes as seen by workers, the attribution of issue-specific causes by an outsider is rather unsatisfactory. How workers interpret their situation is the relevant question. Moreover, suspensions or demands for wage increases do not always lead to strikes. What distinguishes the strike situation from apparently similar situations? In order to understand this, we have to look at the vocabularies employed in situations where strikes appear probable.

Vocabularies in Support of Strike Action

In moving towards a strike, workers have to create a rationale which justifies such a course of action (Hiller, 1969:esp. 49-65). Generally speaking, workers do not happily undertake strike action. They have to work out some definition of the situation which justifies such a step. Some workers are more ready to adopt collective sanctions than others. The reasons for strike action may vary between different groups of workers or different individuals. For example, in our plant reasons for supporting strikes against mobility have varied between different groups of workers. Those immediately involved in the proposed move have typically been concerned with lower earnings, strange work, and being 'buggered about'. Others have been worried because they believe those who are mobile achieve certain 'unfair' advantages, notably the avoidance of lay-offs, and sometimes higher earnings and more pleasant jobs. Others, notably stewards, have opposed mobility because it challenges a variety of shop and union rules. Still others have expressed concern at the way in which management have been able to use mobility as a strategy to reduce the unity of the domestic organization.

Rationales also vary more generally. While some workers object to the immediate situation, some stewards may be concerned with the institutional position of the domestic organization. Others see the situation as part of a larger structural conflict between 'capital' and 'labour' (e.g. Pope, 1942; Eldridge, 1968). Vocabularies may similarly change during the course of a dispute. For example, in the annual negotiations when management only offered a wage increase as part of a package deal involving MDW, the primary foci of discontent were the implications of the new pay system, and the 'cheek' of the company in attempting to attach 'strings' to what had become a legal norm of £1 plus 4 per cent. When management offered to re-open negotiations before the strike, there was still a good deal of support for its continuance. Some workers and stewards felt that they should still strike in order to 'show the company' and in order to maintain the strong collective identity and unity which had been built up. Some stewards were tempted to continue the strike because management had directly informed workers of the resumption of negotiations, thereby ignoring the right of the union to inform workers of such matters.

The rationales involved in strikes or near-strikes may, then, be complex and changing. In table 4.1 we have listed the reasons put forward by workers for action in the 24 near-strikes we observed on the shop-floor. The most dominant vocabularies attribute blame to management. They are seen to be breaking agreements, 'conning', or adopting a hard line. In addition, management are often seen as ignoring men's effort, goodwill, or intentions (cf. Hiller, 1969:50-53). Together, these reasons account for nearly 40 per cent of all the legitimations for strike action. They were put forward in every case of a strike or near-strike we observed. Such arguments were also common in the few staff disputes we observed. In one case, one of the leading members stated:

The company are using methods which were used before the war . . . We fought [in the war] to get the little Hitlers out of the way. Now the company's threatening us. I've worked twenty years for [the company] and I'm the most knowledgeable in my area, and the company treats me like this, it's disgusting.

Workers frequently argued that management not only adopt an aggressive approach but also actually break agreements. The exact interpretation of agreements, particularly custom and practice, is often complex. The following example illustrates this point. One week, a section's bonus fell dramatically. Before this, an informal agreement had been made between a manager and the section that if they attempted to maintain a certain level of output they would be guaranteed a relatively high bonus level. The fall in bonus occurred when management ceased to operate by this informal agreement. The section were very near to strike action, arguing that management had broken the agreement. Management argued that a let-out clause had been included in the informal agreement, a point which the workers denied, pointing to the statement of a particular manager in support of this view.

Such disputes do not, however, only occur over custom and practice or unwritten agreements. They appear to be equally

TABLE 4.1

WORKERS' REASONS FOR STRIKE OR NEAR-STRIKE ACTION

	Number	%
Management breaking agreements, 'conning', adopting hard line	30	27
Fairness, comparisons with other work groups	18	16
Mobility, manning, job description	14	12
Management ignore men's efforts, goodwill, and intentions	14	12
Loss of money, security	10	9
Shop, section, group rules and decisions	5	4
Safety, conditions	4	4
Technical problems in work	4	4
To increase earnings	4	4
Other reasons	4	4
Reasons relating to national strike	5	4
Total	112	100

SOURCE: Observation: 24 shop-floor cases.

common over more formal agreements and their interpretation. For example, a group of workers had some time previously experienced redundancies. Some of their number had been given other jobs in the plant, but an assurance, in the presence of a full-time official, had been given that these men would have the opportunity to return to the group when (suitable?) vacancies arose. They now learnt that a new man was to be employed; they objected that this was contrary to the agreement. Management replied that the man had specialist skills and hence the agreement did not apply. The workers retorted that they had been performing this specialist work for years, and that if the new worker's sole skill was in this area then another agreement relating to mobility between tasks would be broken. The men threatened strike action, but were persuaded against it by a convener in the interests of workers laid off who would lose lay-off pay if there was a strike.

Vocabularies relating to management breaking agreements and adopting a 'hard line' are often associated with some idea of fairness, this being typically based upon comparisons with other, broadly similar groups and ideas relating to the reward-deprivation balance (Hiller, 1969; 50-53). This is the second most common type of vocabulary. Hence, in the case of the staff dispute mentioned earlier unfairness was seen to exist at an individual level, so that one member complained:

The company are pushing us to do more and more work . . . and now we have to do a third of [*X*'s] job. I resent this because I'm [on a low grade] and they're on [a much higher grade]. Also [a departmental member] has got promotion by transfer to another department and he's now on [a higher grade], and he's less efficient than me.

The idea of fairness is also often important in the disputes of lower-paid groups, not only in relation to wage increases but also in relation to receiving mobile workers from higher-paid sections who, while doing the same work as the low-paid, receive the wages of their previous section. Mobility, in fact, is not only an important issue in itself but also leads to grievances relating to fairness more generally. Hence, one of the major reasons for opposition by assembly to receiving mobile workers is that in the past, when assembly has been laid off, these workers have returned to work on their own sections. As one steward stated:

We will only take this labour if it is permanent; that is the rule within the shop. It's not fair that these blokes should come in when they run out of work through working weekend overtime and, to keep their bonus up, their sections just send them down here. They send down all the rubbish — last time half of them were half-dead. But then, when we get laid off, they're allowed to go back to [their own shop]. We should be allowed to choose who goes back.

More immediately instrumental reasons are relatively unimportant within the context of all the reasons put forward. Moreover, security of earnings and loss of money appear twice as often as the desire to increase earnings.

One other type of reason deserves some brief mention. Included among 'other reasons' are a number of references to the general attractions of getting out of the workplace. Some commentators have suggested that this is an important factor in strikes. Workers simply want to express the frustration they experience in work and escape from it for a while. Our observation suggests that this is rarely a dominant factor. However, it does sometimes figure as an additional reason for strike action. For example, in talking about a possible strike several workers agreed that it would be a case of 'hands up and all out in the sun'.

At first sight, such reasons appear trivial, but in our view this is wrong. One major deprivation in work is being confined in a noisy, sweaty workplace. Many of the workers we talked to were very aware of this and said that if it were not for their domestic commitments they would leave the plant and find open-air jobs, at least in the summer. Hence, when the weather is fine, this deprivation is likely to increase. Given other arguments in support of a temporary cessation of work, this might well be 'the final straw' for a few workers. However, its importance should not be exaggerated. We can find no relationship between strike frequency and the temperature or hours of sunshine.

We have so far considered individual reasons for strike action. But our argument has also been that the multi-causal nature of strikes has to be taken into account. For the statistically-minded, we found that an average of five types of reason existed for each strike or near-strike we observed. Again, two examples illustrate the variety of considerations underlying strike action.

In a dispute over mobility, the workers directly involved objected to being shifted to new jobs. They did not like the work involved, and felt that their colleagues were letting them down. In addition, since the move was an alternative to being laid off, they would receive the earnings of the section they were sent to. This would involve a drop in earnings. The members of the section which was to take these men similarly felt aggrieved. The mobile workers had in the past returned to their previous jobs if work on their new section ran short. Often the mobile workers received the earnings of their permanent section which might well be higher even though they were doing the same work as those in the new section. Mobile workers, therefore, were often not welcome, and in this instance it was also argued that the section short of work were sending men who were sick or infirm (see the example above). In other words, they would increase the effort required of those normally on the new section. Members of the section which was short of work were aware of these grievances on the part of the receiving section and their own mobile members. In addition, they themselves began to feel that it was wrong for their fellows to be 'shoved around'. Such views were largely fostered by the stewards. The latter also emphasized that management were artificially creating the shortage of work in an attempt to develop ill-feeling among workers and so break plant unity. In addition, stewards argued that management were breaking agreements in the way they set about moving these workers.

A similarly complex situation existed in the case of the proposed employment of a new man discussed above. The men put forward the following reasons for strike action: long-term insecurity associated with rationalization; management breaking an agreement; the workers' own skills which management were ignoring; the risk of management preventing traditional job flexibility; the lack of consultation over management's proposals and management's more general failure to discuss matters with the men. This apparently simple dispute over the employment of one man therefore embodied a host of problems concerning past events and fears for the future.

These examples, which are fairly typical, show the variety of vocabularies and rationales involved in strike action. An apparently similar case has been put forward by many writers. They argue that strikes are due to a build-up of minor frustrations. We would agree with this view in so far as it means that any single reason in isolation may not lead to strike action. For example, falls in earnings do not consistently lead to strikes: 19 per cent of the piecework sections which have experienced no quarterly fall in bonus of the last two years have gone on strike, but none of those experiencing falls totalling a third or more of average bonus have done so. But at the same time we would disagree with this 'cumulative frustration' thesis because it ignores the crucial process of building the various frustrations into a coherent system of explanation. Previous events have to be reinterpreted to demonstrate 'bad faith' on the part of management. During the movement towards strike action, particularly if this occurs over a number of days, this process of interpreting past events is often clear. Things which at the time were considered merely coincidental now become a defined as part of a larger strategy on the part of management. Such reinterpretations might include mobility, apparently technical problems, and so on.

One of the crucial factors in the working out of these vocabularies of motive is the attribution of blame to management. The process of interpreting events more generally is important to this. The great majority of the strikes or near-strikes we observed would normally be described as 'wildcats'. But, when we look more closely at the issues, we find that workers have been blaming management for many of the underlying causes for some time. In 54 per cent of the 24 strikes or near-strikes we observed on the shop-floor the underlying issues have been a continual source of discontent for several months. Furthermore, in half of the 24 strikes or near-strikes the groups concerned had taken strike action over exactly the same issue in the past.

One case which demonstrates both these characteristics is the question of mobility. It has long been a source of contention in the plant, and has become especially prominent in the last few years. In part, this has been because of more frequent disruptions to production requiring the reallocation of labour or lay-offs. But in addition, and more importantly, two years previously a new lay-off pay agreement was signed which provided for lay-off pay at the rate of 80 per cent of average earnings if disruption to production were not due to disputes within the plant. As a consequence, management have become far more keen to shift labour to different jobs rather than pay them £40 per week for sitting at home. Further, in periods of lay-off management's concern about strikes tends to be rather different from other occasions and they have sometimes attempted to refuse to pay men during lay-offs, arguing that disputes within the plant have interfered with production. The unions have often argued that these disputes do not exist, or that they have had little, if any, effect upon production.

At the centre of these arguments over mobility, and disputes or near-disputes deriving from them, there has often been a disagreement over the meaning of the lay-off agreement. This problem of interpretation has been the subject of debate between the conveners and management, and the domestic organization has on several occasions sought guidance on interpretation from the national officials who made the agreement. This disagreement partly reflects what might be termed the beginnings of the 'career' of a formal agreement, particularly one of such importance, having major implications for other practices within the plant.

This 'career' of a formal agreement involves two features. The first is a process in which the agreement acquires general legitimacy. Hence, many stewards and workers were highly ambivalent about the lay-off agreement, so that it was often referred to as 'the blackmail charter' (in another plant, a similar agreement is commonly known as the 'blackleg's charter'). Second, and underlying this first point, the formal agreement in itself requires interpretation within an already existing network of rules and norms. This involves, among other things, assessing its relative priority over other rules, particularly custom and practice, and developing some consensus upon what the various clauses within the agreement mean. We found arguments that, for example, the interpretation of a particular clause by management was contrary to 'the spirit and intention' of the agreement.

The signing of a formal agreement is only a starting-point: case law has to be developed, and this occurs through debates and disputes, which serve ultimately both to develop a consensus upon the interpretation of specific clauses, and a network of informal agreements and custom and practice which make the agreement meaningful in particular contexts. This process was as yet incomplete, as far as the lay-off pay agreement was concerned. In the interim, disputes had occurred over it and related issues; and, moreover, from stewards' and workers' viewpoints these were often attributable to management 'try-ons'. In this way, then, we can again see the intermeshing of issues in the career of an agreement. We would expect that in the longer term such disputes would decline over this particular question; indeed it would appear that, since our fieldwork was completed, a greater consensus over how this agreement is to be acted out has developed.

Such consensus does not develop simply through debate. Also important is the utilization of power, which involves the mobilization of resources and is an organizational process. While we were in the plant certain shops developed policies on lay-off pay and mobility for the first time, and were ready to impose sanctions in an attempt to carry them out. This was part of a more general process which involved developing a plant-wide consensus upon certain problems relating to the agreement; several months after the completion of our fieldwork, therefore, two plant-wide strikes occurred over these questions, whereas before they had led to significant splits within the domestic organization. The issue had been reinterpreted, and recipes of action had been developed. This had occurred through the workings of the organization, and a crucial factor in this more integrated approach to the problem had been the need to maintain unity in the face of management's attempt to change the payment system.

In this section we have been concerned with the variety of rationales and vocabularies employed in support of strike action and have emphasized the way in which conflicts may focus around reaching a common interpretation of a new agreement. However, vocabularies are not merely employed in support of strike action. They are also used against such sanctions. In the next section we turn to a consideration of such rationales.

Vocabularies in Opposition to Strike Action

Strikes are generally seen as a means of achieving a more or less clearly specified goal. In this respect they form one of a range of strategies. However, one or two stoppages which we observed were not of this kind. That is to say, workers did not cease to work as a conscious means of imposing pressure upon management. Rather, the stoppage of work occurred as a direct result of workers being involved in arguing with management over a particular issue. For example, in one case a group of men claimed that a particular job was unsafe. They demanded that management either made the job safe or guarantee them full compensation in the event of injury. Management explained that they could not immediately make the job totally safe but they would do their best to rectify the situation as soon as possible. In the meantime they could not give rock-hard guarantees, but they requested that the men should, with due caution, continue to work rather than cause a stoppage. While the workers were arguing with several members of management who had by now gathered around them, and while they were explaining that they did not want to stop the track, they did in fact do so. They were so busy arguing over the work that they stopped production. This stoppage might be seen less as a strike than 'a pause for discussion' (Turner *et al.*, 1967:53). In this case, the stoppage was not a strategy.

In many strike situations the stoppage is seen as a sanction upon management. It is a means of reinforcing the rejection of a situation rather than the act of rejection itself (Lane and Roberts, 1971:16). Consequently, one can look at two types of vocabulary in opposition to strike action. The first concerns the legitimacy of the workers' demands, and the second the selection of the strike as a means of pursuing those demands. In the near-strikes we observed, only about one-fifth of all arguments were of the former kind (Table 4.2). In part this is because on most sections workers themselves, opinion-leaders, and/or stewards (especially the Q-E and conveners) would squash issues which were clearly 'non-runners'. But also, when the majority of workers are ready to undertake strike action, anyone arguing that their case is weak is unlikely to be able to dissuade them from strike action. Where others do oppose the strikers' case they generally back their arguments up by reference to policies and rules made by such bodies as the mass meeting or JSSC, or by reference to union principles. These criticisms were put forward mainly by stewards, particularly conveners and the Q-E.

Workers' own hesitations over strike action were mainly in terms of the general norms against strikes. More generally, there appeared to be a hesitancy over striking, particularly when small groups were involved. They were often reluctant to put them-

TABLE 4.2

REASONS FOR NOT UNDERTAKING STRIKE ACTION

	%	
General norms against strikes:		
Not make themselves focus of attention	5	
Be reasonable, show goodwill	5	10
Availability of alternatives:		
Use procedure	11	
Possible compromises	4	
Q-E/conveners negotiate, 'fix' things	20	35
Problems in strike action:		
Management 'setting men up'	5	
Timing of strike, efficacy	7	
Lead to hardship for other workers	13	
Endanger unity and collective strength	11	36
Criticisms of case:		
Problem is workers' own fault	2	
Workers' demands contrary to union principles	9	
Workers' demands against democratically made		
policies/rules	8	19
	Total	100%
	No. of reasons	76

SOURCE: Observation: 24 shop-floor cases.

selves in a focal position in which they alone would be confronting management. Moreover, some workers were concerned that they should show 'reasonable' and 'responsible' attitudes and not take strike action. Such views were particularly common among the staff. Many of the clerical workers associated strike action with an aggressive instrumentalism seen as 'typical' of the shop-floor. They could not see the responsibilities of their roles as clerical workers as consistent with such strategies.

Few workers specifically referred to the costs of strike action in terms of lost wages. This largely reflected the short-term nature of the strikes or near-strikes we observed. However, the plant-wide near-strike resulting from the annual negotiations is not included in the table. This would have been a much longer strike, and we did find some workers expressing hesitancies in this case because of the financial hardships involved. These, however, often focused upon the approaching holidays rather than day-to-day hardship.

Of greater importance in the majority of strikes or near-strikes were objections relating to alternative means of achieving goals and the problems involved in undertaking strikes. Such arguments largely reflected the nature of the strikes or near-strikes we observed. As we show more fully in the next chapter, strike proposals of a particular kind were generally put forward by workers themselves or populist stewards. Objections to strike action tended to come from leaders, and particularly from the Q-E and conveners. On occasion they would be supported by the full-time officials.

The major alternative proposed by conveners and Q-E members is that they themselves will take the matter up and sort things out. Such proposals, where necessary, might be preceded by the suggestion that the steward concerned should himself take procedure as far as he could by himself. The conveners and Q-E, however, might well promise to use all the means at their disposal to overcome the problem. Essentially, this involved the use of their full range of contacts and the exploitation of their strong bargaining relationships. Hence, they might well have an 'informal chat' with a higher member of management if they believed that one of his subordinates was being obstructive. Moreover, the fact that the workers concerned were seriously contemplating strike action might well be an important lever which the conveners or Q-E could employ to persuade managers to reach a suitable agreement. Such pressures strategically employed by the conveners and Q-E were not always successful. In such situations they might return to the members, stress the impossibility of achieving their full demands and seek a practical compromise or 'more room for manoeuvre'.

The other main type of objection to strikes, again primarily from conveners and Q-E, concerned the problems of the strike itself. These were basically of two, often related, kinds. The first was that strike action would fail to achieve the ends sought by the workers. One such reason often concerned the timing of the strike (Hiller, 1969:125-32). For example, in one case a Q-E member emphasized that a strike would be futile before the men knew whether or not management would actually refuse a higher level of manning on a job. This had happened before, but the Q-E member argued that they would have to wait and see. In another case, a convener stressed that strike action at that time would be futile because of a high level of stocks.

The strikes or near-strikes we observed typically involved small numbers of men but frequently led to the lay-off of many other workers. The conveners and Q-E were particularly aware of these wider implications of small disputes. At times, notably when demand was low or there were shortages of supplies, the conveners and Q-E suspected that management were purposely 'setting the men up'. Accordingly, they would advise against strike action.

The second reason for criticizing resort to strike action concerned the implications of small, sectional disputes for other groups of workers and for the domestic organization. As we have said, small strikes could often lead to the lay-off of hundreds, if not thousands, of workers. In addition, if workers were already laid off, then strike action could lead to them losing lay-off pay. Moreover, a one-day strike would lead to the loss of lay-off pay not for one day but for the full pay-week. The conveners and Q-E were particularly concerned with these hardships which could result from sectional action.

These effects of strike action upon other groups of workers could also foster divisions within the union organization between those laid off and those who were ostensibly the cause of the lay-off. Such frictions could also occur for other reasons, for example, between those sending and receiving mobile workers. In an attempt to overcome these problems, plant-wide policies might be developed. On occasion, mass meetings might decide the reverse of the policy proposed by the JSSC. Nevertheless, such decisions were reached democratically and therefore had to be carried out. The conveners stressed the importance of such rules to potential transgressors. In addition, they emphasized the divisions within the organization which could result from such breaches and the possibility of retaliatory action by those who suffered from such action.

For much of our period of observation, however, the dominant theme for members of the shop-floor organization was the need to oppose management's offer in the annual negotiations which included a new payment system as a condition of any wage increase. Basic to successful opposition was the creation and maintenance of an organization-wide unity and strength. Sectional action could endanger unity and reduce strength: it therefore had to be avoided, even when strike action would generally have been considered both legitimate and effective (see Part II).

An example of Q-E and convener opposition to proposed or actual strike action may usefully be given, and we shall consider a case which has already been discussed in terms of the workers' reasons for strike action. It concerned the employment of a new man contrary, in the men's view, to an agreement made during a previous redundancy. A convener knew that there was a possibility of strike action by the department. On two consecutive days he held meetings of the workers concerned and after several hours of discussion was able to persuade them to withdraw their threatened action. The convener was particularly concerned with the loss of lay-off pay for several hundred men which would result from the strike. However, he made little mention of this, and instead concentrated on the workers' case.

The convener argued the following: they should be careful not to victimize the new man for it was a union principle not to let individuals suffer; they could not stop the man being employed now: he had been 'on the books' for several days, he had worked his notice at his previous job, and they had already accepted him. Some men argued they should insist on the union being consulted before new men were laid on. The convener pointed out that there was no such agreement in other departments and that management did not have to consult; he argued that a one-day stoppage (all that they were proposing) was no good. While he sympathized with them, if they were going to go out they should go out for good. What difference would a day make to management?

The convener's role was somewhat limited in the meetings. Every so often he made a point or answered a question, but primarily it was the shop discussing the issue, and the convener stressed that it was up to them to make their decision. When he opposed those demanding a one-day strike, they told him that he should not speak, and certainly not try to persuade people since he was not a member of the shop. He argued strongly against this: he was a duly elected convener representing the full-time official; he was giving them the facts; he merely wanted to correct statements which had been made. The other tactics he used included pointing out to the chairman (the steward) who should speak next, cutting into people's statements, stepping back out of the 'ring' of men after he had spoken, raising his voice, and 'the procedure game'. For example, one man put a resolution that they should have a one-day strike, another that they should have a sit-down. The convener told the chairman that he could not take both resolutions, since they were the same: both involved a stoppage of work.

In this section we have considered the vocabularies employed in opposition to strike action. We have seen that these also tend to be multi-faceted and that they primarily relate to the nature of the larger situation, in terms of other workers and the larger organization. Such arguments are put forward primarily by the conveners and Q-E. This is not, of course, to suggest that more individualistic considerations against strike action do not exist. Of course they do. But we have been concerned with near-strike situations. Such situations do not arise if there is widespread opposition to such action on the part of workers. Consequently, we see that where action is likely to occur it is the conveners and Q-E who play a major role in restraining strike action. Moreover, the vocabularies they employ stress the nature of collective organization and interest.

The Use of Collectivist and Individualistic Vocabularies

In the previous two sections we have looked at the types of vocabulary used in support of and in opposition to proposed strike action. We have seen that the rationales for and against strikes can vary a good deal, and in particular that reference to collective ideals and trade union principles is not necessarily in support of strike action. In this section we consider more fully the use of collective as distinct from individualistic rationales.

We can broadly distinguish two types of rationality in strike situations. The first is directed towards the interests of workers as individuals. The second is directed towards the interests of workers as a collectivity. The former may employ collective means but towards goals of an essentially individualistic nature; the latter involves both means and goals which stress the group identity.

Collective rationality typically involves a degree of collective consciousness. Indicators of this are the lack of reference to purely individual interests, the placing of a high value upon unity and the importance of collective interests, and a widening of opposition to management beyond the specific issue in dispute. When we look for such collective consciousness in our 25 strikes or near-strikes, we find that references of this kind dominate strike vocabularies in only seven cases. (The arguments in support of strike action also tend to be somewhat different. Management 'misdemeanours' and the protection of workers account for 71 per cent of reasons for strikes where there is a significant degree of collective consciousness, compared with only 34 per cent in other near-strikes.) Table 4.3 suggests that a relatively high level of collective consciousness tends to be associated with particular levels of strike action. Hence, in none of the disputes at work-group level was there a great expression of collective consciousness. Rather the individually defined interests of the workers were similar. In such strikes or near-strikes the workers often appeared to feel very isolated, and statements such as 'We don't want to stop the track' or 'What else can we do?' were common. The majority of section-level disputes were of a similar kind. Those where a significant level of collective consciousness existed tended to be on large sections of a hundred or more workers. In one of these cases, however, the expressions of collective consciousness on the part of the strikers or near-strikers were directed almost as much against the rest of the domestic organization as against management. Collective consciousness appeared to be important not only in many strikes or near-strikes by larger sections but also in all of those which occurred above section level. Such a rationale or vocabulary is often a precondition of strike action by a large number of workers (Hiller, 1969:49–54). This is probably because from individualistic perspectives workers would be unlikely to identify sufficiently with each other. The various conflicts of interest between groups, past 'failures' on the part of others, and more general self-interest tend to defeat even a temporary coalition. The development of a collective consciousness helps to overcome this problem. In Part II of this book we look in detail at the 'educational' process involved in the mobilization of collective consciousness. Its importance can, however, be seen in the history of disputes concerning mobility which, we have noted, had led to a good deal of conflict among sections and departments. The continuation of small, sectional reactions to the question of mobility fostered an *ad hoc* disunited approach to the problem. Attempts by the JSSC to get the mass to strike over the question failed on several occasions because other groups of workers were unwilling to lose wages for the sake of the particular group which was at that time confronting difficulties

TABLE 4.3

COLLECTIVE CONSCIOUSNESS IN SUPPORT OF STRIKE ACTION

Level of strike or near-strike	Collective consciousness significant:		
	yes	no	total
Work group	–	6	6
Section	3	12	15
Above section	4	–	4
Total	7	18	25

SOURCE: Observation.

over mobility. However, after success in the near-strike over the annual negotiations, a high level of collective consciousness and unity continued. It was then that a JSSC recommendation for a plant-wide policy on mobility, and strike action in support of it, was carried by the mass meeting.

Another factor in the association between larger strikes and collective consciousness is the role which leaders, particularly the conveners and Q-E, play in such disputes. For leader stewards make most use of the vocabulary of union principles, and are able to mould and shape workers' perspectives. But such leaders do not merely employ references to collective interests to foster strike action. They are an important means by which they dissuade groups from taking collective action. In such situations, there is not the same 'excitement' and sense of elation as has been noted in situations where collective consciousness supports strike action (e.g. Mann, 1973:50). The emphasis is upon maintaining strong organization and protecting others.

However, there is a further interesting relationship between individual and collective vocabularies of strike action. This relates to the timing of the strikes or near-strikes we observed. We were doing systematic observation in the plant for approximately seventy-five days, but a third of the strikes or near-strikes we observed occurred in only three days. These strikes or near-strikes were on a variety of issues and cannot be seen as directly interrelated in terms of the issues in dispute. What does suggest a link between these strikes or near-strikes is that these three days immediately preceded or followed days on which mass meetings in relation to the annual negotiations were held. In other words, they occurred when collective consciousness was at its height in relation to the company offer. As a consequence, members were far more aware of the 'cons' which management might try. In other words, they were far more conflict-oriented and bargaining-aware. As a result, in some departments there were stoppages for the first time in several months. Moreover, the stoppages tended to be over issues which were quite common but had rarely, if ever, been the subject of strike action in the past.

At the same time, leader stewards were afraid that any sectional strike action could endanger the organization's unity and strength. The more general collective consciousness of workers could be used to prevent sectional disputes with relative ease. In this way, the more general consciousness was the cause of near-strikes by making workers more bargaining-aware, but at the same time prevented the strikes actually occurring or lasting for any length of time because workers were aware of more important and wider-ranging goals and concerns. The relationship between individualistic and collective vocabularies is therefore complex. But it is precisely because of this that leaders are often able to 'manage discontent' (Wright Mills, 1948). In the next chapter we look at the role that leader stewards and others play in the mobilization and 'demobilization' of strike action.

5
Strike Initiatives and Checks

The previous chapter has looked at the range of vocabularies employed in the negotiation of strike action. In this chapter we look at another aspect of this mobilization process, namely who initiates strike proposals and who supports or opposes such moves. This aspect raises questions concerning the networks of influence which various members of the union, both inside and outside the plant, can employ.

The first section looks at the role which different types of person play in the initiation of strike proposals. By initiation we mean the first proposal to employ the sanction of a stoppage of work in support of a demand. In particular, we discuss the role played by various types of member distinguished in our first volume — the griever, the opinion-leader, stewards, both populists and leaders, and the Q-E and conveners. The second section deals with the nature of coalitions which developed around the various strike initiatives and how these affected whether the strike occurred.

Strike Initiatives

At the most general level, we can say that any member of the domestic organization may initiate a work stoppage. He may identify and point out to his workmates a particular problem which is immediately viewed as sufficiently weighty to justify a stoppage. But, in fact, of the 25 stoppages or near-stoppages (including that relating to the annual negotiations) we can identify only one such case. This stoppage occurred at the level of a small work group and related to a safety problem which in the past had both caused injuries and been the subject of strike action. The member who was working on the relevant job — he was neither a griever nor an opinion-leader — pointed the problem out to his colleagues and to the steward; the latter agreed that they should stop work until the machinery had been made safe.

Such a strike initiative on the part of the ordinary member is unusual because he typically lacks the resources to mobilize other workers and because there are other actors who are more reward-deprivation (or bargaining) aware. At the level of the work group, three types of actor are more likely to initiate disputes than the ordinary member. The first of these is the griever.

The Griever

The griever is a person who is particularly reward-deprivation aware. His greater role in strike action is due to his greater readiness than other workers to identify and act upon grievances. Such action may take a number of forms: he may inform the steward or foreman; he may attempt to persuade his fellows that they should not permit the grievance to continue; or he may take some form of independent action, leading to his own suspension, which in turn leads to strike action by his fellows.

The griever is viewed with a certain amount of suspicion by his workmates, largely because 'he's always moaning'. Hence, his grievances rarely lead to strikes, simply because his mates are unlikely to find his grievances legitimate. Moreover, it is not uncommon for his grievances to be directed against other section members. For example, one stoppage of work occurred not in support of a griever's complaint but in opposition to it. This occurred when the griever objected to the method of working agreed upon by the rest of the work group. The latter, the steward, and many surrounding section members all opposed the griever. However, while a small proportion of the griever's grievances may lead to strike action or stoppages, those initiated by a griever are relatively important as a proportion of all stoppages. Of the six work-group stoppages we observed, half were initiated by a griever, as was also one of the thirteen section-level stoppages, so that of our twenty-five stoppages or near-stoppages one-fifth were initiated by grievers. It should be noted, however, that grievers are *not* leftist agitators; indeed, the grievers we met could best be described as either non-political or more right-wing than the majority of workers.

Our first example of griever-initiated strikes relates to a dispute over whether a particular task was part of a section's work. In this case, a section member with a particular job had been undertaking this task without complaint. Indeed, over a period of months, two or three members had been on this job and undertaken the task in question. However, one day a griever — a man recognized by his fellow section members, his steward, and foreman as a man who frequently complained about things — was put on the job and refused to undertake this task. The foreman instructed him to do it, but he still refused, arguing that it was not part of the job. He was suspended and sought the support of his fellows. The section met and agreed to stop work until he was reinstated. They agreed that the task was not strictly part of the job, hence the griever's refusal to undertake it was perfectly legitimate and accordingly the suspension illegitimate.

This example demonstrates a number of points about griever-initiated strikes. First, the man does not have a very high status within the group — he does not typically create strikes by the mobilization of resources which are peculiar to him. Indeed, the strike occurred less because of his legitimate (in the eyes of his fellows) grievance, than because management acted in a manner which was seen to be unjust. Second, the greater deprivation awareness of the griever is clear — several other workers had recently done the same job but had not refused to undertake the task nor had they even complained about it to supervision or the steward. The griever served to highlight this question through his own and the consequent managerial actions; the section as a whole were loath to stop work — as is indicated by their finally voting unanimously for the griever to return to work under protest — but felt that they could not permit the suspension of a section member whose actions were both legitimate and in the interests of the section as a whole.

Another griever-led stoppage we observed was of a rather different kind. In this case the griever created the stoppage by persuading his fellow workers that the job was unsafe and could lead to serious injury. The foreman admitted this, but asked that the men should continue to work until it was possible to rectify the hazard. The griever initiated opposition to this proposal — emphasizing to his fellows, the foreman, and the steward the full safety implications, and demanding from management a guarantee of full compensation in the event of an accident. The other members of the work group were not keen to stop work, but the determination of the griever found support from the steward who agreed that there was a safety problem, and did not rule out the possibility of a stoppage; he told the griever, and later the work group, that 'It's up to you what you do.' Indeed, the stoppage occurred almost accidentally, as the steward negotiated with a manager, and the work group, led by the griever, argued with the foreman.

Again in this case, the griever highlighted a problem and his mobilization of his fellows occurred because he was ready to take a stand, whether they did or not. He stressed the possibilities of accidents and the resultant drop in earnings, and gained the partial support of the steward. This same safety hazard also affected another group of workers to the same degree; it is of interest that there was no griever in this work group and they did not even complain about the safety hazard. Indeed, it was the steward who pointed out that the same problem applied to this group and demanded that the foreman 'see to it', without any complaint at all coming from this group.

On occasion then, the griever initiates a stoppage of work, primarily by means of articulating a commonly felt grievance (see Paterson and Willett's discussion of 'exemplars' (1951)). By the mere act of articulating it and being ready to act upon it, he can draw other workers into a stoppage of work — either because of managerial reaction or because he is able to find support among other workers or from his steward.

The Opinion-Leader

The griever mobilizes resources only in the way that any other member can do so, by persuasion. Indeed, grievers often have more difficulty in this than would other workers simply because they have a reputation of 'always moaning' and hence are treated with a good deal of caution by other workers. This is not a problem which another type of section member — the opinion-leader — has. By definition, he holds a more general sway among at least certain of his fellows, and hence has resources which he is able to mobilize. These two categories of the griever and the opinion-leader are not totally exclusive: a few opinion-leaders tend to have a high grievance rate but the way in which they 'grieve' tends to be rather different. In the first place, their grievances are seldom solely or primarily oriented to their own situation. They typically grieve on behalf of groups or coalitions; they therefore do not have the same reputation as moaners. Second, their articulation of grievances tends to be directed more frequently towards the steward or the section as a whole. In this sense also, then, the opinion-leader is more collectively — rather than individually — oriented.

The standing of an opinion-leader rests upon his collective orientation and the resources with which his ability and consequent network provide him. In this role, his colleagues often see his task to be bargaining-aware and to articulate grievances on their behalf. So, for example, in the case cited above where a stoppage occurred against a griever, this was led and handled by an opinion-leader. This type of worker is the second type within the section who has a greater tendency than the ordinary worker to initiate stoppages. Effectively, and generally below the level of the section as a whole, he acts as an informal shop steward. Such opinion-leaders are crucial in determining whether a steward is actually able to lead his members. In the case of some smaller sections, particularly, it is often not the steward but an opinion-leader who has this ability to lead and control his fellows.

Of the stoppages of work at work-group level, we have already seen that half are initiated by grievers. The remaining three were initiated by opinion-leaders. In addition, seven of the thirteen section-level stoppages were initiated by opinion-leaders. It will be remembered that grievers caused only one section-level dispute. The contrasting spheres of influence of grievers and opinion-leaders can be seen in the level at which disputes initiated by each of them tend to occur. The ratio of work-group to section-level disputes initiated by grievers is 3:1, while for opinion-leaders it is 3:7. In other words, the latter tend to have a wider system or network of influence than the griever; it is also one which is more permanent and reliable and less issue-specific. For some members, at least, an issue is more likely to be seen as legitimate *because* it is identified and raised by an opinion-leader (cf. Paterson and Willett, 1951; Karsh, 1958; Kapferer, 1972). This is, of course, even more true of leader stewards. This resource — the ability to mobilize, in turn based upon a certain degree of dependence and deference — rests ultimately upon the reputation of the opinion-leader and the stable pattern of his network.

An example of stoppage initiated by an opinion-leader occurred when a foreman requested that the men concerned work individually on a job whereas it was custom and practice for the men to undertake the task in pairs (largely because of the lifting that was involved). A dozen men were involved altogether in this question, and the foreman addressed all the men concerned in the job, but the reaction came from the opinion-leader. Whereas several of the men were, initially at least, ready to comply with the foreman's instructions, the opinion-leader refused, arguing that this was contrary to custom and practice. It was his lead that the members followed. Indeed, during our period of observation, there were about half a dozen problems with this particular work group, some relating to problems between the work group and supervision, and two among the men themselves (in both cases these were when new men were brought into the work group). In every case, it was the opinion-leader who played the key role in identifying and highlighting the problem in relation to management, or in arbitrating between work-group members (in one case, seeking the support of the steward). Hence, in this particular instance, the members accepted the opinion-leader's refusal to work the job in the manner requested by the foreman. When the latter maintained his position, it was the opinion-leader who told the men to stop work and who called the steward in. The steward supported the opinion-leader, telling supervision that their instruction/request was contrary to shop rules; the foreman complained that this was not a very co-operative approach, but accepted the opinion-leader's and the steward's arguments and withdrew his instruction. The men continued their work.

In this instance, and in the case of several others which we briefly mentioned above, we can see that the opinion-leader's advice was taken by his fellow members of the work group. Unlike the griever, he neither had to indulge in any lengthy process of persuading his workmates of the legitimacy of his case, nor had to go out on a limb himself in order to make the point. The other members of the work group accepted his lead, and this was facilitated by his close contacts with the steward. Indeed, this particular opinion-leader was an important support to the leadership of the steward concerned; hence the steward's dependence meant the opinion-leader's sway with his workmates was that much greater, and at the same time the latter was important in terms of creating the dependence of the steward. The ability of the opinion-leader to mediate authoritatively between the steward and his work group provided him with independent resources which he was able to employ, in this instance, to cause a stoppage of work.

The second example we take comes from the staff side. A group of staff had exhausted procedure with their regrading claim over additional work and were awaiting arbitration, delayed by problems in the union over the selection of an arbitrator. A good deal of annoyance was felt over this delay by many of the clerical workers concerned. During this period management instructed one work group to undertake further additional work, which the workers concerned saw as part of the job of a more highly paid group. Led by an opinion-leader, they refused to do the work. In part because it was typical of staff behaviour, and in part because they saw the unions as the cause of the delay, they made few efforts to contact their steward. Indeed he was informed by management and only then addressed the members on the question. But his advice to take the matter through procedure rather than endanger the union organization as the dispute spread (because of management instructing others to do the work) was rejected; this opposition was led by the opinion-leader, and it was upon his advice that the work group affected agreed to go home. In the same way, when the conveners a day or so later sought a return to work with certain assurances, it was the opinion-leader on whom they focused their efforts and it was he who persuaded the others to return to work.

In this case, then, we have a situation in which an opinion-leader had greater influence with his work group than the steward. This was because of the limited resources which the domestic organization on the staff side tends to have; most importantly, the stewards are not generally the focal point of the networks of leadership. Hence, in this particular instance, the opinion-leader was not only able to persuade the work group to strike, but also to persuade the section to withdraw their claim from the arbitration process. While the leaders of the domestic organization were loath to adopt a strong stance, they did advise against both the walk-out and the refusal to go ahead with arbitration; but in both cases they initially failed. It was the opinion-leader who held sway.

The Steward

The third type of section member who has above-average ability to initiate strike action is the steward. It is, of course, his formal responsibility to protect the interests of his members; in furtherance of this role, he has access to the larger domestic organization and to management (although to varying degrees). A leader steward, at least, occupies a more central position in the influence network within the section. However, against the crude stereotype of the steward as an agitator and trouble-maker, more recent opinion suggests that the steward is, generally, 'a lubricant rather than an irritant' (Donovan, 1968:102). Nevertheless, there are situations in which stewards may feel that strike action is the only means of achieving a satisfactory solution to a grievance.

In the case of our twenty-five stoppages or near-stoppages,

twelve were initiated by stewards; in other words, they account for the initiation of more stoppages than any other type of actor. However, we have distinguished between different types of steward, and different levels of their operation in terms of the domestic organization. In particular, we distinguished between populist and leader stewards, and amongst the latter we identified a group of stewards who were especially influential at plant level and effectively formed an inner cabinet with the conveners. We termed these the quasi-elite (Q-E).

Strikes at section level occur more frequently where there are populist stewards than where there are leader stewards; 87 per cent of section-level strikes over the period from January 1972 to August 1973 were accounted for by sections where there were populist stewards, compared with 13 per cent where there were leader stewards. It has to be remembered that these figures relate to strikes as defined by management, and hence exclude the great bulk of work-group-level disputes of brief duration. However, if we compare these management-derived strike statistics with our observational data on section-level stoppages we find the same pattern; of our fifteen section-level disputes, twelve occurred where there were populist stewards, and only three where there were leader stewards. Moreover, when we look at who initiated these strikes, we find that, in all three stoppages on leader stewards' sections, it was the steward who initiated strike action. In contrast, populist stewards led only half of their sections' disputes. This contrast has to be seen in terms of the control which the two types of stewards have; there is no evidence to suggest that leader stewards have fewer problems, and hence less reason for strike action. The important point is that the leader steward is often able to restrain his members from taking strike action, and initiates the negotiation of issues himself more frequently than does the populist steward. Leaders' members therefore have less opportunity to take matters into their own hands.

We have also made reference to the Q-E and the conveners. These operate in the main from a plant-level perspective, and they tend to initiate strikes at plant and departmental levels. (Where a Q-E member initiated strike action in his *own* section, his influence and role are primarily those of a leader steward, and are classified accordingly.)

When we look at the strikes at different levels, and the extent to which they are initiated by our three types of steward — populist, leader, and Q-E (including conveners) — we find that, of our twenty-five stoppages or near-stoppages, stewards initiated no work-group stoppages, but accounted for more sectional-level stoppages than any other type of actor (nine out of fifteen). However, neither grievers nor normal stewards initiated any of the stoppages we observed above section level — this was the sole preserve of the Q-E and the conveners and, in one case, of the larger unions and the TUC. We consider such stoppages more fully below. Before doing so, however, we shall look at two steward-led stoppages.

The first example is perhaps the most remarkable in that the stoppage occurred merely for a section meeting for which management had refused permission. Before it started only one of us, as an observer, and the steward knew that the stoppage would last only a few minutes. But, in our view, it was perhaps the most noteworthy stoppage we observed since it demonstrated the considerable influence of a leader steward. For he was able to get all the members of his section to leave their jobs immediately with very few of them asking why, and none of them knowing in any detail what the problem was. The story was as follows.

The steward had been negotiating the level of bonus with a manager, but had failed to achieve the minimum level which he saw as acceptable — the ten-week average. (This was important since lay-off pay was calculated on the basis of the ten-week average. If those working were paid below this level it meant they might be earning a lower rate than those laid off received for not working. This was seen as unjust. In addition, if the section often received less than the ten-week average, then that average itself would fall.) The steward emphasized how strongly he felt about the matter and sought management's permission for an immediate section meeting. This was refused, whereupon the steward declared his intention of holding the meeting anyway. The steward walked to his section, a large one with about eighty men on the shift, and merely walked through the area shouting, 'Section meeting outside — leave the [job].' Only one or two members asked why. The steward merely replied, 'Bonus — come on, everybody out.' Everybody left their jobs, with jokes about 'It's nice to be out in the sun' as they gathered outside, and questions as to why they were outside. Only one member expressed any hesitancy about walking out (when he was already out): 'I hope we're not doing anything to endanger lay-off pay.' Those around him were unanimous in their advice: 'Shut up about the blackmail charter.'

It was only outside that the members learnt the reason for the stoppage. The steward had not discussed the problem with any of the members beforehand (although he had with a couple of other leader stewards). Very few of the men even knew that the steward had been negotiating with management, and even fewer, if any, that the subject had been the bonus. And yet, when the steward told them to, they all left their jobs and went outside.

The other examples of steward-initiated stoppages which we observed were of a less dramatic nature, in that members were aware of the reasons for the stoppage before it occurred. In other words, these stoppages were either basically over long-standing problems or issues over which the section concerned had stopped work in the past. This is most obviously the case in stoppages relating to piecework negotiations. In such situations, the steward, frequently aided if not led by opinion-leaders, has often played an important role in identifying the grievance and developing the members' expectations. In some cases, the steward was elected precisely because he, as an opinion-leader, was active in developing the claim, raising workers' horizons, and promising to make those horizons a reality if he were made a steward. In this situation, the very standing of the steward is dependent upon success, and this can be an important pressure upon him to foster and initiate a stoppage rather than compromise in the face of toughness from management.

One case we observed fitted this description exactly. The section had been involved in piecework negotiations for some months, and at times their output had been comparatively low in an attempt to impose pressure upon management. Negotiations continued until it became clear that management had made the best offer they were permitted to by their superiors; but this failed to match the minimum figure acceptable to the section. The steward returned to his members and, on his advice, they stopped work. They later returned to work on the advice of the convener.

This is a more typical steward-initiated dispute for a number of reasons. First, it concerned a long-standing problem about which members and stewards felt strongly, and in the main they agreed on their aims and goals. Particularly with populist stewards, it is often difficult to distinguish their views and those of their members; they are section members much more than are leader stewards, and they exemplify rather than mould section opinion (Paterson and Willett, 1951). This explains what might appear to be a contradiction — namely that stewards whom we call populists, implying that their leadership is relatively limited, tend to initiate strikes more frequently than do leader stewards. In part this apparent contradiction is a definitional one: by leadership we mean the readiness and ability to adopt policies and strategies which initially at least may be contrary to those desired by the bulk of the membership. In the context of strikes, it means that leaders, unlike populists, prevent members from stopping work when they wish to do so, and that they can initiate strike action when at first the members are opposed to it. The initiation of strikes does not necessarily imply the same degree of leadership; by this term we mean that an actor is the first to promulgate the idea of strike action — it typically involves some persuasion, but not the remoulding of workers' attitudes so typical of leadership. Hence populist strike initiatives are typically in a direction where the bulk of the members are already prepared to go. The leader is much more of a strategic animal; he tends to use the strike weapon more carefully and to time its use with greater skill.

Strikes above section level are relatively rare because they invariably require the support of the Q-E and conveners who are often able to find alternative means of achieving their goals. In all three cases which we observed of strike or near-strike action above section level, the Q-E had to be actively involved in moulding and shaping the opinions of the membership. We need not go into greater detail here, for in Part II we look in considerable depth at the activities of the Q-E and conveners in the development of a massive majority among the membership supporting strike action over management's offer in the annual negotiations. The other two stoppages or near-stoppages which we observed demonstrate a similar pattern: lengthy discussions between members of the Q-E and conveners over the policies which should be pursued and the need for strike action; the use of informal means as well as departmental stewards' committees to develop and formalize policy recommendations and to persuade other stewards to follow the policy, and, through these networks and their links with the members, to achieve a vote in favour of strike action from the members concerned.

Resources, Initiators, and the Level of Strike Action

Before going on to look in rather more detail at the resources of these different kinds of strike initiators it is useful to summarize by means of Table 5.1 the levels of strike or near-strike action we observed and who initiated them. The classification of actors is based upon more general observation as outlined in our previous volume.

TABLE 5.1

LEVEL OF STRIKE OR NEAR-STRIKE ACTION AND STRIKE INITIATORS

Stoppage or near-stoppage initiated by:	Level of stoppage:			Total
	Work group	Section	Above section	
Griever (and member)	3	1	–	4
Opinion-leader	3	7[a]	–	10[a]
Steward	–	9	–	9
Q-E/convener	–	–	3	3
Larger union	–	–	1	1
Total	6	15	4	25

SOURCE: Observation.
NOTE: a.The figures do not add up, because in two section-level disputes the initiative for the stoppage came jointly from the steward and an opinion-leader; in these two cases, both steward and opinion-leader have been classified as initiating the stoppage.

The table shows that the level of influence of the different kinds of strike initiators varies considerably. The griever, who accounts for a relatively small number of stoppages or near-stoppages, is influential almost solely at the level of the work group. In the one case we observed where a griever initiated a section-level stoppage, two points are relevant: first, the section was very small and could almost be seen as constituting only one work group; second, the griever initiated the stoppage not through a normal process of persuasion but by getting himself suspended.

The opinion-leader has more influence than the griever at the level of the work group, and initiates as many stoppages at work-group level. But he also has a good deal of influence at the level of the section as a whole, particularly where the steward is a populist. Hence, the opinion-leader is involved in the initiation of almost half of the stoppages or near-stoppages we observed at this level. He is only marginally less important than the steward in the initiation of strikes. When we look at more specific situations, however, we find that the opinion-leader's influence tends to be greater where there are populist than where there are leader stewards, and where sections are small. For no ordinary stewards, either populists or leaders, played an initiating role in work-group stoppages on the one hand, nor, on the other, in stoppages or near-stoppages occurring above section level. Stoppages at department and plant level were the sole preserve of those whose roles, either formally or informally, provided them with resources at these levels — the Q-E and conveners, and the larger unions.

The reasons for this pattern have already been suggested, at least in relation to grievers and opinion-leaders. The grievers' influence rests essentially upon their deprivation awareness, although this is limited by their typically individualistic orientation and their reputations for trouble-making and moaning. The sorts of issues which they highlight tend to be of a very parochial nature, and the limited nature of stoppages initiated by them is fostered by the typically limited and *ad hoc* nature of their networks of influence. By contrast, opinion-leaders and stewards have wider networks of influence, which tend to be of a more stable nature (Bailey, 1969). In addition, they typically have the respect of many of their members, and are generally defined as reasonable men concerned less with individual gain than with the defence of collective interests. Stewards, and to a lesser degree opinion-leaders, are expected by their fellow section members to be bargaining-aware and to look out for the collective interest. In this sense, they start off with a considerable advantage over other members.

The leader steward, and the opinion-leader, in particular, have the advantage, or resource, that not merely is their role defined in this way but they also have channels through which they can more easily influence significant numbers of members. On a large section, a leader steward can achieve such influence very economically through his supporting network of opinion-leaders.

This is, of course, even more true of the Q-E and the conveners. Not only are they leader stewards in relation to their own sections but they also form the focus of the networks of other stewards. Their close mutual contacts and the influence they derive both from this and often from the incumbency of formal positions are important. In addition, the Q-E and conveners, and to a lesser degree, other leader stewards possess wide management contacts whereby they can improve the chances of successful stoppages by means of good timing and skilful use of 'the ways of doing things' within the plant (Boissevain, 1974). Indeed, because of the latter, they less often need to resort to strike action.

Finally, we observed one near-stoppage initiated by the TUC and the larger unions. This was the 1973 May Day strike in opposition to Stage Two of the Conservatives' Counter-Inflation Policy, involving wage restraint. The detailed rationale for such action is well known, and will not be discussed here. In fact, the plant did not strike but the important point is that the initiative for a strike was external to the plant, and came from a group of officials who are frequently accused of having sold out, and of being opposed to the use of collective sanctions. It shows that the initiatives for the stoppages or near-stoppages which we observed came from a large number of levels, ranging from the individual member to national officials.

As we are primarily concerned with a sociological analysis of strike activity, the significance of personalities, though considerable, is treated primarily in relation to the networks of influence, and hence the social structure in which they are located. This social structure is not, of course, a 'formal' organization; for example, three of our five types of strike initiator are not recognized 'formally'. Their involvement in the social structure provides them with networks of influence and thereby an above-average ability to affect others' perspectives and the vocabularies they employ. Finally, social structures are not static, so that the emergence of new leaders may change the pattern of strike activity.

Patterns of Support and Opposition

Given our essentially organizational perspective, it is natural to ask what role the other types of actors play in strikes initiated by any one type of actor. It is obvious that the support of the members has to be achieved, but one of the major means of doing this is to gain the support of these other influential actors.

In strike situations specifically, we can most easily see these systems of influence at work in a very crude way by means of Table 5.2. It should be emphasized that this table is merely seen as an approximate summary of a variety of complex social situations; the numbers involved have a purely impressionistic value.

From the individual scores in Table 5.2 we can build up two further, crude indices of the amount of support which different types of actor achieve for their strike initiatives, and of the significance of each actor's influence in the broad strike pattern. It can be seen from the row 'total influence mobilized' that the griever, even when he successfully initiates stoppages, mobilizes very little support; opinion-leaders tend if anything to have little sympathy with their cases if they are involved at all, and stewards

76

demonstrate very little support, compared with their support for other strike initiatives. The same is true of the Q-E and conveners. This lack of influence explains the very low level at which grievers' strike initiatives are typically successful.

TABLE 5.2

THE SYSTEMS OF INFLUENCE IN STRIKE SITUATIONS

| Role of other types of actors | Strikes or near-strikes initiated by: | | | | Total influence score |
	Griever	Opinion-Leader	Steward	QE/Convener[a]	
Griever		n.a.	n.a.	n.a.	n.a.[b]
Opinion-leader	-0.25	+0.72	+0.76	+0.84	+2.07
Steward	+0.375	+0.90		+1.00	+2.275
QE/Convener	+0.125	+0.20	+0.44	+0.84	+1.605
Larger union(s)	0	-0.05	+0.11	+0.33	+0.39
Total influence mobilized	+0.25	+1.77	+1.31	+3.01	
No. of disputes initiated	4	10[c]	9[c]	3	24[d]

SOURCE: Observation.

NOTES: The table was constructed as follows. For each dispute, we have looked at the role played by the other types of actor involved. Where an actor supports the strike initiative, a score of 1 is given; where he supports the grievance(s) but seeks other means of resolving them, a score of 0.5 is given. Opposition to both issue and strike scores -1, while non-involvement scores 0. For each type of actor and for each type of strike initiative, these figures are added together. Hence, for example, of the strikes initiated by an opinion-leader, the steward supported issue and strike in 8 cases, and the issue alone in 2 cases. This gives a steward score of 9 out of a maximum possible 10. In order to control for the different number of disputes, the maximum support in all the disputes of a particular kind is said to be 1.00, and the actual support score adjusted accordingly; in this case it is 9/10 or 0.90. In other words, the higher the figure in the table, the greater the typical support of such an actor.

a. The Q-E/Convener category involves a number of actors who may or may not support each other. For this reason a score has been given of the overall support/opposition of other Q-E members/conveners involved in a Q-E/convener-initiated dispute. For this category, also, the steward and opinion-leader categories included a number of actors, as does the latter for steward-initiated disputes. Here, again, the same practice has been adopted.

b. In terms of influence exerted by grievers in strikes not initiated by themselves, they have generally even less influence than other members — in terms of such strikes, they have therefore been excluded from the analysis.

c. In two of these disputes, initiation was jointly by the steward and opinion-leader. Both have been accredited with leadership of each dispute in the table, and as having the support of the other actor.

d. Excludes the larger union-initiated dispute.

By contrast, opinion-leaders achieve high levels of support particularly from their stewards and from other opinion-leaders in their sections. But, again, support from outside the sections tends to be small. Hence, their influence is largely limited to the sections on which they work. However, what this does mean is that while they may not achieve much extra-section support for their strike initiatives, their influence within their sections for supporting strike initiatives on the part of their own stewards and the Q-E/conveners can be significant.

It would seem at first sight that stewards achieve less support for their strike initiatives than do opinion-leaders. This is in large part a weakness of the table construction; for all steward-initiated strikes occurred at section level and hence other stewards were not directly involved. We therefore have only three categories of actor who can potentially support them, rather than four as in the case of opinion-leaders. If we control for this, then the total influence mobilized by stewards is virtually the same as that for opinion-leaders (1.74). The similarity of the figures is because the bulk of steward-initiated stoppages are led by populist rather than leader stewards.

Of greater importance is the crucial role of stewards in strikes initiated by other actors. Their total influence score is higher than that of any other type of actor. If adjusted to allow for the built-in bias (see above), the figure becomes 3.033, much more than that of any other type of actor. We may suggest that, over the broad pattern of strikes, stewards are crucial to successful initiation. In large part, this relates to their function as stewards, and the key 'gate-keeper' role with which this provides them. Work-group or section-level disputes, if they are to achieve support from the Q-E/conveners or other groups, have to go through the steward. In the same way, strikes initiated at higher levels typically require the steward's co-operation if they are to be supported by his members. But such apparent or potential influence on the part of the stewards may not be so great in reality. The populist steward is dependent both on the Q-E and conveners, and on his members, and hence is unable to exploit the degree of independence which the gate-keeper role potentially provides him with. It is exactly upon this role that the real influence of the leader steward rests.

The Q-E and conveners' influence in disputes does not appear to be particularly high. In part, this is because we have not allowed for the differing degrees of importance of the various disputes. Most work-group stoppages are extremely brief: they are over in a matter of minutes. It is not surprising, therefore, that the Q-E/conveners are not involved. Hence, they were involved in only one of our work-group-level stoppages. Moreover, our counting system for Table 5.2 is such that we score only 0.5 for peacemaking attempts—that is to say, support for the issue but not for the stoppage. It is this style which is typical of Q-E/convener involvement in section-level stoppages. Of our 15 stoppages or near-stoppages of this kind, members of the Q-E and/or the conveners became involved in 13. In these, they opposed the issue in one case, supported one stoppage, and in the case of the other 11 adopted a peacemaking role.

TABLE 5.3

SYSTEMS OF INFLUENCE AND THE INCIDENCE OF STOPPAGES — SECTION-LEVEL DISPUTES

	Stoppage occured	Stoppage did not occur
(a) Direction of steward influence:		
Support/lead	6	8
Peacemaker/opposed	-	1
Total	6	9
(b) Direction of opinion-leader influence:		
Support/lead	6	9
Peacemaker/opposed	-	-
Total	6	9
(c) Direction of Q-E/convener influence:		
Support/lead	1	-
Peacemaker/opposed	3	9
Not involved	2	-
Total	6	9

SOURCE: Observation.

The influence of the conveners and Q-E can be seen most clearly by looking at the ways in which different groups exercised their influence and whether the stoppages did in fact occur. Table 5.3 suggests that for a situation to lead towards a near-stoppage — that is, a situation where the members are ready to strike — generally requires the support of both steward and opinion-leaders. Hence, in the case of the 15 section-level near-stoppages, opinion-leaders

79

supported or led all of them and in only one case did the steward fail to do so. And yet, in only 6 of the 15 cases did the strike actually occur. In every one of the other 9 cases a member of the Q-E and/or convener did not support the idea of a stoppage (cf. Bailey, 1969; Boissevain, 1974; Kapferer, 1972). This influence is not total in half of the cases where strikes did actually occur, the Q-E/conveners adopted a similar role, but failed to stop the strike. It would, of course be surprising if conveners or members of the Q-E could prevent all such disputes; in all but one of the 3 cases where strike action occurred against the advice of the conveners and Q-E there was an additional factor in the dispute which had occurred since their most recent involvement. In one case, a worker was suspended, while in the other management refused what the workers saw as a legitimate claim for a special payment arising from a change in the conditions of work. In both cases, these were the manifest reasons for the stoppage, and the stoppage occurred before the Q-E/conveners could become involved.

The Q-E/conveners' influence in section-level disputes, then, is generally crucial. As we have argued, in part this is through their ability to persuade members of the inadvisability of strike action or the need to moderate their demands. In part, it is because, by means of their status and wide range of management contacts, they can often win compromises from the company in favour of the section. Moreover, section-level stoppages seldom last for more than a shift or so because members of the Q-E or conveners manage to persuade the men to return to work — by essentially the same means as they prevent near-stoppages actually becoming strikes. An example of such action occurred when one section had received significantly lower wages than normal one week. The section, led by their steward and an opinion-leader, were threatening strike action. The steward consulted a member of the Q-E, who told the section to wait while he attempted to overcome the problem. He went to see several managers without success, and so discussed the problem with a convener. They both told the section not to act precipitately, and had informal discussions and formal nego-tiations with various members of management. The result was that they swiftly achieved an improvement in the level of earnings for the section for that week, although they had to engage upon more lengthy negotiations in an attempt to resolve the basic problem.

The Q-E and conveners, then, play a crucial role in whether or not section-level stoppages actually occur; their influence is far greater than Table 5.2 suggests. However, the development of the pressure towards strike action typically occurs within the section itself, and it is the steward and opinion-leaders who play a crucial role in this process. The Q-E/conveners' role is primarily one of checking the expression of the grievance in the form of strike action. But, frequently, they can also be seen as playing an important role in the development of a situation in which strike action is likely. This is through their role in persuading sections to attempt to renegotiate their piecework values — they do this through a long process of persuasion in which they are primarily demonstrating possibilities and raising horizons, and changing workers' definitions of what they can legitimately expect. These new aspirations are often an important factor underlying threatened strike action, although minor problems may be the actual precipitating factors. It is a case, then, of a temporary failure on the part of the Q-E/conveners to 'manage discontent' — although, typically, they regain their influence before the stoppage occurs.

In the same way that conveners and the Q-E can prevent stoppages at section level through their network of contacts, they can frequently mobilize larger groups of the workforce to strike action through this same network. It will be remembered that all of the Q-E/convener-initiated stoppages or near-stoppages were either at departmental or plant level. They therefore require for success a much greater and more complete network of influence, since many more workers were involved than in simple section-level disputes and because perceived interests were more likely to conflict. It can be seen from Table 5.2 that the Q-E/conveners do indeed mobilize more influence in support of their strike initiatives than do any other types of actor; they win support from other members of the Q-E, other stewards, opinion-leaders, and even the larger unions. All of these groups demonstrate a higher level of support for Q-E/convener-initiated stoppages or near-stoppages than for any other type of actor-initiated stoppage which we observed. It would be wrong to suggest that such attempts by the Q-E/conveners are always successful; certainly they are not. But it is also typically the case that a departmental-level or plant-wide stoppage does require far more mobilization.

In this chapter we have looked at the role which different actors play in the initiation of the idea of strike action and the process of mobilization which may develop from such initiatives. In particular, we have shown that the manner in which strikes develop or are avoided is intimately related to the distribution of power and influence within the domestic organization. The same is also true of the more limited forms of collective action discussed in Chapter 3. Indeed, from the viewpoint of the steward these often have the advantage that he can initiate them without requiring his members to engage in dramatic and possibly costly action. But in the main they still involve collective decisions similar to those we have outlined in relation to strikes. Opinion-leaders and stewards are often dominant, and it is not unusual for conveners and Q-E members to attempt to remove overtime bans in order to prevent the lay-off of other workers or, occasionally, to facilitate bargaining with management. Processes of negotiation therefore occur among workers, although systems of argument in favour of overtime bans, for example, tend to place rather less stress upon the broader notions of management-worker conflict. Moreover, there is sometimes more discussion of the efficiency of various forms of collective action, although this is less than might be expected for two reasons. First, as we have noted, some forms of collective action derive almost naturally from the issue in dispute. Second, in a strongly organized plant where collective action is common, the strengths and weaknesses of different forms of sanctions are part of the common stock of knowledge, particularly within the steward network.

6
The Dynamics of Strikes

In this chapter we bring together the two themes which formed the centre of our attention in the two previous chapters. In Chapter 4 we looked at the variety of vocabularies employed in near-strike situations. We saw that, for a strike to develop, a process of defining an issue and creating a case for a work stoppage generally had to occur. In that process, objections to the idea of strike action were also important. Negotiations occurred concerning the legitimacy of a demand or grievance, and often about whether a stoppage of work was an efficacious or reasonable means of pursuing the case.

Such negotiation occurs within a context of social power and influence inside the domestic organization. In Chapter 5 we found that certain types of actor played disproportionately significant roles in determining whether or not a group should strike. Moreover, such influence might be in favour of, or in opposition to, a work stoppage. The vocabularies employed varied between actors, and in Chapter 4 we noted that wider organizational concerns and reference to trade union principles were particularly employed by the conveners and Q-E.

In this chapter we discuss in rather more detail the dynamics of the movement towards strike action, involving the exertion of influence and resort to a variety of vocabularies. We take a number of examples of near-strikes, looking at the roles played and the vocabularies employed. We consider three strikes or near-strikes. The first of these is a stoppage at work-group level over a safety issue. The second concerns a section striking over the suspension of a man who refused to undertake a task which he and his fellow section members said was not part of their job. The third is a near-strike by a section relating to a long-term demand for a new payment system. In the first two of these strikes or near-strikes, the domestic organization as a whole did not become involved. In the last it did. Finally, we draw together our more general arguments concerning strike activity.

A Work-Group Stoppage

The work-group stoppage we consider was initiated by a griever in a work group of five men. When the men began work one morning on the track, certain components were missing; this made the work of the group difficult and dangerous since they could not easily get into the vehicle to perform their allotted tasks. The griever noted this and after complaining to his fellows went to complain to the steward. The latter agreed that it was dangerous and asked the foreman to see that the components concerned were replaced. The griever returned to his station but the components had still not been replaced. He pointed this out to the other members of the group, who also felt that it was a safety hazard. The griever again went to his steward, emphasizing that the components had still not been fitted and that the job was dangerous. The steward went with the griever and, after looking at the situation, called the foreman over and pointed out the problem. The foreman explained the reason for the shortage of components, but asked that the men should continue to work while he acquired makeshift alternatives to the missing component from another department. Led by the griever, the work group told the steward that they wanted assurances in case they hurt themselves. The steward informed the foreman of this condition for continued working. The foreman said that such an assurance was beyond his powers and went to the departmental manager to discuss the situation.

The manager called in the steward who explained the men's views and asked for a guarantee that the company would compensate the men if they were injured. The manager admitted that a safety hazard existed and that the company 'will help the men to take care', but he could give no guarantee. The steward insisted on a guarantee — 'Assurances aren't enough, we've had them in the past.' He went on to cite previous cases where such assurances had proved worthless. The manager replied that the company could not possibly give a guarantee but 'by recognizing the safety risk, the company is admitting liability.' The steward stressed that the problem could also affect other groups who could not possibly be expected to undertake their tasks in the face of such a safety hazard. The manager agreed.

The steward finally said that he wanted a witness to the manager's assurances. The manager expressed surprise but agreed. The steward left and found another steward whom he brought in after briefly outlining the situation. The argument was repeated, with the new steward stressing that no matter how careful the men were, if they were doing the job all day some error was very likely; if a drop of oil got on a man's shoes he could easily slip and break a leg. The manager agreed that this was possible but still refused to give a guarantee.

Meanwhile, the foreman had been trying to persuade the men to continue working. The men had refused, for as they discussed the matter among themselves they became increasingly conscious of the risk of an accident. The foreman came to report this to the manager who suggested to the steward that they should have the men come into the office to discuss the matter. The steward said that it would be wrong to bring the men into the office because this would subject them to too much pressure. For it seems to be generally accepted that entry into an office — management territory — is a means of imposing pressure upon workers. (Stewards and managers may often argue over where a discussion between them should take place. If they are on weak or delicate ground, each prefers his own territory; the foreman his office, the steward the shop-floor. Some stewards believe this to be important because clearly beating a foreman in front of other workers is good for the steward's position and the morale of the workers.)

Consequently, the two stewards, the manager, and the foreman went over to the work group. The manager tried to persuade them to continue working. The men refused. Even though the foreman had now got another department to make a substitute for the missing component, the men were not ready to continue working since the substitute would not be completed for several hours. The discussion continued, with managers and foremen trying to persuade the men, and the men recounting previous injuries, the problems involved in entering the vehicle, the risk of forgetting the component was missing because they were used to it being there, and the risk of slipping with oil on their shoes. By this time an audience from the rest of the section, whose work had stopped, had gathered at a distance, and there were now seven members of the management present. Seeing the stoppage, they had come over to see what was happening.

One of the conveners was walking through the shop and the

steward called him over and explained the situation to him. (Such chance encounters appear to be quite important in affecting the outcome of near-strike situations.) The convener said that there were risks of stoppages in several other areas of the plant and that 'We don't really want any stoppages now because of the mass meeting' (over the annual negotiations). The convener suggested that the best thing would be to get the Safety Officer, and he went to phone him. Meanwhile, the manager was still trying to persuade the men to continue to work — 'You've either got to work or stop the track.' The men replied that they wanted to do neither.

Much to the disgust of the men, the first statement made by the Safety Officer on his arrival was an expression of concern over the stoppage of the track. But he did agree that a safety hazard existed. The convener told the steward that he should fill in an official grievance form 'so that there's a record in case of any problems'. The steward told the men this, but they were still hesitant about working.

Meanwhile a foreman had phoned the Methods Department and two men from there now arrived to look at the problem. Another foreman also brought some components which he thought might be suitable as temporary substitutes. They fitted one of these and one of the men tried it out. He and his colleagues were still not happy but finally the steward persuaded them to use it, stressing that with a grievance form completed they would be 'covered' in the event of an injury.

The steward and foreman discussed manning details concerning the fitting of the substitute component and agreed that an extra man would be required on the work group to relieve the pressure on the men. The foreman went off to find the additional man required. As he did so, two other stewards came over to find out what was happening. On hearing which component was the cause of the problem, they pointed out that a large stock of these existed in another section. The steward told the foreman who checked the components and found that they were suitable, and the problem was over. The stoppage had lasted about half an hour.

A Section Stoppage

A griever was also central to the section-level stoppage we consider here. It occurred on a machine-shop section when jobs were rotated and the griever was moved to a new job. He argued that taking crates of components off the rollers running from his machine and stacking them on to pallets was not part of the job. He had told the foreman this who argued that it was. The previous men on the job had been doing it, to which the griever replied that they had only been doing so to help the material handler who was not fully fit and whose job it really was. The foreman insisted that the stacking was part of the job, and so the griever went to his steward and explained the situation.

On finding no change in the foreman's position, the steward went to one of the conveners. The latter told him to take the matter as far as he could in procedure, and if no satisfactory conclusion was reached, then the convener would take the matter up. The steward was unable to achieve any success with more junior management and so the convener raised the matter with the relevant departmental manager. Management insisted that stacking was part of the job and produced the views of other managers and foremen as evidence. The convener and steward repeated the men's argument. The manager finally warned that unless the griever did stack the crates he would be suspended.

The convener and steward returned to the section. Groups of the men had been discussing the issue and they all agreed that it was not strictly part of their job. Furthermore, the men were especially annoyed because they viewed management's action as taking unfair advantage of their kindness in helping an unfit man to continue in his job. As a consequence, when the convener called a meeting of the section they decided that if the griever was suspended they would down tools. They argued that they could not possibly permit the griever to be suspended when he was in the right, and when the point at issue was something which was of relevance to the whole section (for others might equally be instructed to undertake the task in question).

A stoppage therefore occurred late in the afternoon when the griever was suspended. The convener went back to management to see if he could solve the problem, but without success. The next morning the section had resumed their sit-down when the convener came to report back on his meeting with management.

The convener explained to the men that management had refused to discuss the matter further. Their argument was that while the material handler did stack crates on near-by jobs, his job did not involve, and never had involved, the stacking in question. The men rejected this. Certainly they had done the job over the last few months as management argued, but they insisted that this was not part of 'normal working' as management claimed. This point was strongly emphasized, as were also their attempts to help the sickly material handler and the practice in other areas of the machine shop. Detailed technical discussions of changes in the length of rollers and the consequences for effort were discussed for some time, until the convener finally asked them what they intended to do. He explained that the manager concerned would not be available for half an hour or so, but he would then discuss the matter with him again. In the meantime did they intend to 'sit around or what?' At the instigation of an opinion-leader the section decided to continue their stoppage until the convener had negotiated with management, especially in view of the fact that a man had been suspended.

Events had moved rapidly from the initial refusal of the griever to stack completed components. The delay involved in waiting for management provided an opportunity for the members to show the convener the details of the job in question. After this, he tried to phone the departmental manager, but without success, and so he went with the steward to discuss the matter with another manager. The latter said that he had done all that he could. He had checked with work study and the manager in charge of material handlers and both had said that stacking was part of the machinists' job. The steward insisted that the problem had been raised with the manager on several occasions in the past, but he denied that this was the case, although a similar problem had arisen on another job nearby. The convener and steward questioned this. The foreman, who was also present, said that stacking had always been part of the job and the chargehand, who was also contacted, agreed with this view. The debate focused on this question of fact until they finally agreed to see the departmental manager who had now arrived.

The departmental manager began by stressing that strictly he could not talk while the men were on strike, so that 'Strictly this meeting is not taking place, it's unofficial and off the record.' He then said that everybody he had asked said that stacking was part of the machinists' job. The convener denied this, stressing that 'The men say different.' The manager argued that, if they were correct, 'You're really talking to the wrong people. I've got no authority to employ or change the jobs of indirect workers.' The convener agreed but stressed that the manager was also involved. Finally, it was agreed that the steward should ask the material handler whether he had ever done the stacking. (The manager later explained to us that he had proposed this rather than calling the man into the office 'so that it could not be said that management had put the man under pressure'. He had been asked by a steward on the shop-floor.) The steward returned to say that the material handler denied ever doing the job. The convener said he would have to return to the men, and the manager sympathized. One solution was to check the details of the job description with work study, but this was impossible that day because they were on holiday. Finally, the convener and manager agreed that, if the men went back to work, they would undertake a thorough investigation of the issue.

The convener and steward returned to the section and held a meeting. They reported their negotiations and pointed out that the material handler denied ever stacking crates. Several workers retorted that the material handler was lying, and pointed out that when they had worked on the job they had never done the stacking. They reiterated the point that they had merely been helping a sick man. The convener argued that they had to discover the truth and somebody was clearly lying. The arguments were reiterated until finally the convener stressed once more that there would be no investigation until they returned to work and that they would gain nothing while they were 'off the clock'. The griever insisted that he was still unwilling to stack, but an opinion-leader who had until now backed the griever volunteered to take the job. Arguments were reiterated, the opinion-leader made it clear that he was not ready to be 'saddled' with the job permanently and it was agreed, on the suggestion of the steward, that the griever should be asked to stack, but 'under protest'. The griever objected but the convener pushed the matter to a vote and it was unanimously agreed that the griever be asked to stack under protest and that they return to work. An investigation began several days after the resumption of work.

A Section Near-Strike and the Domestic Organization

The next near-strike we consider had a long history. It concerned a group of indirect workers who for many months had been demanding that they have an incentive scheme. In support of this they had imposed a restriction on new work. This had led to the suspension of a man and a consequent strike. Conveners and full-time officials had been actively involved in persuading them to return to work because the strike had led to a major lay-off in assembly. The group involved felt they had been let down because the conveners and full-time officials had promised to try to gain an incentive scheme for them but had so far failed to achieve satisfactory proposals. Government legislation and the course of the annual negotiations suggested that there was little hope of the section achieving their demands in the near future (see Part II).

The particular issue with which we are concerned has to be seen within this larger context. Following from the strike, the section imposed a limit on overtime. This raised problems concerning stocktaking which, in the face of production problems, management hoped to undertake over several days. That would involve this indirect group in rather more overtime than they were prepared to work. Management called in the conveners and outlined their stocktaking plans. In view of the possible problem with the indirects, management asked that the conveners should not simply outline the stocktaking plan at JSSC but should also have a word with the indirects' stewards concerned. The conveners suggested ways of overcoming the problem but management did not think them practical. The conveners finally agreed to see the indirects' stewards since any restriction could endanger pay for those currently laid off.

The convener concerned therefore approached the indirects' stewards and stressed that any refusal to comply with management's proposals would sabotage lay-off pay. The stewards were sympathetic but non-committal. They did not discuss the matter with any of their members on this day, although they and their members continually discussed their demand for an incentive scheme, their critical attitudes towards the rest of the domestic organization, and their need to fight for their demands.

The next day, however, the stewards did discuss stocktaking with several opinion-leaders. They agreed that the company was trying to do it 'on the cheap' because it was normal for production to halt for such an exercise, but now this was not proposed. Such discussions led to the conclusion that they should not comply with management's plans, and the conveners were told this when they asked what the men intended to do.

At the JSSC meeting later in the day the conveners outlined management's stocktaking plans and the possibility of problems arising from the indirects' overtime restriction. There was little discussion of the matter, however, at the meeting itself. After the meeting the indirects' stewards concerned discussed the issue with one or two other indirects' stewards, most of whom sympathized and some of whom offered the support of their members in the event of any dispute. Some members of the Q-E suggested to the conveners means of avoiding the problem but these were seen as impracticable when proposed to management. Similarly, managers in the indirect area were concerned about the stewards' intentions and whether they had been pressurized by the JSSC to work normally. On hea ring that no such pressures had been imposed, the managers themselves stressed the damage the indirects would do to their fellows by endangering lay-off pay.

It was normal for the indirects' stewards to hold a section meeting after the JSSC to report back to their members. This they arranged for the next day. As they went round informing members of the meeting they again discussed the stocktaking situation with various opinion-leaders. They stressed the need to maintain the overtime restriction and the need to be ready to withstand the pressures which they thought the conveners would inevitably impose upon them. They found general support for this view from the opinion-leaders and subsequently referred continually to the situation when chatting to members. There was a common vocabulary which found support in these chats and in the section meeting itself. They agreed that lay-off pay was a company weapon and that the conveners would do all in their power to preserve it. It was argued that this was typical more generally because the domestic organization was dominated by pieceworkers and everything had to be done to keep assembly happy. Indirects were ignored all the rest of the time, but when stocktaking came round then everybody was concerned with them. Such articulations of their feelings led to the stewards suggesting, and finding support for, the possibility of a total stoppage. Certainly they would not work the extra overtime and they would insist that if any meeting had to be called to discuss the restriction the conveners themselves would have to call it.

Throughout the day the indirects' stewards discussed whether and when the conveners would 'pressure' them, and the probability of their calling a JSSC meeting on the matter. In fact, the conveners did discuss the situation. They checked the lay-off pay agreement and concluded that management 'must be hard-pushed' if they were going to refuse lay-off pay. But there was a case which management could put, and the only solutions were to raise the matter at national level and get the section to lift their restriction. The indirects' stewards later came to see one of the conveners. He pointed out to them that management did have a case in terms of custom and practice, and that he had seen management who had now made it clear that lay-off pay was in danger. The stewards of the section questioned the inevitability of the lay-off but the conveners stressed management's intention and their power according to the agreement.

Only on the third day did the issue begin to 'hot up'. The stewards of the section came to see the conveners and argued that if any pressure was put on the section, 'The lads won't work just to spite everyone' — 'The lads are saying balls to lay-off pay.' The conveners emphasized that management did have a case and that it would hurt the company if they had to pay lay-off pay. They appealed to the stewards to 'let common sense prevail', and warned that one of the full-time officials had advised them to man up the jobs. (This official had been contacted by the conveners to raise the interpretation of the lay-off agreement at national level.) At the same time a meeting of the assembly stewards was being held; it was their members who would suffer most if the section went on strike. It was agreed that in line with a previous JSSC resolution they would seek a meeting of the JSSC. The assembly members of the Q-E went to see one of the conveners who explained the situation and pointed out that the stewards of the section feared that any pressure would merely aggravate the situation. But he finally agreed to a JSSC meeting the next day.

At this meeting the conveners explained the situation, referring to the company's strategy and arguments, the JSSC resolution, and the views of the stewards concerned. They 'appealed to the stewards to encourage the men not to strike and to lift the restriction'. Pressure began to be put on the section.

Assembly Q-E member: The stewards should have a meeting and point out to the men that they're jeopardizing lay-off pay. I've spoken to several [section] people, and they say they agree with dropping the overtime ban.

Section steward: We've no intention of calling a meeting of the members because last time we were shot down — you [the conveners] will have to call the meeting.

Various evasive strategies were discussed but there were technical difficulties which made these ineffective. Pressure on the stewards increased:

Q-E member: I don't care about the lay-off for myself personally, but I am concerned about people being pushed around because of egotistical disputes . . . the stewards should tell the section. It is not beyond the [power of the] conveners and stewards — lift the restrictions.

Convener: The important point is to hang on to lay-off pay. It's no use grumbling about blackmail — this is part of the game, it's only natural.

A steward: Lay-off pay is the company's shop steward. [The section] should accept this and say they'll lift the ban. If only they stay in, 'the company can do nothing — it's not asking much and otherwise there will be blokes on the dole.

Q-E member: I sympathize with the [section] stewards but they've got to go to a meeting and use a bit of cunning; the [section] are not fools — they will accept the situation.

It was agreed finally that a meeting of the section should be called.

Before this meeting the stewards were cynical of the outcome. They agreed that they should ensure that opinion-leaders were 'lined up', and contacted several of them to ensure that the motion to continue their action and to threaten a strike should come from a respected opinion-leader. When told of the section meeting, members were cynical of assembly and critical of the conveners and agreed with the stewards' plans: 'Oh, the conveners are coming when the whole factory is involved. Well, in that case stuff them and we'll have a strike.' The possibility of a total stoppage was widely discussed and, when members applauded such ideas the stewards told them to 'do your stuff at the meeting'. They were concerned that if a resolution was not put quickly in the meeting the conveners would be able to persuade the section to withdraw all sanctions.

The conveners were aware of this 'anti-convener' attitude on the part of the section. This was one reason why they had been trying to avoid a confrontation with the section. The latter was blaming the conveners for the lack of movement towards an incentive scheme, and a vicious circle had developed — their imposition of sanctions meant that the conveners could make no progress with management who would refuse to negotiate under duress. Before the meeting the conveners were still testing out other means of overcoming the problem. One of the full-time officials was contacted to raise the question of the interpretation of the lay-off pay agreement at national level; he was also told that manning up the jobs was not possible because only accredited storemen could undertake the stocktaking audit. The conveners went to see the industrial relations manager who argued that management had already been forced to change their production schedules because of the probable restriction, and therefore even if it was not lifted lay-off pay would not be paid. They saw the section stewards to see if it was possible to employ some other strategy; the stewards thought it was possible, but when they saw the departmental manager he denied this.

The conveners therefore went to the section meeting. One of the stewards explained that the JSSC had demanded the meeting, and he then introduced the conveners who were hissed. The conveners argued that they should ensure that those laid off were paid because this would 'hurt the company', and that they had beaten the company on this in the past. They pointed out that their jobs could be manned up, and the section should be reasonable and sensible on this matter. Several of the section members were hostile: 'Keep the ban on'; 'What about our incentive scheme?' The stewards were asked for their opinion and they replied: 'We're not backing the JSSC recommendation; they [the JSSC] merely said we had to hold a meeting. We will back whatever the section decides.' There were cheers and shouts, and the conveners were critical of the stewards' behaviour; the stewards pointed this out to the section and there was uproar. The vote was 2:1 against lifting the threatened strike.

The assembly members of the Q-E came to see the conveners; were they to get lay-off pay or not? The conveners told them about the section meeting, and management's statements that now, no matter what, lay-off pay would not be paid. The Q-E members demanded another JSSC meeting, in line with the JSSC resolution, and the conveners agreed to this.

The next day at the JSSC, the section stewards were strongly criticized. One of the conveners pointed out that he had warned the JSSC that the section might keep the ban on—the section had been 'anti-convener': 'The stewards did not support the recommendation [of JSSC] and showed no respect for the conveners . . . Our own lads have cost us this [lay-off pay], not the company.'

Other stewards continued this criticism of the miscreant stewards: 'Stewards who back their sections should resign.' 'My section decided there should be a mass meeting over this.' 'We should discipline these stewards.' 'Stewards have got to support JSSC, even if they disagree — otherwise there is no point in having one.' 'We should man up [the jobs of those striking].'

Finally it was resolved that the stewards should go back to the section and get them to reverse the decision, and, if it did not, JSSC would reconvene and possibly take the matter to a mass meeting.

The reconvened section meeting was very subdued. One of the

stewards explained that the JSSC had asked for another meeting because they had failed to put the JSSC recommendation to the section properly the day before. There were few questions, although one member aggrievedly pointed that that 'You represent us and not the JSSC.' The steward emphasized that lay-off pay would be lost if they did not lift their threat, and the section finally agreed to do so. No strike or any other sanction occurred. Stocktaking was done according to management's proposals, and those laid off were paid.

An Overview of Strikes

In the previous sections we have described three strikes or near-strikes in an attempt to emphasize the complex ways in which vocabularies are developed and negotiated and decisions consequently made. We have seen how different types of actor play a crucial role in this process and the way in which the range of persons involved can vary widely. Hence, in the work-group stoppage relatively few were involved, while in the near-strike we have just described many groups were active. Not only were the conveners involved but so also were the JSSC, the full-time officials, and the assembly stewards. Strikes therefore may involve large parts of the domestic organization and the larger union even when they are proposed by relatively small groups of workers.

One other group is also important, namely management. In part because of our more general concerns in our research, we have paid relatively little attention to them since we have focused upon the dynamics of the domestic organization. But it is clear from the descriptions of strikes or near-strikes that on occasion they play an important role. Obviously, if management are ready to concede workers' demands, then particular strikes will not occur (although, of course, such action may lead to strikes in other areas). But their role is often much more than this. In the course of a movement towards a strike, and during the stoppage itself, they can often have an important impact. Sanctions upon workers, such as suspension, may become the focus of proposals for strike action. Rejections of alternative means to resolve problems may leave workers with little choice but to strike if they are to achieve their ends.

Similarly, as a stoppage approaches, or even during the course of it, managers may mobilize their resources either to withstand the strike or to avoid it. In the case of the work-group stoppage

95

described above, for example, managers out-numbered strikers by two to one at one point. The managers were all trying to find solutions to the problem or persuade the men to return to work. As one worker looking on cynically commented, 'Look at all of them trying to get the glory of getting the blokes back to work.' In the same way, the stocktaking issue shows the way in which, realizing the possibility of problems if they tried to implement their plans, management attempted to persuade and impose pressure upon the conveners to resolve the difficulties.

It is not unusual for management to attempt to employ the internal systems of influence and interests of the domestic organization to facilitate the achievement of their goals. Members of the domestic organization, as we have noted, often attempt to employ the same strategy in relation to management organization. As a consequence, some members of management and the domestic organization may form coalitions against others. The pattern of alliances in near-strike situations can be complex.

In this way we can begin to see the relationship between the two organizational themes we have stressed throughout the first part of this book. The organizational processes involved in moving towards strike action depend upon the more general patterns of organization and organizational centrality which we have discussed in earlier chapters, for these provide established avenues and recipes of action, and involve a variety of resources and sanctions.

At the same time, strikes and near-strikes can change the larger organizational pattern, as is indicated by the indirects discussed in relation to the stocktaking issue. An increasing division had developed between them and many of the production and other areas of the plant, because of their strike action and the failure of others to support them. At another level, strikes may change actual patterns of work organization, payment and so on. In this way they can affect the institutional position of the union and hence its resources.

Strikes and the threat of strikes are often therefore an intimate part of the organizational pattern and development within a workplace (Hiller, 1969:11; Lane and Roberts, 1971:16). They both reflect and influence workplace organization. It is from this perspective that we have discussed strikes in this and previous chapters. In Part II we adopt the same approach to a much larger near-strike.

Part II
The Strike That Never Was

7
The Development of Claim and Counter-Claim

So far we have discussed strikes and near-strikes primarily in general terms. We have emphasized the importance of organizational processes and union centrality in understanding strike-proneness and the movement towards particular acts of striking. However, our interest in the latter aspect has so far been concerned with relatively small, short-term strikes or near-strikes which are typical of the car industry, and indeed industry more generally. Large plant-wide stoppages do occur, however, involving major problems of creating and maintaining a plant-wide unity and solidarity. It is for this reason, and because of their often dramatic nature, that detailed studies of strikes have typically concentrated upon stoppages of this kind.

From our perspective a large-scale strike is clearly of considerable interest. Such strikes are likely to involve a very lengthy and complex process of negotiation, and the organizational resources involved are likely to be considerable. We can look at strikes of this kind from two perspectives. First, consistent with the previous chapters of this volume, we can assess the utility of an organizational approach to strikes. Second, we can see such a major action as illuminating the processes of leadership within a domestic organization.

We focus on both of these areas of interest in our discussion of a near-strike which involved the whole of the shop-floor domestic organization. This arose out of the annual negotiations when management offered the legal maximum wage increase only if the labour force accepted a change in the payment system from piecework to measured daywork (MDW). The Office of Manpower

Economics defines MDW as a payment system in which 'the pay of the employee is fixed on the understanding that he will maintain a specified level of performance, but the pay does not fluctuate in the short-term with his actual performance. This arrangement relies on some form of work measurement or assessment, as a means both of defining the required level of performance and of monitoring the actual level' (1973:8). The stewards were opposed to such a change on the terms offered. Having failed to achieve anything in negotiations, they determined on strike action and such a move was finally accepted by the membership. However, within hours of the commencement of the strike, management offered to re-open negotiations which finally resulted in the payment of the legal maximum wage increase without any change in the payment system.

This near-strike occurred during the operation of a government incomes policy. In late 1972, the then Conservative government imposed a standstill on incomes, termed Stage One of the Counter-Inflation Policy. Stage Two, which was introduced in early 1973, was in operation during our study. Increases which had been delayed by Stage One could be paid but, in future, pay increases were permissible only at twelve-monthly intervals. Any award to a group should not total more than 'the sum which would result from the payment of £1 per week per head plus 4 per cent of the current pay bill for the group, exclusive of overtime'. In addition, some movement towards equal pay for women was permissible, as were also certain improvements in basic hours, holidays, pensions, and redundancy pay. No person was allowed to receive a pay increase of more than £250 in the year.

Our research on shop stewards provided us with a unique opportunity to study the movement towards a strike situation on such a scale. However, our observational work did not begin at the start of the negotiations; for the early period of events we are dependent upon documentary material and interviews conducted at the time. Our actual observation began at the first negotiations over the new payment system. At a previous meeting management had merely detailed their proposals, and the JSSC had rejected them in principle a few days before our observation began. In terms of key 'formal' points in the history of this issue, our observation began three weeks before a failure to agree (FTA) was registered, four weeks before the JSSC decided to recommend strike action, and about ten weeks before the mass meeting voted in support of strike action. A diary of the main 'formal' events between the beginning of local negotiations and the mass meeting's acceptance of the terms of the agreement is shown in Table 7.1.

TABLE 7.1

A DIARY OF MAIN EVENTS

Week 1	First local negotiations — discussion of plant industrial relations.
Week 6	Local negotiations — union-side reject MDW. JSSC reject company proposals.
Week 9	Local negotiations—union-side reject MDW. JSSC agree wage increase to be across the board.
Week 10	Local negotiations lead to an FTA.
Week 11	Local negotiations clarify reason for FTA. National negotiations review FTA.
Week 12	First company document to workers.
Week 13	JSSC agree to recommend strike action. Second company document to workers. First steward document to workers.
Week 14	Third company document to workers.
Week 15	Fourth company document to workers. Second steward document to workers.
Week 16	JSSC agree date of mass meeting. Fifth company document to workers. Mass meeting agrees to strike action.
Week 17	JSSC agree to recommend to mass suspension of strike action. Mass meeting agrees to suspend strike.
Week 18	Local negotiations resume and lead to agreement.
Week 19	JSSC support agreement and recommend it to mass. Mass meeting accepts agreement.

The Structure of Negotiations

The company operated a system of annual negotiations. That is, between these formal negotiations once a year they tried to refuse to reach agreement over any claims which did not meet certain criteria; for example, piecework sections could not negotiate new piecework values 'where no change has taken place in method, material or means of production'. The annual negotiations, therefore, formally provide the opportunity for the unions to seek both general and sectional increases.

101

In addition, the process of negotiations was formalized in a somewhat complex manner, in two ways. First, a fairly clear, set timetable for negotiations existed. Second, certain elements were seen as the province of company-wide bargaining, and other issues as that of plant bargaining. These two levels came together in two ways. The first item in the formal timetable of negotiations was a Delegate Conference, consisting of the union negotiating teams from each of the plants and the relevant national union officials. This body met approximately six months before the end of the term agreement to discuss the local claims and to develop a national claim. The proper subjects for national bargaining concerned conditions of employment: hours of work, overtime and shift premia, and fringe benefits such as pensions and holidays. Other matters, particularly wage increases, were the subject of plant bargaining. In the past, plant and national bargaining had occurred concurrently, and plant agreements had to be ratified nationally. In the event of a failure to agree locally, the issue went to national level. (The terms 'company-level' and 'national' are used interchangeably.) The aim was to have made a new agreement by the end of the period of operation of the previous term agreement.

It is possible, therefore, to distinguish three stages in the negotiation process. The first of these is the development of the claim on the union side. This involves discussions within the domestic organization and the Delegate Conference, and the work undertaken in support of the claim by the larger unions, and particularly their research departments. Also, management may be expected to be developing their ideas as to how the payment system should be changed or modified in this period. Clearly they will generally be reacting primarily to the unions' claim. But also certain changes may be proposed by management to details of the piecework agreement. In our year of study, management prepared major new changes in the method of payment.

The second stage of negotiations can be seen as the actual negotiations when claims are answered and modified, compromises made, and agreements reached. The third stage is the acceptance — or rejection — of the agreement by the membership. If the agreement is rejected, then there is a return to the second stage of the process.

Employing this somewhat approximate three-stage model, we first look at the process of developing claims and ideas relevant to the negotiations. We consider the development of the union claim, and then look at the process by which management reached their counter-proposals.

The Union Claim

We have already suggested that the annual negotiations provided an opportunity not only for the plant as a whole to seek improved earnings, but also for sectional groups to pursue their own specific claims. Such claims could be expressed in three different ways. The first of these was not merely to put in a claim but also to pursue the claim through procedure during the operation of the previous term agreement. This was the strategy employed by the maintenance workers, who were seeking a system of payment linked to the toolroom, and a significant increase in earnings associated with it. By the time of the negotiations proper they had exhausted procedure. The advantage of this method was that there was a norm that those sectional claims which had been right through procedure tended to have preference. By November, the planned date of the Delegate Conference, the maintenance workers had therefore established their claim.

So also had certain other groups of indirect workers. But they had not exhausted procedure. While the indirects had also made clear their claims for systems of piecework payment (and in some cases upgradings as well), they had not actually employed procedure to the limit. Therefore when the union side to the annual plant negotiations met, one full-time official described the situation as follows: 'The aim was to decide priorities for the various groups, particularly the stores — but we decided they should not take priority because they hadn't been through procedure, and there were more deserving cases, such as maintenance.'

The third means of establishing a claim was to present it solely for the annual negotiations. The majority of the 31 sectional claims presented were of this kind. Many were for very small groups of workers. The assembly-shop stewards began to discuss what their demands should be in August, seven months before the current agreement expired. They set up a sub-committee to discuss the question and by the beginning of the next month they had discussed their claim with the conveners and had reported their proposals to the assembly shop as a whole.

Other groups also undertook similar exercises. In some cases this was done by sections and, where stewards met on a shop basis, claims were co-ordinated. While the assembly stewards as a group took an early initiative on a shop-wide basis, some sections in the machine shops developed their own particular demands. The machine-shop stewards did not bring these claims together until early December — several weeks after a plant-wide claim had been developed by the JSSC and after the Delegate Conference.

The various claims reflect, of course, the dominant concerns of workers at a variety of levels. At the level of the plant as a whole, the following general demands were put forward: a substantial increase in wages; a new non-contributory pension scheme; a shorter working week; an extra week's holiday; and a better lay-off pay scheme and increased holiday payments.

These demands reflected general pressures of inflation and the sorts of wage increases achieved in the district. In addition, improved holidays and shorter hours can be seen as more general demands which have been typical of trade union aspirations for many years. The pension-scheme demands reflected similar aspirations which were all the stronger because of the age distribution of workers. The demand for improvements in the lay-off pay scheme reflected the problems we have noted in Part I over this question.

This problem also found expression in another demand. The assembly shop's primary concern was to become defined as low earners, because of frequent lay-offs, and hence receive favourable treatment. The assembly stewards argued that, while in theory they were skilled workers on a relatively good weekly wage, in practice their situation was considerably less favourable. They had few opportunities to boost their earnings significantly through piecework negotiations, and, more important, frequent lay-offs meant that their average weekly income was relatively low. Some assembly workers averaged only about two-thirds of the earnings they would have received over the year if they had been working a regular 40-hour week. They therefore demanded that they should receive the highest increase which any group received. This demand was voiced to the conveners at the JSSC and a resolution for a 'token strike to further the claim' on the day the officials met the conveners was proposed at an assembly stewards' meeting but defeated.

The dominant interests of the machine-shop stewards similarly reflected a concern with those who were less well off. Hence, they sought the following: low-earning sections should be made up to a new bonus level; there should be a higher bonus norm for future piecework negotiations; jobs three years old or over should be considered for retiming by management. In addition, they sought improved payments for waiting time, a common rate to be paid across the shop 'to enable the company to use fully the mobility of labour clause', improved payments for certain groups, and a number of changes in the details of piecework practice.

The toolroom, concerned with differentials, also sought the highest award of any other group, while a variety of other indirect groups sought higher job gradings and links with piecework groups. Two of these groups' demands were to become particularly important: those of the millwrights for a link with the toolroom, and those of the stores and associated groups for upgrading and piecework.

The task of the JSSC was not merely to develop a plant-wide claim but also to integrate and adjudicate between these various claims. A number of discussions were held and a sub-committee was formed to consider the question of pensions. Some elements of the plant-wide claim were the proper subjects for company-wide bargaining according to the agreed procedure. Primarily in order to reach agreement on the · company-wide claim, a Delegate Conference of representatives from the various plants along with a number of national and local full-time officials met in late November. It also provided an opportunity for an exchange of ideas on the plant negotiations. One full-time official described the Delegate Conference in the following way:

The Delegate Conference receives a report from the secretary of the NJC [National Joint Council — the negotiating body at national level] on the questions which have gone through procedure. The Conference also details the individual priorities of the individual plants and their general feelings. With the guidance of the officials, the individual plants decide their priorities. There is no voting and it's up to each plant to decide what it goes for — but there is an exchange of ideas, it gives the officials an idea of where members want to go, and it's possible that one plant learns ideas from the others.

Important for our plant was that the Delegate Conference agreed that the pension scheme which they alone wanted could be negotiated locally. This was accepted largely for two reasons — first, our plant had been pushing this claim for a number of years, and, second, other plants did not really believe that the claim could be successfully achieved.

In addition, it was agreed that at the company level the unions would seek the introduction of a 35-hour week without loss of pay, and the establishment of an additional week's holiday, together with additional days' holiday.

Our domestic organization, therefore, was involved in the development of claims for particular groups, for the plant, and for workers in the company as a whole. The details of the company-wide claim were largely developed by the union research departments. This claim involved a great deal of 'backroom work'; reviewing the performance and prospects of the company internationally; and arguing for a shorter working week in terms of favourable effects upon output, productivity, and labour costs, on the basis of studies in a variety of countries and also in terms of 'a qualitative change in society'.

The development of the union claim relating to the plant had taken up a large amount of time on the part of stewards and union officials; it had also been agreed by the membership. The time from the first formal discussion among assembly stewards to the actual submission of the plant-level claim was six months; if we see the pursuit of procedure by the millwrights as primarily directed towards the annual negotiations, the development of the claim took an even longer time.

The Management Counter-Claim

We have argued above that it is not merely the unions who develop claims. In part, the management in our company may be seen as exceptional in the extent to which they traditionally put forward counter-claims; the agreements reached always included a number of quid pro quos developed by management in exchange for wage increases and other benefits. To a degree, their counter-claims were dependent upon the exact nature of the union claim, and therefore invariably had to await the receipt of the latter. But, for the annual negotiations which we studied, they had spent three years developing a set of proposals for replacing the piecework system with MDW.

The origin of this idea may be seen as part of the more general trend away from payment by results in engineering. But, more specifically, management were concerned with two points. The first of these was the number of disputes which they believed to be directly attributable to piecework (this was a point which the unions were to question in the negotiations). Such disputes were seen as the result of the wide dispersion of earnings resulting from piecework drift, and led to management concern with disruptive effects upon production. In their view, elimination of piecework would lead to less disruption and hence improved output. In other words, what they saw as a more equitable wage structure would lead to higher production levels. (Such views were, of course, common more generally; e.g. Donovan, 1968; H. A. Clegg, 1970: 168–85; NBPI Report No. 65.)

The second factor favouring the change was the problems which piecework raised for management in terms of introducing change. Under the existing payment system, the full advantages of innovation were not achieved because of the necessary, and often long, process of negotiating new piecework values. The result was that change was very often slow. This was a particularly important consideration because a new model was planned for a year or so's time, which would involve major changes. It was feared that under a piecework system a new model would lead to significant increases in wages, as had happened at the last model introduction. The managerial problems of piecework became more acute with the major changes proposed, and hence the perceived advantages of a new payment system became that much greater. As one manager rather delicately explained, 'It was developed because industrial relations and line management saw problems with the payment system because of the unfair differentials in earnings and in view of the future.' Or, more succinctly, 'There was the problem of piecework drift and cost when the new model came in. We agreed MDW was the only way round the problem.'

The basic idea of switching to a time-based payment system was developed by the director of industrial relations and the manufacturing director, who had also previously worked in industrial relations. They had put the idea in their five-year plan and it was accepted at corporation level.

Once the basic idea had been accepted, more members of management became involved in formulating the policy in greater detail. Most of the more senior managers we spoke to had had some involvement in details, but among more junior managers some said, 'I had no involvement in MDW; I didn't know anything about it until the men did. I think that's bad.' Such involvement as many managers had was somewhat marginal: involving, for example, questions about the possible effects on production; the possibility of getting rid of setters; all workers being on one production rate; and the detailed costings of particular aspects.

The groups of managers primarily involved in the formulation of the proposals were industrial relations, work study, and to a lesser degree those in factory accounting. These groups were particularly concerned with the formalization and increased control of managerial behaviour. It would appear that work-study experts formed the core of the planning group, although, in the words of one manager, 'The question passed up and down the organization'. Work-study managers undertook surveys of the British experience of MDW and made a number of trips to company plants in the USA which were undergoing a transition from piecework.

The payment system selected was one which management hoped would reduce delays in introducing changes in production by cutting out any form of negotiation: 'To avoid a carry-over from piecework where everything was negotiated — [the system of MDW we chose] would probably lift effort.' Not only did this proposed change in the payment system have potential implications for production which were considered in some detail, but also it was planned to change the ratio of foremen to workers. Previously the ratio had ranged from 1:7 to 1:160. It was now seen as desirable to achieve a norm of 1:30, and before the negotiations many new foremen had been appointed. This was to have some importance in the negotiations themselves and also served to confirm in the minds of many stewards what had by August 1972 become 'really an open secret' (in the words of one manager). The unions had on a number of occasions asked managers if the company intended to introduce MDW and had met with denials.

Of possibly greater significance was the proposal to incorporate with MDW a new costing system, with every job standardized under a synthetic standard minute system. This involved not merely a great deal of work on the part of work study but also of course on the part of factory accounting. It was the detailed planning and implementation of the new costing system that accounted for the bulk of the latter's involvement.

On the management side, the planning of their counter-claim involved both the details of the MDW system and its wider repercussions for the organization, and the development of a strategy for the implementation of the scheme as far as probable worker reaction was concerned. Industrial relations became importantly involved in this area. Management conceived of two distinct phases in the process of negotiations. The first stage concerned negotiations to accept the principle of MDW: as one manager explained, 'We saw little trouble here.' The second stage was envisaged as the negotiation 'of standards, and how much money and for what':

We had expected to have to pay an average of £5 per man, and significantly more to some groups. Here we expected a really big fight and we were prepared to stand a long strike on this — we had had two years to prepare and had plenty of vehicles stacked away in various places.

The preparation for strike action on the part of workers was also carefully planned. In the earlier stages of preparation, market forecasts suggested a very low demand at the time of the negotiations, so low, in the words of one manager, 'that if there was no strike, there might have been a six-month lay-off'. This would have meant paying 80 per cent of average earnings to all those workers laid off. Even so, certain managers were involved in forecasting the likely cost of the expected strike, and also, as a manager put it, 'in the strategy for protecting the market for the company'. This involved finding locations for storing vehicles so that during the expected strike orders could still be met.

Like the 'best laid plans of mice and men', the management strategy suffered serious disruption because of the Conservative government's counter-inflation strategy. Stage Two of this strategy limited wage increases to £1 plus 4 per cent. Exceptions to this were permissible for the movement towards equal pay, and — an issue which became important in the negotiations — certain improvements in pensions. In addition, increases totalling £1 plus 4 per cent were meant to include any piecework drift not clearly related to increased effort. The previous year's drift was to be taken as the indicator of drift in the year following.

The legislation had a considerable impact on both management and unions generally. Our observation of full-time officials in negotiations covered the initial period of the legislation, and it was clear that officials and management were uncertain as to its meaning. Our fieldnotes record the views of one official:

I've read the White Paper. I carry a copy around with me but I'm not quite sure what the exact implications of it are. I've 'done' four or five works conferences since [the introduction of the policy] and things have been rather unclear. The only thing we can do is negotiate wage increases for whenever the limit ends.

The initial reaction of management in our plant was that any chance of introducing MDW had disappeared with the legislation.

The maximum they would be able to offer workers would be £2.86, and with other companies recently (before the incomes policy) paying as much as £8.00 for MDW, they felt initially that they could do nothing. 'But then', as one manager explained, 'we hit upon the idea of redundancies in assembly as a feasible method.' A fairly complex 'package' was therefore devised. This rested upon two key points. The first of these was that the £1 plus 4 per cent which was legally permissible, once piecework drift and other offsets were taken into account, was reduced from £2.86 to approximately £1.60. Second, paragraph 26 of the White Paper permitted increases in earnings associated with increases in output per head under existing payment schemes. Hence if redundancies occurred in the assembly shop while output was maintained, then more could be paid since output per worker had increased. The management therefore hoped to overcome the limits on wage increases in order to increase the attractiveness of their proposals, while at the same time reducing the attractiveness of rejecting MDW by emphasizing that the alternative legal wage increases were relatively small: 'We thought we could sell it on the grounds of the offsets against the £2.47 leading to a wage increase of only £1.60 compared with MDW giving £4.81 for some and the promise of more to come.' (The figure of £2.47 is reached by deducting from the £2.86 the cost of the additional holidays which were negotiated nationally, and by including canteen workers who were originally excluded from the 'package'.)

The management proposals were therefore presented in the negotiations as follows:

Stage I: The achievement of a better balance of earnings through:

(i) A reduction of 182 in the Assembly and Paint Shop areas by voluntary early retirement and redundancy.

(ii) A maintenance of current production levels which would result in an increased bonus yielding £4.79 on average. This increase would have the effect of increasing the current average earnings in the Assembly and Paint areas from £45.71 to a proposed new earning level of £50.50.

(iii) The Machine Shop conversion to MDW would not be based on the current average earnings of £48.87 but on the improved Assembly earnings level of £50.50.

Stage II would involve making an agreement for conversion to the new payment system; agreeing a new grade structure; establishing the grade rate for the new structure; allocating the money available under Government policy to go as far as possible in this agreement to move to the new grade structure; determining dates for the start and finish of Stage I and the date for conversion to MDW and the new grade structure.

More generally, 'the company', in its own words, 'sought the following significant changes by means of MDW':

(a) The introduction of a rational grade pay structure.
(b) The acceptance by employees of full work measurement in all areas, together with the acceptance of proper work standards and allowances.
(c) Introduction of fixed tea breaks.
(d) Introduction of a production component counting function.
(e) Acceptance of *full* mobility of labour.
(f) The elimination of the Chargehands' role of assigning and guiding labour in all departments except Facilities and Engineering.

This offer was seen as a 'total package', although particular elements within it were subject to negotiation. The detailed proposals were drawn up by work-study experts and then industrial relations, work study, and the manufacturing director 'thrashed out the package offer'.

In sum, the unions had developed an essentially conventional claim, apart from the inclusion of a retirement pension/grant, while management had prepared in great detail a set of proposals oriented primarily towards a major change in the payment system. However, these proposals were not actually revealed to the unions until March 1973, when the company was to reply formally to the unions' claim at plant level. Before this, negotiations had taken place at national level. Two points are of importance in these negotiations for what happened at plant level. First, a procedural form was agreed whereby national negotiations would be completed within thirty days so that the available cash for distribution was clear at local level. Sixty days were allowed for local negotiations, after which 'the NJC shall review all negotiations [in the various plants] and determine its involvement'. Second, a number of days' additional holiday were agreed, the cost of these having to be set against the legal maximum wage increase of £1 plus 4 per cent. These set constraints upon the local bargaining which we discuss in the next chapter.

8
The Beginnings of Local Negotiations

We have seen how the unions developed a claim at local level and management also prepared a counter-claim. By the beginning of 1973 both of these claims were well advanced but it was not until early February that the unions formally presented their claim to management at plant level, and it was a month later before management revealed their proposals.

The conveners, along with the senior stewards of the electricians and sheet-metal workers, formed the domestic representatives at the plant-level negotiations. In addition, the local full-time officials of all the unions with more than a handful of members were involved. Formally national officials could also be present, but in fact on no occasion did they attend, and a Regional Official of the AUEW chaired the union side. The local negotiating team included four members of the NJC. All of these met together at the beginning of 1973 to discuss the claim and, in the words of one official, 'to identify the key points of the claim'. The unions also considered the impact of the incomes policy which made clear the room for negotiation. For the first time ever, they knew the size of 'the pot', or the maximum amount of money which the company was willing or able to pay out. This had been confirmed at the first NJC meeting when the unions had asked the company if they intended to recognize the incomes policy and the Industrial Relations Act. (Most of the unions involved had formally refused to recognize either.) In line with more general company policy, management had replied that they were a law-abiding firm.

By this time, union officials and many of their members had become accustomed to the view that what was the legal maximum for wage increases was in practice a legalized norm. The importance of this will become clear later, but at this early stage the unions were less concerned with the overall size of wage increase than with the question of how the £1 plus 4 per cent should be distributed among the membership. As one official explained:

The problem was how we should distribute it. If we dealt with all the anomalies, there would be little if anything left for a straight increase. This is where the retirement grant was so important, as a substitute. This was because, really, a mass meeting could only support a straight increase where everybody was getting something. But, even then, if it was a straight percentage increase, then the lower paid would complain and might go into dispute; if it was in cash terms, then the skilled would go out because of the erosion of differentials. You just can't win.

It is here that the various means of establishing claims discussed earlier become important, and the negotiating team agreed to place a lower priority upon particular groups, particularly stores.

The incomes policy also had another effect upon the unions' position. Improved pension schemes were understood not to be permissible under the legislation and, given also the company's stance on the law and the distinction between areas suitable for national or local bargaining, the idea of a pension scheme became converted into a claim for a £2,000 retirement grant to be paid to all those retiring, no matter what their years of service with the company.

Management's Concern with the State of Industrial Relations

The union claim was formally placed before the company in early February. Normally this was a largely formal occasion, followed by a fairly lengthy adjournment for management to prepare their reply. But, at the initiative of management, a somewhat heated discussion developed on the state of industrial relations in the plant.

Management's concern related most immediately to the stores. Several days earlier the storemen had initiated a policy of blacking all 'new work' and refused to supply cover for absenteeism, in support of their claim for the introduction of a piecework incentive scheme. When a worker was suspended for refusing to handle what he considered to be new work, a strike ensued. This strike (other than a 4-hour resumption of work on the advice of the conveners and officials which quickly ended when 'new work' was again presented to the worker) lasted for several weeks. At the negotiations the company also reviewed a number of other recent disputes in the plant, and emphasized the deleterious effects upon production and other workers. The unions argued, in turn, that a large part of the trouble could be attributed to the newly appointed foremen who lacked the requisite industrial and human relations skills. Management doubted this, and sought to emphasize that the action undertaken was unconstitutional and that it was the duty of the officials to control their members.

With the continuation of the stores dispute, the company postponed the date of the next meeting 'pending the resolution of the [stores] dispute'. The formal justification for this was the company policy never to negotiate under duress. Part of the annual claim related to stores, and accordingly the maintenance of company policy demanded a postponement of the proposed meeting.

By the time of the next NJC meeting in early March when the progress of plant negotiations was to be reviewed, no developments had occurred. The stores were still on strike, and no further meetings had been held at local level. At the NJC meeting, management tabled a document relating to the dispute. After detailing the stores dispute, the document continued (unless otherwise indicated, the quotations in this chapter·are from the minutes of the negotiations):

The Trade Unions and Management are well aware of what has been happening within the . . . plant over the past eighteen months. From 1st November, 1971 until 23rd February, 1973 we had planned to assemble vehicles in 65 working weeks. Vehicle assembly performance during those 65 weeks has been appalling.

Number of weeks on full production	27
Number of weeks on 75%	12
Number of weeks on less than 50%	20
Close-down weeks	6

or the equivalent of only 44 working weeks out of the 65.

Management went on to argue that most of these losses were due to internal disputes and restrictions, and listed a number of these. They also questioned the unions' arguments that disputes were attributable to inexperienced supervision. They emphasized the loss of earnings to employees, the company's declining share of the home market, that over 1,700 men were currently laid off, and that 'lay-offs will now extend progressively.' The company statement concluded by emphasizing the unconstitutional nature of the stores dispute and its effects upon the annual negotiations. The company had attempted to:

Secure a resumption of normal working through the recognized processes that exist between the Company and the Unions, and they have failed. The departmental Stewards, the JSSC, the Conveners, the Local Full-Time Union Officials, and the National Officials have all recommended a resumption of normal working.

The circumstances are extraordinary. We have proposed to the . . . Conveners, subject to the co-operation of the Unions, to re-start production without Stores and Line Feeders. This will require the full co-operation of employees and, in particular, volunteers with a knowledge of stores activity to undertake the [Stores] work.

The Conveners are conveying our proposal to the JSSC this morning.

We are respectfully asking what action the Trade Union side of the Council is prepared to take to resolve the immediate problem of the stores, and to achieve a resumption of normal working, which will enable local discussions to take place on the problem of 'new work'.

According to one union official present at the meeting, 'there was uproar, the unions arguing it was against all union principles.' But no commitment or detailed reaction to the document was made by the unions. However, within a short time the strike ended, in part because of the efforts of stewards, conveners, and officials, and in part because of the strains which a long strike invariably imposes upon the strikers themselves.

Some time has been spent upon the discussion of this dispute in the negotiations because its very occurrence demonstrates the strength of feeling of some members over their sectional claims. It also demonstrates the extent to which other groups of workers, notably those in assembly, suffered from lay-offs and, consequently, the logic of assembly's own claim. But, from management's perspective, the highlighting of this dispute and the effects of disputes more generally, particularly as a reason for delaying plant negotiations, was a useful ploy since it was precisely on this sort of problem that they hoped to 'sell' MDW to the unions. Indeed, much of the documentation provided with reference to the stores dispute was to be used a few weeks later as an argument for the proposed change in the payment system. Moreover, the resumption of the dispute a few hours after the men

115

had returned to work, and over the same issue, suggests that one aim of management was to weaken both the unity and strength of the shop-floor organization in preparation for the confrontation they expected. We have no further evidence for or against such a view.

Management's Presentation of their Proposals

Several weeks later, with stores working again, negotiations continued and management replied to the union claim, employing in part the arguments above. In support of their claim, the unions had pointed to the increasingly favourable trend of sales and profits of the company, and their members' contribution to this. In reply, the management argued that company performance was by no means as good as the unions suggested, that such improvements as had occurred were primarily attributable to improved markets abroad, and that, far from making a significant contribution to company profits, the UK plants had experienced serious disruptions. Some of these were attributable to the state of the British economy, but many were due to internal industrial disputes.

The company reply then turned to the specific proposals in the union claim. They rejected the claim for a retirement grant on the grounds that the cross-subsidy involved in a non-service-related scheme did not 'represent the best return'. Second, they argued that pensions, as a major condition of employment, should be negotiated nationally and they were 'not prepared to depart from that position'. Management similarly argued that shift-working payments were a subject for national negotiations.

Before answering the 'predominantly wages features' of the union claim, the company reply reviewed the current and future situation at the plant. The development of production plants in other countries meant that Britain would continue as a significant producer only if such production met requirements and was achieved at a competitive cost. Our plant was seen to have advantages in terms of proximity to efficient suppliers, a skilled and experienced labour force, and a skilled and experienced management. But,

The Company had one major liability which was offsetting the assets, namely the . . . piecework system. The piecework system had the following adverse impact:

116

(a) It produced a wide disparity in earnings for direct workers largely unrelated to effort and performance. This caused resentment and discontent and produced conflict and interruptions to production.

(b) The company lost production when new features and facilities were introduced because employees on NOP [Not on Piecework: this refers to jobs on which piecework values have not yet been agreed. The workers concerned are paid average earnings.] deliberately restricted output until a piecework price was agreed.

(c) It was virtually impossible to plan a completion date for a major product change and the resumption of full production because of the endless negotiations which had to take place on piecework prices . . .

There was no doubt that both sides of this bargaining table were concerned to ensure the long term future of the plant. Even if no concern was expressed in respect of the future, then both employees and management were well aware of what had been happening on the plant in the past eighteen months.

Management then went on to review the impact of disputes as they had done at the NJC meeting, and concluded:

If this liability of piecework was not eliminated it required little imagination to see what the future held:

(a) . . . the replacements for the current range of models would be sourced elsewhere . . . The effect upon employment here would be catastrophic.

(b) As material costs equalized in the Common Market, the UK's principal asset would be eroded. The UK Company had to increase its efficiency if it was not to price itself out of the market.

Attempts to overcome the problems of the piecework system of which both sides were aware 'had now ceased to be effective'. According to the minutes:

Both employees and management therefore had a common interest in eliminating disputes. This could only be achieved by a more rational and equitable method of payment.

In reply to the wages feature of the claim the Company therefore wished to negotiate with the Trade Unions an agreement for the conversion of the . . . plant to Measured Daywork.

The company therefore proposed to change the payment system and explained how this was to be achieved and how it was permissible under the freeze. Detailed proposals on areas for redundancy and payments for voluntary redundancy and early retirement were given. In addition, management argued that 'The proposals either met in full, or made a substantial move towards, many of the aspirations identified in the Trade Unions' claims.' For they provided a wage increase; it overcame disparities which was the aim of the union proposal to link indirects to the movement of piecework earnings; it solved many of the thirty-one outstanding claims and anomalies; improved waiting-time payments would result, and by improving the base rate the increase would improve shift payments. In addition, while legislation 'prevented the achievement of an ideal conversion', the proposals made 'the best possible initial agreement' and 'a target for complete implementation when possible'. Documents containing the details of these proposals and arguments were handed to the union representatives.

A few days later we interviewed a number of the officials, and we were therefore able to gain their initial reactions. As one official described it, 'Last Monday [the day of the meeting] the company dropped a bit of a bombshell.' After asking a few detailed questions, the unions sought an adjournment. According to one official, the discussion in the adjournment covered the following areas:

The company had increased the number of supervisory staff — the conveners and I thought there had been some purpose in this . . . The company must have planned MDW for some time, but had been denying it. I, and the conveners, thought the company had worked out their plans long ago and were just waiting to strike while the iron, and their bargaining position, was hot . . . the unions were powerless to act . . .

In answer to the company, we said we doubted if it would be acceptable to the stewards. You see, we knew it was only the first offer of the company. Over the years, the bargaining has followed a set piece; we claim, the company formally replies and after the first two meetings we get down to the bargaining.

So, after the adjournment, the unions told the company that we couldn't commit ourselves to the principle of the deal and we'd have to go to the JSSC without any recommendation at all.

This itself was a major break with tradition. Many years ago, it had been agreed that only the final agreement would be taken back to the JSSC and the membership, because leaks of plans and feelings to management had been suspected. But it was decided to take the question of MDW back to the JSSC, because it involved a major issue of principle. It also seemed to reflect other factors. As the official quoted above suggested, the unions felt themselves to be in a weak position given the constraints of the incomes policy. It was also felt that the shop-floor was not strong enough to resist the company, given substantial lay-offs recently without pay. Further, there appeared to be a general feeling that if a company was determined to introduce MDW, unions generally lost if they tried to resist; this was certainly what had happened in other plants in the area. Finally, there were other problems. MDW was contrary to the policy of many unions, and therefore officials and conveners could not be seen to recommend it even if they wished to. But at the same time it was felt that many members would gladly accept the cash offered without thinking of the implications. Union principles and member wishes might well be in conflict; a strike was therefore unlikely. The solution was to take the matter back to the JSSC without any recommendation. One official explained this:

Many unions are hypocritical; they say they're opposed to MDW, but they negotiate it. Management knew that if they offered enough money, they could buy out the opposition. This was the real question at [the plant] — how much would the men get for the switch. This is really wrong because concentration on the immediate cash prospects often leads to problems in the longer run. But union officials are often happy to go along with this because if the members see the money they don't care about the problems which the officials foresee, and the officials are often willing to accept this because it gets the problems off their backs . . . I'm sure MDW will be introduced. There's no real problem with the freeze because you can just pay retrospectively.

The unions, after the adjournment, therefore asked the company what they would offer if MDW was rejected. According to the minutes 'The Company stated that its offer would be in accordance with the Government's restraints of £1 plus 4 per cent.' The outstanding claims would almost certainly be rejected, and they would only consider a 'topping up' of the current pension scheme. Management added that 'It was important that the Unions understood that the Company would have come forward with an MDW proposal irrespective of the existing Government restraints.'

The meeting ended with the unions stating that they would take the question of MDW to the JSSC for a decision, and the company agreed to provide copies of their proposals for the stewards if they were required. In addition, the next day the conveners met the management and had the details of the company proposals explained to them more fully.

Two days later a special meeting of the JSSC was called at which the conveners 'reported the state of negotiations', explaining that they and the officials felt the JSSC should be consulted before any further talks took place because of the issues involved. On being informed of the company proposals, the assembly members of the Q-E in particular reacted strongly since not only were many of them more generally opposed to MDW but also they saw their shop bearing the brunt of the proposals. After a lengthy discussion it was resolved 'that we reject the company proposals on MDW and we instruct our officials to re-negotiate with the company with the emphasis on the £2,000 retirement pension'. Since they rejected MDW in principle, it was agreed that they should not even receive copies of the company's proposals.

This apparently strong rejection on the part of the stewards reflected at least two strands of thought. The first was the most obvious one, that it really was a total rejection of MDW in principle. The other strand of thought was explained by an official as follows: 'The JSSC said, in effect, "We won't start talking [on the company proposals] until the company starts talking on our £2,000 retirement grant that we claimed." That was the *quid pro quo* of the JSSC that the conveners were told to follow.'

There appeared, however, to be relatively little concern over the negotiations among the stewards at this time. On the one hand, as became clear later, many thought that £1 plus 4 per cent was still available, as suggested by the concentration upon the retirement grant in the JSSC resolution. The stewards pointed out that elsewhere in the area the legal maximum had become an automatic wage-increase norm. They interpreted the company's reply on the alternative to MDW as offering the legal maximum. At the same time, as one of the officials quoted above suggested, the company proposals were seen by some as merely an opening gambit. The problem from this perspective was how the £1 plus 4 per cent should be divided among the various groups in the plant.

After their initial rejection of MDW in the middle of March, the JSSC merely confined itself to considering the ramifications of the incomes policy, and the assembly stewards, whose members would be affected most by the company proposals, did not discuss the question at all in their meetings. The machine-shop stewards did discuss the annual negotiations. They proposed that other company plants be contacted over the retirement grant. One steward suggested that a meeting of the members be called 'to get a feeling' about MDW, but this was rejected since it was contrary to normal practice during negotiations. While it was agreed that the machine-shop stewards would purchase pamphlets on MDW, they were not sufficiently concerned at this time to take up the offer of stewards from another plant to come and discuss their experiences with MDW.

The initial reaction to the proposals, therefore, was one of manifest rejection on principle. In reality, however, it would seem that the strength of feeling on the question was not great. Some certainly thought that the company was not particularly serious; the consensus appeared to be that they should wait and see what the company offered once their proposals had been rejected by the JSSC. There was little mention of the possibility or probability of confrontation.

9
The Search for Compromise

It was just after management had revealed their proposals that our full-time observation in the plant began. For the rest of the period, therefore, we are able to use not merely documentary materials and interviews but also our observational data. As suggested at the end of the previous section, feeling over the MDW proposals was certainly not running high when we began our observation. Hence, one convener discussed the question in the following terms:

I'm against MDW, but it would solve many problems for management, like the haggling over piecework . . . But they could only negotiate manning . . . The real problems are the freeze and assembly having to pay for the wage increase; then there's the question of complete flexibility. As conveners our lives would be easier, but the stewards wouldn't have much to do . . . The real problem is the money.

The Testing Process

At the end of March the NJC had reviewed progress in the plant bargaining and had agreed that 'The term of the existing Agreement . . . could be extended for a further eighteen days to allow discussions on a new Agreement to progress.' Accordingly, a further meeting was held at plant level several days later. Before the negotiations proper began, the union side met and discussed the situation. One convener explained the decision of the JSSC and the general feeling in the plant:

The main problem is the number of bods who will be made redundant — there needs to be more money •on offer if there's going to be redundancy . . . There's a feeling that the Company is wanting MDW but is giving nothing. While it's been rejected, a lot of people are talking about it as inevitable.

The uncertainty of the union position was confirmed by one official: 'The Company document is thrown out — but for how long we don't know.' They as negotiators were bound by the resolution of the JSSC. They could not negotiate over MDW: but given the uncertainty of shop-floor feeling they could envisage a change in their mandate. One official stated, 'I doubt if there'll be a strike.'

This view that feelings might well change rested not only upon the limited feeling against the MDW proposals but also upon the fact that otherwise it would be impossible to meet the thirty-one claims and give a general and substantial wage increase. But there was only one course open to the negotiators at present; that was to investigate the possibility of management improving what was thought to be their alternative offer: 'Management have said the alternative is £2.50 and two days' holiday . . . we've got to concentrate on the £2,000 grant . . . we'll have to see if £2.50 is the maximum or not.'

When management entered the negotiating room, the unions therefore emphasized the rejection of the Company's proposals and went on:

So there's still our claim to be met. There are a number of questions — is £2.50 the final offer? There are the thirty-one claims to be satisfied: there's the question of the restrictive clauses; there's the grant — if you granted this, a lot of problems facing us would be looked at in a different light.

Management questioned the accuracy of the union report on shop-floor feeling: 'Did the shop-floor understand? . . . Because we've had playback which indicates a mixed reception to our proposals . . . it's clear that some people misunderstood.'

There was then an adjournment for management to consider their position. The company was now in a difficult position: the JSSC resolution formally rejected MDW in principle, and management, it will be remembered, had not expected this but rather a fight over what they would pay for MDW. The situation was somewhat ironic, for we have seen that in fact the feeling on the shop-floor, at least as perceived by many of the union negotiating team, was generally in accordance with management's

123

prediction. The unions themselves were hinting at the possibility of the shop-floor accepting MDW if an improved offer was made, but given their mandate they could not openly negotiate on these terms.

Management did not appear aware of these nuances behind the statements of the unions. Indeed, after the negotiations, one manager stated that they perceived no signs of division within the union negotiating team. They therefore believed themselves to be facing a situation in which the JSSC resolution did *not* reflect true shop-floor feeling and where they felt they had still to push MDW. This conviction on the part of management was to become an important factor later.

On the resumption of negotiations, therefore, the key management negotiator repeated management's proposals and emphasized that any alternative offer, limited to £1 plus 4 per cent, would not solve many of the claims and, with offsets, would be a small increase. But he added that he would only make such proposals 'if I had a wild rush of blood to the head'.

One official in particular was trying to persuade the unions to accept discussion of MDW but this was confused by the second strategy which management adopted; for they questioned the accuracy with which their proposals had been transmitted to the stewards and members: 'I'm going to do something now which I have never done before. I am not convinced about the communication [of our proposals] to the shop stewards, because there was uproar when they were in the [local] paper.'

For the unions, the issue was now one of an outsider criticizing and questioning the working of their organization. Before this explicit statement by the company, one or two officials had been hinting at the possibility of a deal: 'The basis of rejection, I think, was the view that "we're not having this for £2.50."' Now the reaction was very different. Management were told: 'If you want [MDW] you sell it to the workers. But you accept the repercussions if you want to do it — I won't take the way you've treated us . . . Now what is the answer to our claim?'

Management replied that there would be no improved cash offer, and that a retirement grant was a subject for national negotiation. The unions disputed this latter point, arguing that it could be treated separately, that consequential claims from other plants were unlikely on the basis of past experience when holidays had been negotiated locally. Management argued that a grant would be subject to the incomes policy; the unions questioned this, and also pointed out: 'There are ways of getting round that . . . anyway, the company's got to say yes before the government can say no.'

In an adjournment, the unions discussed the position. The view was expressed that the size of the company offer was not really due to legislation, and some of the officials suggested the possibility of part-financing the retirement grant since it appeared that management were now ready at least to talk about the grant. The conveners rejected this idea for the present, unless there was more money available: 'I know the members are not willing to give up the whole of their wage increase for the grant.' While there was, therefore, a readiness to move their position, the unions were uncertain simply because they did not know what the cost of the grant would be. On the resumption of negotiations, they therefore asked management if they could cost the grant, without this implying any commitment. Management agreed to this, but said it would take a week to do. The unions also raised the question of the outstanding claims but the company refused to move on these.

In an adjournment, officials again raised the possibility of discussing MDW 'because of the way the negotiations are going'. The conveners were hesitant but agreed that it might be possible to take to the members a 'package' of £2.50 plus the £2,000 grant and discussion of a new payment system: 'But we won't recommend it'. Several of the officials agreed, stating they would not recommend such a package either, but they would accept the decision of the men. 'But if we don't recommend it we can't be blamed when things go wrong.'

There had, then, been a significant move on the part of the union side, but this was not pursued fully by management in these negotiations. This was because the unions had raised the interpretation of the lay-off pay agreement by management in relation to a dispute in progress. Management, after considering their position in the adjournment, did not make any clear move towards the unions' demands that those men who were currently laid off should be paid, but said that they would inform the conveners of their decision the next day. The ensuing argument over this ruined the opportunity for management. However, all was not totally lost. According to the minutes, 'It was agreed that the Trade Unions would review their position and the Company, without commitment, would report back to the Trade Unions on the cost of [a retirement grant] scheme at a meeting arranged [for a week's time].'

A Possible Basis for Negotiation

Discussion of the state of the annual negotiations among stewards and members now became somewhat more common. Informally, the next day the conveners discussed the situation with various members of the Q-E, explaining what had occurred in the negotiations and attempting to assess which groups were most likely to oppose the formal JSSC resolution. In particular, it was felt by the Q-E that either the possibility of negotiating MDW should be delicately investigated or that all sectional claims should be dropped and the wage increase paid across the board. The latter served to satisfy the demands of some of the most powerful groups in the plant, notably assembly and the toolroom, but the conveners and Q-E were worried that other groups — stores, maintenance, and the drivers, in particular — might oppose such a move.

Two days after the meeting with management, a special JSSC was called to report on the state of negotiations and to investigate the feelings of the stewards. The conveners reported that management had not really changed their position, and that given this there was little prospect of achieving the whole of the claim. They did not raise the question of MDW specifically for a number of reasons. First, they themselves were not in favour of it and did not want to find themselves in a position where they might appear to be recommending it. Second, if they had done this, the stewards could legitimately challenge them for going against the JSSC mandate. They therefore stressed to the stewards the implications of the situation which they were facing; since they believed £2.50 was available, they pointed out that with this limited amount of cash on the table it would be quite impossible to meet the sectional claims, and stewards should realize this. A lengthy discussion ensued and the 'hard-liner' stewards argued that they should seek more than £2.50. One convener replied, 'I agree, but it would be possible only if everyone else did the same. If the miners won't fight the government, then there's little hope for anyone else.'

The result of the discussion was an acceptance that only £2.50 would be available. It was therefore resolved:

That we accept the company undertaking to cost the £2,000 retirement grant benefit and give a reply at the next meeting, and we move that all monies forthcoming from the Wages Agreement this year be equally divided between all the hourly paid personnel at [the plant].

Only seven of the 120 or so stewards present voted against this resolution. The fears of widespread challenge to the dropping of the sectional claims were therefore not realized, but the conveners were still aware that the members more generally might question the JSSC decision. Shop meetings were held that lunch-time in the machine shops and the assembly shop, at which the conveners and members of the Q-E explained the state of the negotiations and the JSSC decision that any increase should be across the board. In addition, they stressed that the retirement grant was legal and could therefore be paid by the company. There was general support for the JSSC recommendation.

The union position was, then, essentially reaffirmed. There was to be no discussion of MDW, and in the production areas an across-the-board increase appeared to be acceptable. But this was not true of all the indirects. The maintenance men, on hearing the JSSC recommendation, sought a meeting with their official at the earliest opportunity and contacted him with this view in mind without going through the conveners. Indeed, they later informed the conveners that on the day that the negotiations were to continue they would be awaiting the attendance of the official at a meeting.

They were indeed waiting when the officials arrived for the negotiations. The conveners explained the situation to them and it was agreed that two of the officials and one of the conveners should meet the men. The officials sympathized with the maintenance men's case and had previously given a commitment to promote it in the current negotiations. Moreover, 'We cannot refuse to see them — the members have a right to demand to see their officials.'

At the meeting the officials stressed their sympathy with the maintenance claim. 'But', one of the officials continued, 'the facts of the matter are that since that time [that we met you] there has been a freeze imposed and the shop-floor have decided that any wage increase should be across the board. Our hands really are tied.'

Although, the official said, he was amazed at how law-abiding the unions had become, the fact of the matter was that no one had taken on the government. If the maintenance men chose to, he would back them but he could see no chance of success. In answer to questions, the officials emphasized that there was no way round the legal maximum — 'the best brains in the unions' had not discovered any loop-holes. The maintenance men would merely have to make do with £2.50; it was necessary to realize 'It's not a just world, and you've got to face that.' The maintenance men could not be described as happy with this situation; indeed, immediately after the meeting several of them were talking in terms of imposing a work-to-rule in support of their claim. But they were not so angry that they thought in terms of any more dramatic form of action which would have endangered the pay of those who were laid off.

After this meeting, the officials and convener returned to the negotiations where management gave details of three possible schemes for a retirement grant. After checking on certain of the details, the unions sought an adjournment to consider the position.

The conveners argued, and the officials accepted, that the only possible scheme was one which provided for payment of the grant no matter how many years of service. Discussion really concentrated, however, on the question of whether or not the unions should agree to workers part-financing the scheme. The conveners rejected this possibility 'at present', and so, in an attempt to 'reach a negotiating position' one of the officials again raised the question of 'a change in the wage structure':

Convener: We've tossed that out. We refused to talk about it.
Official: They [the company] understood us to be rethinking our position on restructuring . . . Our position is, then, no MDW but we want £1.15 [the cost of the grant scheme] plus £2.86. That's the situation we're asking for? [Nods of agreement.] I'm not saying we're wrong.
Convener: I don't ever recall saying MDW for a pension.

The official stressed the need to persuade the company to accept the grant in principle, but it was agreed that workers part-financing the retirement grant would not yet be raised. When management returned, therefore, the unions argued:

[The grant] is the most important factor and the money we are dealing with. Shop-floor feeling is strong enough to lead to difficulties. On April 19 we can break down. So we wish you to offer, in addition to the money, the £1.15 scheme to be met by the company.

Management rejected this demand but did offer to negotiate a retirement grant, to be paid for by the workers as part of a total package including the end of piecework.

In the subsequent adjournment, the unions found themselves essentially in the same position as at the end of the previous negotiations, but views were now somewhat different:

Convener: We reject the company offer — we're being manoeuvred by the company to talk MDW. We're working ourselves into a box.

1st Official: The company are moving, and MDW is negotiable. If there's a failure to agree, the company can implement [their proposals] and the shop-floor may or may not fight.

2nd Official: The only addition is the grant. We've got no authority to negotiate, we've got to go back to the shop-floor.

3rd Official: We can't be seen to negotiate. I'm worried; every time we go to the shop-floor, if I were a steward I'd begin to think the conveners were trying to sell MDW.

2nd Convener: We've got no licence even to talk MDW — if the workers want it, they'll have it . . . As yet, everyone has accepted that there will be no MDW — [the company] is giving us nothing. There will be many problems — we've told the shop-floor MDW may overcome them — but they say 'no'.

3rd Official: Do we fail to agree or report back to the shop-floor?

1st Convener: It would be dangerous to go back because they would ask what we've been doing and we'd say talking about MDW.

The Shock of the Legal Maximum

A major decision had to be made by the unions. But one of the officials raised a question about the assumptions on which they had been operating up to that point: 'On the question of a failure to agree [the company] hasn't offered £1 plus 4 per cent yet.' A debate ensued on whether or not this was so, and finally one of the officials went to inquire about it from management. He returned to state:

£1 plus 4 per cent is not on the table without the [MDW] package.

2nd Official: That's not funny, refusing to give the legal [maximum] . . . I told maintenance that was on.

Convener: It's intellectual harassment.

1st Official: We'd better fail to agree as of now — it will be better for a dabble.

Management returned and restated that their offer was a total package — 'I'm not prepared to consider any other alternative.' The union side argued that the company had previously offered the legal norm/maximum, to which a manager replied:

I said [that would be the case] if I had a rush of blood to the head . . . I only drew a comparison.

Official: We are registering a failure to agree.

Manager: I'm surprised.

The failure to agree had resulted from a serious mis-understanding because one side saw the £1 plus 4 per cent as virtually an automatic right and the other saw it as something to be negotiated. It is certainly idle to speculate; but the course of negotiations up to this point was such that the union negotiating team, and probably the shop-floor more generally, had certainly not thrown out the company proposals. It is remarkable, therefore, that the unions were dabbling with the company proposals even though they thought £2.50 was available. Management were surprised at the failure to agree. The next day they contacted the chairman of the union side to propose a further meeting, ostensibly with the purpose of clarifying the reason for the failure to agree, but certainly some members of the union negotiating team interpreted this as an attempt to resume negotiations.

Such a resumption was seen in different ways. Some of the union negotiating team at least hoped that it would mean an offer of £1 plus 4 per cent. But at least one convener, in discussions with members of the Q-E, feared that management would again attempt to raise their proposals and that the officials would 'fall for it'.

The way in which this new meeting was arranged is of interest. It first involved the company phoning the chairman of the union side to seek a new meeting in order to clarify the reason for the failure to agree (FTA). The latter rang the other officials and finally told management that they were agreeable to a meeting if the conveners agreed. Management then informed the conveners that a further meeting was arranged; the reaction of at least one convener was that the reason for the FTA was perfectly clear, and that a further meeting would serve no useful purpose. He feared that the company was 'conning' the officials, although another convener told several members of the Q-E that he agreed that 'the union side was not clear on the reason for the FTA'. The conveners phoned their local officials, and learnt that at least one of them was opposed to the additional meeting.

Over the next few days, the conveners discussed the situation with members of the Q-E. One in particular was suspicious that the officials were too ready to compromise with management, and he reiterated the dangers of MDW, notably low pay and loss of control. But even this convener confided to a member of the Q-E that the real problem was that 'The men might accept it; it's the men's right to decide, but we cannot recommend it.' Such a possibility was at least delayed if the unions refused to discuss the company proposals.

Confrontation was now becoming a greater probability, as was reflected at the next week's JSSC meeting. One convener gave a report of the negotiations, stressing that management had not even offered £1 plus 4 per cent, and continued, 'I'm afraid that the management are getting at the officials — we're at the top of a slippery slope and we're about to slide into MDW.' This convener, and other stewards, again stressed the dangers of MDW, and the fact that a retirement grant was legally permissible since another company had already made a similar award: 'There is something wrong if [this other company's] officials can get a grant, but ours can't. And some of them are the same people.'

For the first time, the stewards seriously considered being forced into a strike, and many were worried by this prospect: 'I'm afraid there's going to be a confrontation; management are taking a very hard line . . .' 'Management are stockpiling ready for a fight . . .' 'Management are getting difficult [in piecework negotiations] . . .' 'Management will stand firm because they've got to pay for all their new foremen.'

The stewards' concern with this possibility was in many respects quite natural; not only had they been wrong in their assumptions but also no group positively enjoys the prospect of a strike, particularly on such a scale, when management have been able to plan their strategy. One convener tried to calm many stewards' feelings of 'righteous indignation', stating, 'If there is going to be confrontation, it's no good if it can only last one day.' In addition, he was hesitant to take the question to the men:

The decision might go the wrong way. I've had a lot of people come to me privately about MDW; a lot in the machine division would go with it. They tend to forget that if piecework goes in assembly it'll soon get them as well . . . People should come out openly about how they feel about MDW. I'm afraid that the men might well vote for it.

This quote shows clearly that the ambivalence which had existed since management declared their MDW proposals still existed; the conveners and Q-E still feared that the earlier management contentions might well be perfectly correct. Largely because of this

131

the only decision reached was to have another meeting of the JSSC immediately after the next meeting with the company.

There was a certain degree of guarded optimism when the union side met immediately before the negotiations. The chairman explained how the meeting had arisen and said that in his view the reason for the failure to agree was perfectly clear: 'Because £1 plus 4 per cent was only there if we accepted MDW'. But the latent possibilities were argued by one official:

If [the company] is rethinking, then we should take every initiative to achieve what we were told to achieve . . . if we can get £1 plus 4 per cent and the retirement grant on the understanding that we are prepared to discuss the wage structure, I think we've got a recommending situation. If we fail to agree there will be chaos or the alternative is a possible confrontation, and I wouldn't like to see that.

This possibility was discussed, but rejected finally when one of the conveners summed up the position:

We should clear this up — whether MDW is introduced is irrelevant — that's up to the members. Confrontation is possible, and I've said this to the JSSC, and may lead to MDW. But I won't recommend MDW . . . we would lose control. MDW has been rejected by JSSC. If the members want it I believe they will have it. But at present MDW is rejected. The company want MDW . . . but they won't get it without a confrontation.

One of the officials who favoured negotiating MDW had, before the meeting, been in contact with other members of the negotiating team and had gained what he interpreted as their support. But he did not receive this at the meeting, and later when he asked why not he was told that, given convener opposition, there was no point in backing a loser.

When management entered and were asked whether they had 'moved', they merely replied that 'We are in a position to negotiate our proposals.' A debate ensued whether £1 plus 4 per cent had ever been on the table, and the unions further argued that 'the credibility of these negotiations' was at stake unless the company made an improved offer.

The unions asked for an adjournment and continued their previous debate. The considerations involved can best be seen by quoting from our fieldnotes at some length:

1st Official: If we're not careful, our asking questions will lead to us negotiating. Are we negotiating?

2nd Official: That's not quite true . . . unless we negotiate, the alternative is chaos, and we'll be selling the indirects down the river.

2nd convener: No. There's been no offer yet except the package, we've got nothing to recommend to the shop-floor. We can tell the shop-floor there are problems about an across-the-board increase, but we're not in that position yet.

3rd Convener: I think [the company] believes the shop-floor is not saying what we are saying . . . he's pushing for us to take MDW to the shop-floor.

1st Official: There is no point in negotiating. We will just demean our position.

1st Convener: I agree. They're trying to find out how weak we are.

2nd Official: How weak are we?

2nd Convener: MDW will only come, if ever, after a confrontation.

2nd Official: We don't normally follow a mandate.

2nd Convener: We're now in a completely new world, MDW. It's different.

The official favouring MDW pushed it to a vote and only he voted in favour. It was agreed that they would fail to agree. When management re-entered the unions declared:

Let us just say we are failing to agree because £1 plus 4 per cent is not on the table.

Management: It is, as part of a package.

Official: We are the ones registering the failure to agree and it was on that.

The scene for confrontation was now set.

10
Steward Commitment to Confrontation

The confirmation of the FTA led to no immediate rise in the 'temperature' of the plant, and only a few discussions on the question occurred. In part, this was because stewards were preoccupied with a variety of other major problems in the plant, namely lay-offs and a number of probable disputes which would serve to increase unpaid lay-offs.

Such discussions as occurred tended to look back at what had happened rather than forward to a strategy to resolve their problems. So, for example, an official and two of the conveners discussed the situation; they were uncertain whether the shop-floor were in favour of MDW and while they had explained the problems — 'we can do no more' — they accepted the possibility that the bulk of stewards did not appreciate the implications of an across-the-board increase. Essentially, it was felt that an all-out strike was unlikely because the shop-floor might well accept MDW, but that would be 'no skin off our nose'; the point was that they could not negotiate changing the payment system because they had no mandate.

The reason for this calmness was many felt that discussions would be resumed. As one convener said to a member of the Q-E, 'I'm disgusted with the course of the negotiations. They can't do anything at national level. It's bound to be referred back for local discussion.' This view was indeed correct. At a meeting of the NJC the day after the confirmation of the FTA, the unions told the company that 'If the Company is not prepared to make an alternative offer of £1 and 4 per cent then it will have to accept the consequences of its action.' The company stated that it would not improve its offer, and the unions concluded by stating that they would 'recommend to the EC [Executive Committee] members of each Trade Union that they support any action taken by the membership concerned, in pursuance of their claims'. At the same time, both the unions and management expressed their readiness to meet if the other side wished. In addition, the company stated that if its offer was accepted before the end of April it would be prepared to make its offer retrospective to the beginning of the month.

While our fieldnotes show that some members of the Q-E discussed the dangers of MDW in the next few days, there was still an implicit expectation that they would receive £2.50. A meeting of the craft stewards, while discussing the dangers of management's proposals, only passed resolutions concerning the breach of the agreement which would be involved if £1 plus 4 per cent alone was paid across the board.

It will be remembered that the assembly shop would have been the area most badly and immediately affected by the company's proposals. But, when at a meeting of the assembly stewards a few days after the confirmation of the FTA, a member of the Q-E introduced a discussion of MDW, it was only after stating that he was surprised that no one else seemed interested.

However, it was here that the first serious discussions of the problem of mobilizing the membership took place. Two members of the Q-E particularly stressed 'the need to fight MDW. We've got to get the men together and educate them against MDW . . . there's a risk that they won't realize the full dangers.' In addition, the assembly stewards were afraid that they would be outvoted in JSSC and agreed that, if necessary, they would insist that only those directly involved (i.e. assembly) could vote on the redundancy proposals included in the company's plans. However, it was agreed that they would not begin to hold meetings to 'educate the membership'. Given that many of the assembly workers were laid off, it would be difficult to ensure good attendance at a meeting, and there would be a problem of 'low morale'. Second, the hope that confrontation would not occur still existed. As one Q-E member argued, 'MDW might not come in . . . We've been caught before [telling the men about things which have then not happened] and looked fools in front of JSSC.'

The Beginnings of the 'Propaganda War'

The situation began to change only towards the end of April, when management made it clear that they intended to attempt to implement their proposals. As had many other companies in a similar situation, they distributed a 'message to all hourly-paid employees' which presented their case for MDW. This document began 'For some time it has been obvious to everyone working at [the plant] that the situation in the factory is far from satisfactory for us all. Even our families have begun to ask if there is no way that progress can be made.' The document went on to list the disruption to production and the consequent dangers to the market, and concluded that 'In the course of time this could mean that the standard of living of all working here will deteriorate.' Under a heading 'what have Employees already lost?', the document pointed out that in the last sixteen months assembly had lost the equivalent of fifteen complete working weeks, others had lost time, and all had lost earnings. Management argued that:

the cause in 89 per cent of cases was a dispute related to disparity of earnings in [the plant]; that is, in one way or another, piecework. In short, it is continual piecework disputes that are causing employees heavy loss of earnings, with the worry that future earnings and employment have been put in jeopardy by loss of production.

Management then detailed their proposals as to 'what can be done', outlining their proposals for MDW 'incorporating a more equitable wage structure, with immediate cash improvements for everyone'; and 'a retirement grant, based on total service'. The document included a wide range of examples of current and proposed rates for different jobs, suggesting increases in several cases of about £10 or more, and in other cases as little as £1.35. It also emphasized that the new rates were subject to negotiation, and that 'future increases would be paid as soon as government policy allows.' The document concluded:

The above proposals go further, in financial terms, than any other method to resolve the outstanding sectional claims.

They will remove grievances and disputes caused by inequalities in earning levels. By accepting them, we would achieve a first and major step towards a fair balance between pay and effort, and greater job security with increased earnings throughout the year.

Two aspects of this document are important. The first is the underlying thinking of management, the second the reaction of the unions and the shop-floor.

We have already noted that management were convinced that the shop-floor would accept at least the principle of MDW. They had been surprised by the first JSSC resolution, and questioned the accuracy of union communications to their members. It also appears that, on the basis of this view and the 'playback' they received, they had been trying for some time to make the unions take the matter back to the membership for a decision. They had so far failed in this, but it was clear that, if the unions were to maintain their present position, a mass meeting would have to be called soon. Management therefore wanted to ensure that their employees — the union membership — received the details of their proposals in the way in which they wanted them presented. For this reason they effectively took up the challenge given to them by one official at an earlier meeting that 'If you want MDW, then you try to persuade the members.' By doing so, however, they were going against a long-standing tradition in the plant that communications of this kind were left to the unions. They had already questioned the efficiency of such communications; now they were attempting to set up an alternative channel.

One of the 'hard-liner' stewards had for some time been forecasting, on the basis of experience in other plants, that the company would begin to 'wage a propaganda battle'. He had therefore been arguing that the unions should also attempt to educate the membership, not merely by word of mouth by also by pamphlets. Many stewards were annoyed at this new move by management, and at the same time this first document of management's — for others were to follow — created a good deal of interest on the shop-floor; numerous members indicated interest in the management proposals and were critical of the unions on two grounds — that they had failed to detail the proposals, and that the unions never seemed able to provide such documentation for their members.

In the next few days there was some discussion of the company proposals among members and among the conveners and the Q-E. There was general agreement within the Q-E and the conveners that, as one convener put it, 'We've got to prepare for a fight and plan carefully. We need to ensure that people understand the situation.' The mass meeting, however, was dismissed by the conveners as a means of doing this for there was 'a danger of disruption'. One convener told a group of stewards that he was 'confident of the members' attitude', and that they should take a ballot, 'to prove to management that the conveners were right about the men'.

Such an expression of confidence in fact exaggerated the convener's own views. With members of the Q-E, conveners typically expressed much less confidence. While the conveners were genuinely uncertain — as were most stewards — of membership feeling, statements of confidence, to populist stewards especially, were a means of fostering opposition. To admit doubts openly would be to take a defeatist stance, and, like confidence, might well be self-confirming.

The Determination of Strategy

At a JSSC meeting at the end of April, the stewards had to make the crucial decision of what they should do. The basic uncertainty which many stewards felt is reflected in our verbatim notes of this meeting. The bulk of stewards, from this point on, could be broadly divided into two groups, both of whom accepted, at least implicitly, that at this time it was by no means certain that the members would oppose MDW, certainly to the extent of embarking upon what could be a long-drawn-out strike. The first group consequently advocated a vigorous strategy of 'educating the membership'. The second group, which never became quite so vociferous (since they could have been accused of going against the JSSC resolution), while they opposed management's proposals in principle nevertheless advocated negotiating MDW as a long-stop, so that even if there were to be a strike, and they lost, they would not return to a situation where management could do as they wished. For it was argued that no one had ever won a strike of this kind and strikers had therefore had to return to a primarily managerially determined situation. At this meeting of the JSSC, the disparity in underlying views began to develop.

The stewards were formally told of the FTA in the negotiations and its ratification nationally. There was an immediate demand from one of the assembly Q-E members that 'We call a mass meeting and recommend strike action in favour of £1 plus 4 per cent.' One of the conveners warned of the need for caution, for such a decision should not be entered upon lightly: 'We've got three choices: all out; less dramatic action and negotiate; or to put up and shut up.' Only one populist steward, who represented a group of men who felt strongly about their sectional claim, recommended the last course of action: 'I'm against a strike because strikes against MDW have never succeeded. We should just go without any wage increase this year.' This idea gained little support. Similarly, the demand for an immediate strike was quickly silenced on the advice of the conveners and the more militant Q-E members: 'We've got to fight a propaganda battle — management always do.' 'We need literature to counter management's. Many of my members say they don't know the catches in the management statements.' More generally, the conveners and others were concerned whether they really knew what the shop-floor felt, and feared that there would be splits among the membership: 'Dayworkers especially aren't strongly opposed.'

The conveners emphasized that if members did not understand the situation then it suggested that the stewards were not doing their job properly; certainly there was no excuse for any steward not understanding the situation, and perhaps many now regretted not attending a course on MDW which had been arranged a year or so earlier. It was agreed, however, that some form of member education was necessary, and that a mass meeting was not a suitable forum for this. It was finally agreed that the JSSC should produce its own document.

One of the conveners, with the help of two officials, had been preparing such a document over the last few days, and said at the JSSC meeting that, after gaining the agreement of the other conveners, the document would be distributed. He added, 'You see, I don't lead from the rear, despite what some people say.' Support for the idea of a document rested upon a number of considerations: the importance of the issue, the fact that management were distributing 'propaganda' and, third, the apparent attitude of management to the union. Their attitude was reflected in the document and in the fact that 'Management were secretive. They circulated their document while the JSSC was going on.'

The need for propaganda meant that strike action could not be undertaken immediately, despite the fact that several assembly members of the Q-E argued, 'We should strike now while management are unprepared.' Another factor was also important, and was stressed by one of the conveners and several of the Q-E; 'We should wait a while for the mass until everyone's back at work.' 'We should wait because it's bad to start a battle on management's ground.'

Underlying this view, however, was the feeling that they should be cautious. Since it was by no means certain how the membership felt, there was a risk of stewards failing in their attempt to lead the members against MDW; if this happened, management would be in a strong position. A strong lead by the stewards could, in such a situation, mean both a weakening of union leadership by defeat and a longer-term loss of control when a unilaterally determined, and hence harsh, system of MDW was introduced. There were, therefore, a number of views underlying the resolution of JSSC: 'That we recommend to a mass meeting that we give notice of our intention to withdraw our labour in favour of a claim for £1 plus 4 per cent plus pensions along the lines of Phase 2 of the Government legislation.' The conveners finally warned the stewards that they should not go chatting to management about their intentions: 'Management will hear of our plans, but even so stewards should deny it [i.e. the intention to strike].'

In the next few days, the stewards began to discuss the situation rather more; this was particularly true of leader stewards who talked among themselves, attempted to pressure populist stewards in their areas, and chatted about the issue with their members, particularly the opinion-leaders. We can see this activity most clearly by looking at the activities of one member of the Q-E over the next three days.

With one populist steward the Q-E member stressed the importance of the issue and the way in which management had 'set them up. Management are clever. They planned things so that the men have got to fight on management terms and against each other . . . They softened assembly up by lay-offs, because they want MDW for the new models which are coming in.' With a group of other Q-E members he had several conversations about the consequences of MDW; stories were exchanged of the downright physical exhaustion of older workers in plants where MDW had been introduced. Another leader said: 'We don't want a situation like [another company] in the thirties — they had to put their coats on hooks which were lifted up into the roof until the end of the day . . . they used to photograph people, and they even checked how much time you spent in the lav.'

The member of the Q-E chatted to several opinion-leaders on his section. He told one, 'The management document is a con to get the plant to desert assembly . . . their retirement grant's useless and the money is fiddled. We should send [the documents] back.'

An opportunity to do so appeared the same day when a second

management document was distributed by the foremen. The steward ostentatiously tore his document up, and he and others shouted that 'It's a try-on.' One of the opinion-leaders placed his document on a notice board, and wrote over it, 'Whose idea is this? Nixon's or [the managing director's]?' (It was the time of the Watergate and other scandals surrounding the American President.)

The second management document began by emphasizing the disadvantages of piecework and that the unions

have suggested the alternative of negotiating
— a piecework agreement on similar lines to the present one;
— a retirement grant provision of £2,000 unrelated to service.
The reason why we have not put forward an offer on these lines is that *we do not consider that a piece-work agreement would provide an answer to the basic problems which are troubling us all* and would, indeed, serve to prolong them [management emphasis].

Management then went on to list the deductions from £1 plus 4 per cent which 'Government legislation requires. After the deductions, and assuming no new linked schemes, the general increase would average 95p, varying by bonus level from 75p to £1.22 a week.' Examples of the wage increases for different jobs were then listed, and on the opposite page wage increases under MDW. The contrasts showed an average difference between the two proposals of just under £4 a week. In addition, the costs of the retirement grant proposals were compared — the union proposal costing £1.15 a week, 'which would also have to be set against the increases shown above', compared with 45p for the company proposals. Comparisons of increases in overtime and shift rates were also listed, and finally a difference of £4.10 in the lay-off pay for an 'Assembler' was noted.

In the 'Conclusion' to the document, management stated:

We feel that another piecework agreement would:
— do nothing to resolve outstanding claims;
— fail to meet the underlying wishes of those employees now seeking linked schemes or transfer to piecework at improved rates;
— continue for a further period the disadvantages of our present situation with its frequent piecework disputes and losses of production and wages.

They then repeated the advantages of their MDW proposals and concluded (their emphasis): *'Finally, we hope the Trade Unions will be prepared to negotiate on the basis of the Company's proposals.'*

Management were not only trying to persuade the membership; they also began to attempt to assess feelings and reactions among the members. Information was passed up from foremen and others in contact with the shop-floor; in some cases we know that memos of discussions were sent to the management negotiators. One such discussion followed after some negotiations:

Manager: Can we have an off-the-record chat [about MDW]? What was the reaction to the leaflets?

1st Q-E member: They were no good. All the men are opposed.

2nd Q-E member: The men are selling. All the stewards say MDW would be considered if there was £60 in it and no redundancy . . . The document was aimed at weakening assembly . . .

Manager: Yes, it is mainly directed at assembly. But you've got to remember it's been planned for many years.

1st Q-E member: It was put in because of the freeze.

Manager: No, it's unfortunate but it wasn't consciously done by management.

This was typical of the conversations of this kind which we observed. In them the stewards, generally leaders if not members of the Q-E, purposely exaggerated the strength of shop-floor opposition to MDW, and also half-jokingly suggested that the company should improve its offer. Indeed, on the stewards' part, much of it was seen in an essentially joking manner.

The stewards were, of course, by no means confident of shop-floor feeling, as we have seen. Certainly, at least immediately before the second management document, many members were not particularly interested in the situation. For example, at one section meeting the steward asked 'Do you want an account of the negotiations?' And in reply one member, with whom the majority agreed, argued, 'No, we've got more important things to discuss: the rota [for lay-offs].' This example shows that as yet the possibility of confrontation over MDW was not the dominant issue for most members or stewards. Indeed, our fieldnotes show that many stewards, and even more the conveners, were so involved in problems of lay-offs (to which the question of rotas in the above quotation is related) and a variety of important piecework negotiations that they had little time to consider the annual negotiations. Moreover, since many were laid off it was not an opportune time to push opposition hard.

The most serious consideration of the situation therefore occurred in the various formal steward meetings. At a meeting of the assembly stewards the more militant argued strongly that they should produce their own document, on the grounds that, 'JSSC or not, we've got to educate the men and keep management away.' Others argued that, though the document promised by one of the conveners might well not be ideal, they should wait and see what it was like, because 'we need to prevent JSSC from having any opportunity to criticize us.' This risk was particularly strongly felt by many in assembly; we have noted in an earlier chapter that there was a good deal of hostility towards assembly, who would suffer most if MDW was introduced. They had, therefore, to ensure that they did nothing to give other groups an excuse for supporting the proposals largely to 'get at' assembly. It was felt that this was essentially what the management documents were attempting to achieve.

The assembly stewards agreed, therefore, that they would await the convener's document, and then decide on any course of action deemed necessary. But they did decide to continue their own efforts at educating the membership by holding a shop meeting the next day, because, as one Q-E member explained, 'a lot of the blokes think £1 plus 4 per cent is still on the table.'

The Stewards Join in the Document War

The next day the union document was distributed, by the stewards. It began:

[Plant] Joint Shop Stewards' Committee
Reply to the Managements' Statement re Measured Day Work
Background
A claim was put to the Company on your behalf for the 4% + £1, plus a Retirement Grant. Sectional claims were also submitted.

The 4% + £1 has been granted to Work Study and the Foremen. But, for all the Manual Workers the Company's offer is contained in the statement circulated to you. It means we can have the 4% + £1, if we accept their requirement for a new system of payment (the Retirement Grant offered is simply allowing us to pay for our own pensions).

Your Joint Shop Stewards' Committee unanimously urges rejection of the Measured Day Work principle on which the Company's offer is based.

Measured Day Work

Measured Day Work implies a flat rate of payment for a strictly measured amount of work, or level of effort. There is no incentive for those prepared to work faster, or put in more effort. It is based on the myth that someone, somewhere, can tell us exactly what every worker should produce in a given time period.

All the relevant conditions must still be negotiated — manning, track speeds, standard performances etc. — but under MDW the all important money issues would be settled once a year. Bargaining power would be transferred away from the Shop Floor — away from you, the people who do the work.

The Offer

The Company require us to accept their "Proper work measurement, including rating" and "Full mobility of labour", which would give them enormous power, and what do they offer in return? Only the £1 per week and 4% of the total wage bill, which most Companies have given without any strings whatsoever.

The apparent extra income for some Piece-workers would be paid for by a big reduction in labour, which, as the Company wants existing levels of output, means considerably more work for those remaining in employment.

Piece-work

What of the Company's case against Piece-work.

They claim the losses of earnings are due to disputes — that disputes are due to disparity in earnings — that disparity is due to Piece-work.

These assumptions are false.

1. The great majority of recent disputes have not been due to Piece-work. The most serious issues have arisen where Day Work groups have sought incentives, and where the Company has failed to deal with these long-standing grievances (Day Work groups which have gone onto Piece-work have had no disputes).

2. Piece-work as a system of payment does not *cause* disparities in earnings. Weak and inefficient Management can allow anomalies and disparities to occur in *any* system of payment.

3. There is no evidence that MDW would reduce the number of disputes in any factory. Current experience at [two other car firms] indicates that this system of payment encourages types of disputes and industrial action which do not normally arise under Piece-work.

If [the company] Management are so concerned about the level of disputes and "disparity of earnings", let them provide incentives for our lower paid Day Workers.

[Company] Management are rightly concerned at any threat to our reputation and competitive position in all markets. They should remember that the quality on which this position and this reputation have been built has been produced by a labour force geared to Piece-work incentives.

The document received cries of 'About time too' or 'This is more like it' from many members when it was distributed. But many of them, and the stewards even more so, felt 'It's too weak — it needs more punch and detail.'

Several of the Q-E in the assembly shop felt this particularly strongly and agreed that they should write their own document. This was agreed at an assembly stewards' meeting the next day — 'even if it does upset the conveners' — and a sub-committee was formed for this purpose. Similarly, a meeting of the machine-shop stewards voiced some criticism of the document and felt it needed 'pointing up' as far as their members were concerned. It was agreed that there should be a plant-wide committee to prepare documents and that this would be raised at the next JSSC meeting. The stewards had been forced by managerial initiatives to take a clear, public stand. They now had to attempt to mobilize the members behind their document.

11
Mobilizing the Members

On the same day that the first stewards' document was distributed, shop meetings were held in both the assembly and machine shops, with a convener present at each. The conveners and members of the Q-E emphasized the painful experiences of other plants operating under MDW, the loss of money involved in the longer term, and that everyone — not just assembly — would suffer, stressing that 'You'll be the ones who pay for MDW if it comes in.'

While a number of questions were asked at both meetings, only one question indicated any support for MDW. Most stewards were pleased with the members' reactions. As one leader steward stated of the machine-shop meeting, 'The meeting was very quiet, but was opposed to MDW. The reaction of the shop-floor was better than I expected.' Given this boost to their position, the stewards became more confident. As one said to a member of the Q-E, 'Me and my members agree that if MDW had been put to the vote at the meeting today, we would have won the day.' Discussion tended to turn towards the areas where opposition might not be quite so strong. Our fieldnotes record several discussions between stewards such as the following: 'The machine shops are against MDW, but there could be problems from the indirects'; and 'the machine shops and the low paid will endanger the fight against MDW and it could be close.' These two quotes show clearly that there was no consensus among stewards as to the areas of strength and weakness. This in large part reflects the very limited social contact between the stewards from different areas and the traditions of hostility and suspicion.

More importantly, the boost which the meetings gave to stewards encouraged them to continue to educate the membership. Management also facilitated such action since many stewards began to find themselves with little to do because, as they explained it, management were beginning to take a hard line in piecework negotiations as a means of imposing pressure on the membership: for example, one steward pointed out, 'Time study are aiming at low values because of MDW.'

Increasingly the Q-E and conveners became concerned that there should be no sectional disputes which could endanger the unity that was beginning to develop. It seemed best not to attempt to negotiate. The result was, as one Q-E member put it, 'I'm in suspended animation with the attitude that management are taking.' In fact, there was no formal policy of this kind laid down explicitly by management. However, given the investment of the company in the MDW proposals, many senior managers especially were aware of the need not to do anything which might weaken their position. Some managers told us that they, on their own initiative, did begin to 'tighten up on things'. Similarly, on occasion in negotiations a manager would argue to the stewards, for example, 'You're the ones who want piecework and this is it', and refuse to improve an offer.

Problems of Assessing Membership Attitudes

The probability of confrontation was becoming clearer to stewards and to members. Throughout the next few weeks stewards fluctuated in their assessment of member feeling. As the prospect of a strike increased, however, the considerations which the conveners particularly had previously stressed became more central: namely, it was no good undertaking strike action unless they could see it through. The question which concerned many stewards, therefore, was 'would the members be prepared to strike?' and 'could they last out?' Some, at least, were afraid that the answer would be no.

One member of the Q-E now began actively to promulgate the second view mentioned previously, namely: 'I'm worried [about the members]. What we should do is negotiate the best possible [MDW] deal and then go out because if we lose it'll still not be too bad.' Some other members of the Q-E, and a number of other stewards, whilst hesitant about such an approach, could see the logic of it. It made sense in terms of the experience of many other plants who had gone on strike but failed to prevent the introduction of MDW. But also, as a Q-E member told one of us, 'I'm afraid that while there's opposition [to MDW], it would need a long strike [to win] and the mass would vote against that.'

The other group of stewards condemned this view — the Q-E member who was proposing this change of strategy was 'back-pedalling'; such action would mean an at least implicit acceptance of MDW. The steward had no choice but to act according to their principles and adopt a stance of outright opposition.

A number of more junior managers and foremen confided to members of the Q-E that they supported them in their opposition to MDW. But, of course, they could not afford to state their views openly. In some cases, however, they did make informal deals with stewards to alleviate hardships resulting from the tougher line adopted by some of their superiors. Such hidden deals permitted them to maintain good relations with their stewards and workers, but at the same time avoided the risk of reprimands from their superiors.

As members of management in close contact with the shop-floor, however, it is likely that the hesitations and doubts which they heard were passed on by them to their superiors. Some.of the more senior managers therefore sought to elicit the views of Q-E members more clearly. But, again, the stewards' answers were generally aimed more to deceive than illuminate. For example: 'MDW is not on, and we won't discuss it. Management is on a loser and we don't want to ram your defeat down your throat . . . You should leave it to Industrial Relations to find out the views of the shop-floor.'

Nevertheless, the management information network operated well — as we shall see, it was sufficiently good to pick up most of the worries of members so that they could be answered in further company documents. On one occasion, in part because of a slip by a steward, a company document was issued which answered a specific point in a union document before the latter even appeared.

The 'propaganda war' became the primary task of the stewards. Their efforts received a considerable fillip when one of the officials was reported in the paper as being strongly opposed to and critical of the company's MDW proposals. Members and stewards alike commented, for example, 'That's more like it . . . but I'm surprised, I didn't expect it of him.' Assembly were planning their own document. One of the Q-E mentioned this to a convener, who was worried about the implications for unity. At the next assembly stewards' meeting, the convener warned that 'Doing your own document would be silly because it gives the rest of the factory a chance to opt out. You should take it to the JSSC.' A document had, however, already been prepared which listed the dangers of the company proposals, described as 'a modern form of slavery': there would be no day-to-day negotiations; it would mean increased effort, a loss of control, and more disputes; while other factories paid a lot for MDW, their employers 'expect us to pay for it' through redundancy. The assembly stewards thought the document was good, 'because a lot in assembly think MDW would be good'.

On the advice of the convener, however, only one steward opposed taking the document to the JSSC, or forming a document sub-committee from the JSSC. Similar advice had also been given to a craft member of the Q-E who had prepared a document for the toolroom. The three major groups in the plant — machine shops, assembly, and the craftsmen — therefore all came to the JSSC with the idea that the stewards as a united group should prepare documents.

At the JSSC meetings, one of the conveners reported on the general situation, and warned that 'Many think that MDW is OK.' To dispel this belief he read out extracts of the detailed company proposals. He stressed the following aspects: the maintenance of current production levels until new MDW standards had been agreed; there would be no restrictions on work; the chargehands would disappear; all would be subject to full work measurement, including performance rating; management would establish methods and sequences of work; work standards would be used for control purposes; the company would have the right to undertake methods and lay-out studies in all areas; checks would be made to ensure workers maintained standards; a change of work allocation would not be grounds for a change of pay; work study could be undertaken at any time, including during overtime working; strict personal allowances would be operated; in assembly no personal relief would be permitted during the first forty-five minutes of a shift; there would be strictly limited tea breaks, the time of which could be varied and would be determined by management, and indirects would take tea when work permitted in the department to which they were assigned. The convener then went on to outline the procedure on new work standards; each employee would be informed of the work he was allocated to and the required standard. No grievance could be lodged until the new standard had been given a fair trial by competent operators. The grievance procedure would permit only a limited role for the union. The conversion to MDW, he continued, would not require the retention of the

149

section structure; groups would be reorganized in accordance with supervisory responsibilities and work requirements. Training needs would be decided by the company and provided by them: 'All employees will co-operate.' The convener concluded: 'And that's just part of Appendix I [of the company's proposals] . . . It's time the members were told what they've got to give up — and don't forget that was only some of the points.'

Members of the Q-E emphasized to other stewards the implications of some of these proposals. The reaction of many stewards was caught by one Q-E member who asked, 'And where are they putting the gas chamber?' Many stewards felt that the best propaganda they could produce would be the detailed company proposals; the objection that this could not be done because 'we decided we would not discuss MDW' was dismissed, and a sub-committee made up of representatives from the various departments was formed to prepare a document.

The realization of the full implications of MDW had not really struck many of the populist stewards until this meeting. But the conveners' quotation from management proposals 'put the fear of God into them'. It reaffirmed their feeling that management could not be allowed to introduce their proposals. Their feeling that something had to be done was therefore strengthened significantly.

At the same time, however, the earlier growth of confidence in the membership's support for the JSSC policy began to decline. In part this was natural as the members began to realize the implications of opposition and that £1 plus 4 per cent was not an immediately available alternative offer. The local press was also having an impact. More generally, the local media played an important part both in this situation and in others. The company had good relations with the press and therefore events in the plant were widely reported. It was not unusual for members to learn of internal events through an external medium. In this instance, the local paper reported that many wives of members were opposed to strike action. This angered and worried many Q-E members and the conveners; as one of the latter explained to a group of stewards, 'Wives have nothing to do with union business in the plant . . . I think the mass might accept what the company are proposing.'

Stewards were beginning to have second thoughts; they were seldom, however, expressed publicly. Criticisms of the JSSC's total rejection of MDW were voiced, and some felt that they should, from the start, have given the proposals in full to the men. More importantly, the policy of negotiating before a strike gained increasing support. Both of these points were raised in a discussion among stewards:

Q-E member: [The proponent of negotiating] is just saying it's all got to be thought out before we take any action; he's not backpeddling.
Steward: The conveners should not have refused to hand out the MDW proposals to the JSSC.
Q-E member: Possibly that was because no one realized then that £1 plus 4 per cent and MDW were tied up together.

Several members of the Q-E agreed that the idea of negotiating should be put to the JSSC. At the same meeting as decided upon a document sub-committee, therefore, the proponent of the idea argued, 'We should negotiate first because, if you look at other factories which have gone out, they've lost and come back on management terms.' But the idea received little attention at the meeting — the realization of the full implications of MDW swamped it. However, the significance of the statement was that it introduced the idea to stewards who were not Q-E members and who were in other departments. After the JSSC meeting, therefore, two points dominated steward discussion — the implications of MDW and the possibility of employing the 'fail-safe' strategy of negotiating first and then striking.

Education and Strategy

The stewards now began to stress the full implications of the company's proposals to their members. The activities of one leader steward may be taken as an example.

(1) A member informs him that a section member died last week.
Steward:
Even more will die of strain if MDW comes in.
(2) Steward to group of members:
The management proposals are terrifying. They'll have you tearing your bloody ass out rushing up and down the line. There'll be 182 redundant and then as many again after work measurement. I'd rather have my cards.
(3) Steward and member, after discussing MDW: We'll leave and go window cleaning if MDW comes in.
(4) Steward and opinion-leader, in front of a group of members:
Steward: If MDW comes in, I'll leave.

Leader: I'll try for voluntary redundancy. At [another firm] they've had hundreds of disputes [with MDW] so your money really goes down, and you've got to work bloody hard as well . . . I had a row with [the foreman] because he said I wasn't working hard enough, so I told him that was nothing to do with him under a piecework agreement. It'd be different under MDW. The buggers would be breathing down your neck all the time.

(5) Steward to another group of workers: The harrassment of [MDW] . . . I'll leave. Sections will disappear, shop stewards will and the foreman will have absolute control. [Jokingly] I'll stand for the conveners' job — that'll be the only good job in the plant!

Such discussions with members were common while with more trusted members the alternative 'fail-safe' strategy of negotiating before strike action was also discussed. But generally this was a debate among stewards, more of whom began to argue this view. Others rejected it, for while they accepted the logic they argued that once negotiations on MDW began it would be difficult to keep a check on those negotiating it. Some stewards felt this was a serious danger and that 'We've got to keep as tight a rein as possible on the [negotiators].' It is difficult to assess how many stewards favoured the 'fail-safe' strategy; but in these few days we learnt privately the views of thirty-two stewards. Of these, twelve were in favour of it, sixteen against, and four undecided. Most of those in favour were populists. This was not a representative sample, for the bulk of these stewards were in production areas; but, given that the indirects were less strongly opposed to MDW and their stewards were populists, it is at least plausible to suggest that if a suitable opportunity arose, a small majority of stewards might have voted for negotiating MDW formally as a prelude to strike action.

That opportunity did not arise. Instead the JSSC decisions carried the stewards on in their attempt to educate the membership. The document sub-committee met on several occasions in the next week and prepared an eight-page document, but it was to be another week before this was actually distributed. Over this period — until the middle of May — the same debates continued. It is perhaps worth quoting one example which involved seven stewards, five of whom were members of the Q-E:

1st Q-E member: We should negotiate, so that if we lose we'll still be OK.

2nd Q-E member: A strike is the only way.

3rd Q-E member: The men won't last.

2nd Q-E member: That's no problem. Even if we lose at least we as stewards are clean — the men can't blame us.

1st Q-E member: That's not the right attitude — you should care about what happens to the men on the shop-floor.

2nd Q-E member: I agree there are difficulties because the company's in a strong position.

4th Q-E member: That's just not true, stocks don't have a high profit, so they can't afford a strike.

Steward: We've got to strike, we can't negotiate now.

1st Q-E member lists the experience of other plants: We should have negotiated from the start.

2nd Q-E member: You can't trust the conveners and officials — they'd negotiate everything away.

The task of ensuring the support of the membership received a boost from two sources because they required reactions by the stewards. First, a member had written a letter to the local press questioning the reported statement of an official and arguing that the shop-floor had not even been consulted on MDW, let alone opposed it. The Q-E in particular were critical of this; as one said, 'He's only trying to become a foreman . . . Twenty years ago the men would have refused to work with him.' Several stewards therefore began to counter this letter in their discussions with members. Not all were successful, however, on one occasion a member's reply was 'Well, he was perfectly right.'

Second, a third management document appeared in the second week of May, entitled 'Some of Your Questions Answered'. It began: 'We have received a considerable number of enquiries, most of them based on the proposed reduction in the Assembly Shop labour force and the proposed Retirement Grant.' The document then gave details of the voluntary nature of redundancy, the qualifications for early retirement, the number who qualified,.and the benefits they would receive. It then went on to detail the company's reasons for proposing a 'service-related normal Retirement Grant'.

When they received these documents, many of the members laughed and jeered, and on reading it several remarked that 'management are stressing the rewards.' However, as no doubt management hoped, many were interested in the possibility of voluntary redundancy or early retirement. One steward told another that 'There's a queue outside Industrial Relations for voluntary redundancy.' Within the next ten days, the company claimed to 'have already had 214 firm enquiries and requests to be considered'. In other words, the apparent generosity of the proposals served to reduce some workers' opposition to MDW; for example, one elderly worker complained that the unions were costing him hundreds of pounds by their refusal to negotiate. Stewards thought that 'management are buying the men out with redundancy money.' Others, however, maintained their opposition to MDW but still 'put themselves down' for early redundancy, 'in case', as one put it, 'MDW really does come in'. When, a few days later, it was found that several stewards had done this, there was a good deal of criticism and, with the support of a convener, a member of the Q-E raised this at a JSSC meeting, accusing them of double-dealing.

It was also at this time that the stewards began to look more seriously at their strategic position; there was some discussion of the state of stocks which were seen to indicate management strength. But the question was really forced upon the assembly stewards when management requested a large amount of overtime for the weekend. Initially, several stewards refused overtime, even though normally they would have agreed it. When asked why, a member of the Q-E explained, 'It's different now — it all links up with MDW and the members will back us up.'

At a meeting of the assembly stewards this view was modified. While it was agreed that overtime would have to be looked at carefully, only one steward finally voted against doing overtime. While such overtime might help the company to achieve its orders, and while it helped to cover a lack of labour which was seen as purposely created by management, the majority view was that 'There's no advantage in refusing overtime.' Most importantly, it provided an opportunity for the members to increase their savings in preparation for a strike, an important consideration in view of recent unpaid lay-offs.

Stewards' meetings continued to discuss the state of shop-floor opinion, and the 'fail-safe' strategy. The assembly-shop stewards agreed to another shop meeting at which the situation was discussed, 'the need to fight' emphasized, and the men warned that: 'It's management strategy to split us up [by the redundancy offer] — but you are daft if you fall for it because only a few of you would ever get redundancy.' The machine-shop stewards had a rather different priority. The MDW proposals, as we have seen, would have the strongest and most immediate impact upon assembly. But members of the Q-E in the machine shops were worried that their members would fail to realize the impact upon themselves. One of the Q-E therefore spelt out in detail the effect of MDW upon each section. In the ensuing discussion of the risks of the membership accepting MDW and the possibility of adopting the 'fail-safe' strategy, the Q-E members emphasized:

It's the job of a shop steward to educate his members that MDW will mean living with the foreman . . . If the shop-floor are going to agree to MDW, we must at least make sure that they know what they're accepting . . . They can throw out [our recommendation]. We can only tell the shop-floor [the dangers].

During these attempts to educate the shop-floor and assess their feelings, and the discussion of the 'fail-safe' strategy, a fourth management document appeared, entitled 'More Questions Answered'. In it, management replied to eight questions which workers had been asking. They denied using the incomes legislation to introduce MDW 'on the cheap', emphasizing that they were committed to paying further increases 'when allowed to do so' and pointing also to the cost of early retirement. They then went on to assure chargehands (whose jobs were to be eliminated) that they would not be dismissed, and in fact had a number of options open to them. Third, they argued 'there is no evidence to suggest' that 'employees become more and more disenchanted with MDW after it has been introduced' and quoted 'an independent report' which 'states that *the employees themselves* showed "a clear general satisfaction with MDW and feeling that the changeover from previous pay systems was an improvement"'. The document went on to deny that MDW would involve a change in shift working arrangements, and pointed out that under MDW there would exist 'a procedure giving employees and their representatives the right to challenge time studies just as they can under piecework'. The sixth question answered was why the retirement grant had to be paid out of the £1 plus 4 per cent — because it was required by government legislation and 'The Company has no option but to comply'. Seventh, the document denied that a director of another company had described MDW as 'a modern form of slavery'. (This was an argument contained in the JSSC document which was to appear the next day. The local press, in an article on this document war, later confirmed the JSSC quotation.) Finally, the management stated that 'The Company has emphasized that the draft proposals are for negotiation and we hope that the Trade Unions will be prepared to negotiate on the basis of the Company's proposals.' The appearance of this fourth document led to a good deal of criticism of the union by members — when were the stewards going to produce another document? At the same time, members were beginning to ask when the mass meeting would be held.

The Second Steward Document

The second steward document appeared the next day. Its aim was to show 'what you will have to accept in order to attain' the earnings quoted by management. The document listed many of the company's proposals on work study and work organization in a manner similar to that outlined at the last JSSC meeting. It then discussed a number of conclusions. It continued:

Measured day work has been described as a 'Modern Form of Slavery' and this we are convinced is an appropriate description. Significantly enough this description was not given by either a Trade Union Leader or a Militant Shop Steward. It was in fact given by [X] and he was the member of [another car firm's] management who was responsible for the introduction of measured day work into that factory . . .

Measured Day Work is a Fixed Rate System of Payment
This eliminates the day to day negotiations over money which take place under a piecework system. Once measured day work is accepted increases in wages can only be achieved as the result of an Annual Review, and invariably any such increases are tied to productivity deals which include 'strings'. These 'strings' may mean the same track speeds with less labour, or increased track speeds with the same labour. Inevitably they will mean more effort from all the labour . . .

Measured Day Work means Handing Control to the Company
Control of track speeds, labour loading and full mobility of labour, so that what once was a struggle for money now becomes a battle as to how many operators should be on each job, and how much work each operator should do.
It has been proved in plants who have accepted measured day work that this particular battle becomes so intense that it invariably ends in far more shifts being lost over manning than ever were lost in disputes over piecework prices, thus exploding that popular argument by Management that measured day work gives greater continuity of employment.
Giving control to the Company also hands them the right to impose conditions of work which, regardless of the inconvenience to the workers, they consider to be the most effective in order to produce the article.
In many other plants where measured day work has been introduced it

has resulted in an alteration to the shift working arrangements, usually to even shifts on a fortnightly changeover.

Measured Day Work is not just applicable to Pieceworkers

The effect upon Dayworkers and Indirects will be equally as devastating. They too will be subjected to work measurement and stringent supervision resulting in reduced manning or greater work loads. The number of Foremen is increased and they are given greater powers. Whereas under piecework the effort is towards increasing the level of earnings, under measured day work similar effort would be required just to maintain a reasonable job.

In every other plant where measured day work has been introduced workers who thought that they were not involved have grabbed what they thought to be a juicy carrot only to find to their subsequent disgust that the carrot had been replaced by a stick.

Measured Day Work and [the Company]

In the certain knowledge that the consequent increase in efficiency would quickly recoup their initial financial losses all other companies who have introduced measured day work have paid large sums of money to their.workers in order to get it into their factories.

The [company] approach however is something quite unique for they have gone much further than attempting to use the Government 'Freeze' as a means of introducing it on the cheap, they are actually demanding that their workers, by a large reduction in the labour force, finance the introduction of measured day work themselves.

This can be seen by the following:—

The Company are demanding that the Assembly Department and Paint Shop reduce their labour force by 182 operators. These operators including premium times and insurance stamp are currently receiving a wage of £48.00 per week, therefore —

182 operators @ £48.00 × 52 weeks = £454,272.00

Following the reduction the remaining 1,100 operators in Assembly and Paint would each receive £5.00 per week increase *if present track speeds are maintained and the same efficiency achieved.*

1100 operators @ £5.00 × 52 weeks = £286,000.00

This means a net saving in wages for the Company of — £168,272.00

with which to meet much of their financial commitments to the remainder of the plant.

So it can be seen that considering that some of the workers are already in receipt of more than the maximum wage being offered and consequently would receive very little, and with the remainder of the plant receiving the Assembly and Paint Shops saving in wages, the employees are largely financing measured day work for the Company.

The stewards' document concluded by stressing that the

retirement grant which they had sought was permissible under legislation.

The document generally received a good reception from the members. There were some complaints about the delay in creating and distributing a document and the number of copies available. But, nevertheless, the majority of members whom we observed became fully aware of the implications of MDW for the first time. The effect upon the members was comparable to that upon the stewards when the company proposals had been read out at the JSSC.

More importantly, by creating interest in the question the document provided stewards with an opportunity to assess more fully feeling on the shop-floor and to attempt to persuade the members to fight MDW. So, for example, on one section the steward talked to a number of work groups. The men were opposed to MDW but complained that 'The shop-floor hasn't. got any strength.' It was on this point that the steward concentrated:

You compare what things are like now with what they were twenty years ago . . . it was the strength of trade unionists in the old days that won what we enjoy now. Then people were hard up and they fought hard — when I was a kid, I can remember often having broken biscuits for dinner because my old man was out on strike . . . Now everyone's mortgaged to the hilt and they've lost all their strength . . . The trouble is the working class take whatever's thrown at them until they're really down, and only then do they fight back . . . There are signs of a return to the bad old days — you take the way they're paying out [wages] on the night shift — it's all leading up to MDW.

Opinion-leader: I'd leave rather than work under MDW — I couldn't work at the speed of the track all day.

1st Member: You've got to keep the men militant . . . We should branch [impose sanctions on them through the union branch] them if they won't follow section decisions . . .

2nd Member: I'll fight for my principles.

Steward: Yes, you're a good fighter. But [turning to another member] it's people like you — you've got no guts, you're afraid of trouble.

3rd Member: I've got to pay my mortgage.

In the next few days, the steward and the key opinion-leader pushed the dangers of MDW very hard. This particular opinion-leader was a joker (see Glossary) so that a dozen or so men were always gathering around him. The steward and joker held public discussions on MDW and particularly about the need to strike; on one occasion we counted over thirty men listening in to a conversation which included the following:

Yeah, under MDW there'll be a lot of strain; there are five nervous breakdowns on the section now — there'll be even more then. Blokes will get so pissed off they'll be sabotaging the line . . . The ordinary worker isn't out for all he can get — just enough money to give the wife for house-keeping, pay the bills and have a few bob for himself — 90 per cent are like that, and then management try this [MDW] on. But it's a load of cobblers to say that it will mean security — you take [another plant with MDW].

Certainly many stewards were now happier concerning the reactions of their members. At a meeting of the machine-shop stewards there was a good deal of praise for the union document and a feeling that their members at least had 'the right attitude about MDW'. A member of the Q-E concluded that 'When we have the mass meeting we must be sure every steward has done the job we have done in the Machine Division.'

But, even with this optimism about the members, there was still the problem of the relative strengths of the company and the shop-floor. Some stewards at the meeting felt that the JSSC should adopt the 'fail-safe' strategy; others were concerned that the management position was gaining strength for confrontation because of the level of stocks which had been built up.

12
Power, Unity, and the Mass Decision

The stewards' attempts to educate the membership appeared to be meeting with some success. Nevertheless, particularly because they thought the company was in a strong position, they were worried how successful strike action could be. Two factors brought these problems to a head. The first was a re-opening of the question of whether £1 plus 4 per cent really meant £2.50, and the second related to evidence on the balance of power.

The Problems of Government Legislation

The conveners began to point out to stewards that, with the offsets, £1 plus 4 per cent could well mean only 95p. They did so for two main reasons. The first was an attempt to assess the strength of feeling and a fear that if the wage increase really was this low, then a strong demand for the 'fail-safe' strategy of negotiating before strike action would develop. Second, they wished to protect the credibility of the union organization and themselves. There could be little doubt that, if the company chose to present an agreement in a particular way, the Pay Board would demand that a range of offsets be subtracted from the £1 plus 4 per cent. If the membership were to go on strike, possibly win, and then return to find that what they thought was £2.50 had suddenly shrunk to 95p, the reaction against the JSSC and the conveners would be extremely hostile and possibly break the union organization. The latter was something the conveners were unwilling to risk.

They therefore began to discuss the question of offsets with members of the Q-E, and the next day raised it at the JSSC. It formally received support from a fifth management document, which again took a question-and-answer format. It first detailed the way in which particular offsets led to the figure of 95p. It also repeated arguments that MDW would resolve outstanding sectional claims and that there would be no problem in achieving a reduction of 182 men in assembly. It also pointed out that, while one company was always cited as evidence of the faults of MDW, there were companies where it had been extremely successful. There was no reason why conversion to MDW 'should not go just as smoothly here as it did at [another company] and, indeed, as it has at most factories where this system has been introduced'. The company document reminded workers that if agreement was reached before 30 April — a week's time — wage increases would be backdated to the beginning of the month.

The document also returned to the question of a retirement grant. Management now argued that their opposition to sole company financing rested upon a desire 'to protect us against "leap frogging" claims. Unfortunately, this feature was omitted from our previous statement.' It continued:

We agree with your stewards that improvements to occupational pensions are permissible under paragraphs 135 and 136 of the Phase 2 legislation. However, a retirement Grant is not an occupational pension scheme but would be *a new cash benefit* and covered by paragraph 141 of the Phase 2 legislation [emphasis in source].

Unfortunately for the company, the impact of their documents had been significantly reduced. Around the plant, workers had written up the number of pamphlets produced by management and stewards as a football score, 'Management 5, Unions 2.' The new company document met with laughter and joking and, whereas once company documents were read carefully, now they tended to be thrown away. Such reactions were, of course, encouraged by leader stewards. Leaders stressed to their members that management were producing so many documents and were making offers of such a kind that there was good reason for suspicion: 'If management are offering more than the unions are asking and are pushing it this hard then there's bound to be something fishy about it.' (It was generally accepted afterwards by managers, stewards, and officials that the proliferation of company documents was self-defeating.)

The company statements that wage drift had to be taken into account therefore had little effect. But support for this contention by the conveners led to a good deal of concern on the part of many stewards. So, for example, the conveners' statements were raised at a meeting of the assembly stewards, and fostered the contention among some of them that conveners really wanted MDW. We heard this view expressed by a number of stewards. In the case of the assembly stewards, it was agreed that before the next JSSC meeting they would meet to discuss how the mass meeting should be run and how to ensure that MDW 'doesn't come up at the mass'.

The rumour that the conveners were saying £1 plus 4 per cent meant 95p had reached a number of members and among some caused concern, among others led to some support for MDW. In one case, a steward attempted to explain that it was wrong to subtract certain sums from the £1 plus 4 per cent, but several members were now ready to express views such as 'Assembly won't vote to go out', or 'We won't go out — we've got our mortgages to think of, and MDW isn't too bad.'

Some members of the Q-E and the conveners were aware not only of a change in attitude among many of the membership, but also that, as one put it, 'A lot of stewards are leading [the retreat].'

Those most firmly opposed to MDW realized the importance of reasserting the initial JSSC resolution against MDW. At the assembly stewards' meeting before the JSSC, it was agreed that, at the worst, they would have to stress that the mass meeting could not decide the labour-loading in assembly. (This would be implicit in agreeing to the MDW proposals, which involved a reduction of 182 men in assembly.) More generally, it was felt that 'There's a risk that the mass will accept MDW', despite the fact that 'After the JSSC document, the men's outlook changed'. It was agreed, therefore, that they would 'have to give an agenda to the conveners', ensuring that MDW was not raised at the mass meeting and that the claim was for £2.50 and not 95p.

These points were raised strongly at the meeting of the JSSC later that day. The conveners pointed out that £1 plus 4 per cent might not mean £2.50, and emphasized that 'the company is preparing for confrontation'; 'We have to accept MDW or fight. We've got to be clear on that. There will be no problem with the mass if stewards have reported back as they should have done.' Some of the indirect stewards (populists) expressed concern that the £1 plus 4 per cent would mean more for some men than others. The conveners pointed out that the JSSC resolution prevented this. More importantly, the assembly stewards attempted to tie the conveners down to £1 plus 4 per cent meaning £2.50 and, while the conveners refused to accept that the resolution to the mass should specifically refer to £2.50 (since this was not the original JSSC resolution), they did agree that £1 plus 4 per cent and £2.50 were, in their view, the same.

Many stewards were also concerned at the delay in calling the mass meeting; they felt that the members had now been sufficiently educated and hence there was no barrier to calling the mass. They were afraid that further delay might lead to a weakening of member opposition to the company's proposals. The signs of this were already becoming apparent. After a lengthy discussion, therefore, the JSSC resolved: 'That a factory mass meeting to be called at 12.15 Wednesday'.

Mobility, Unity, and Assessment of Power

The assessment of the unions' strategic position also encouraged this decision. We have already noted that production stewards particularly had become concerned about stockpiling by management and whether or not the unions should facilitate this (at the same time increasing members' incomes) by permitting overtime. This situation now became more acute.

The assembly shop had been laid off a good deal in the months preceding the MDW confrontation. But many sections in one of the machine shops had continued to work normally and had built up stocks of parts which meant they were months ahead of schedule. So the company demanded that certain men from one of the machine shops should be transferred to other departments, notably CKD (the packing of components for assembly elsewhere) and assembly.

Management could not have been unaware of the implications of this for member attitudes, for such mobility had been a source of contention during the year; the assembly shop had gone out on strike over the issue twice, but a mass meeting had rejected strike action and therefore implicitly accepted mobility. Further, mobility from the machine shops into CKD annoyed the latter because, while doing exactly the same work, the machine-shop men were paid their machine-shop rates which in some cases meant £10 to £15 more than normal CKD workers received. They therefore threatened to take action if the machine-shop men were brought in under the customary payment method.

Similarly, the assembly stewards were opposed to this mobility because the machine-shop men were treated as temporary labour; that is, if assembly were laid off, these men merely returned to their own sections and hence suffered no loss of earnings.

While temporary labour was a subject of contention for assembly, it was further complicated by two other factors. First, management had failed to replace men who had left assembly; the stewards were concerned about this because of the prospect of MDW. Second, there was the more general question of overtime. As we have seen, overtime in assembly meant that the company would be able to complete vehicles and get them out of the plant. It seemed increasingly sensible to ban overtime. Some stewards had already done this, and wanted a general shop ruling that this be done. But it was defeated when put to the vote because overtime was a question for individual sections so that a shop decision on the matter might well lead to conflicts within the shop. This was decided despite the fact that in some cases management had ceased to seek the agreement of stewards to overtime. At the same time, the assembly stewards had recently agreed that no overtime would be done which was considered to be aimed at covering the vacancies which management had failed to fill. But, as several stewards pointed out, they would look silly if, on the one hand, they refused overtime on the grounds that it was covering vacancies, and, on the other, refused labour (from the machine shops) which would serve to fill those vacancies.

At the same time — and this was a new feature of such situations — the men from the machine shops also objected to being moved. In the past they had done so with few complaints, and the machine shop involved had made no attempt to limit mobility by reducing output or by carrying men themselves. If this lack of action on the part of the machine shop were repeated, then it was clear that the unity which appeared to be developing over the annual negotiations would be dissipated. There was a distinct possibility of sectional action by CKD, and possibly assembly. This would lead either to an all-out strike or to major disputes within the shop-floor organization.

The assembly stewards met to discuss the problem. They suspected management's motives in insisting upon mobility, and, after a long debate and on the advice of a convener, they agreed that they would not seek support from the membership for strike action when the men came into the shop, but rather when they left it. (This would be the crucial test of whether the men were temporary labour. It also, of course, avoided strike action at that time.)

The conveners found themselves in a difficult position. They were opposed to mobility and felt that the machine shop concerned should look after its own men. Permitting them to be sent to other jobs was seen as a somewhat selfish means of maintaining high earnings levels among those remaining in their normal jobs. The conveners accordingly advised the stewards in this machine shop to hold a shop meeting and develop a policy. At the same time, they emphasized to the assembly and CKD stewards that the policy accepted by the mass meeting when it rejected strike action was the full mobility of labour and assembly should accept this fact. But the assembly stewards rejected this view.

Management had delayed the movement of the small number of men to permit the stewards to reach a decision. But they finally decided to put the machine-shop men into assembly. It was a confrontation situation, with the assembly stewards anxiously waiting for the men to appear. But the men due to go into assembly insisted on seeing a convener first of all. They therefore waited, and in the meantime their colleagues in the machine shop agreed a policy of opposition to mobility and decided upon strike action.

As this situation had developed, a good deal of hostility had arisen between the stewards in assembly and the machine shop involved. But at a JSSC meeting the matter had been discussed, and, more importantly, two Q-E members, one from each department, who had been to school together, had chatted and learnt that both departments in fact wished to pursue the same policy. They agreed that 'The company's trying to create inter-shop conflict to fuck up the mass [meeting].'

This management policy, if such it was, had failed because of the machine shops' decision to strike. The danger of a breakdown of the nascent unity had declined. But the outcome of the strike, which lasted a few days, was also another important factor in affecting the conveners' assessment of the possible outcome of a strike. In previous months, strikes against mobility had lasted some time because of management refusal to accept union demands. But this time the situation was different. Within a couple of days management agreed to permit the machine shop concerned to drop their level of efficiency and hence maintain their otherwise surplus labour. The conveners reached the conclusion that management's position was not as strong as they had thought; if a strike was accepted by the mass, they felt there was a chance of winning.

Two other events of relevance led up to the mass meeting. The first was the course of events in another company establishment which was a major supplier to our plant. The union there had reached an impasse with the company in the annual negotiations, and had undertaken various forms of collective action. But for management and the stewards in our plant the situation there was far from clear, and there had been numerous rumours that they had gone out on strike and that, therefore, there was a serious risk of imminent lay-offs. At about the same time as the strike by one of the machine shops, a report of a stoppage at the suppliers seemed to be reliable, and there was a fear on the part of many stewards that their position *vis-à-vis* the company was therefore much weaker. The company might well like a strike because it would mean they would not have to pay lay-off pay. But the conveners rejected this view on two grounds: first, one of them argued to a group of Q-E members that the story was designed solely 'to frighten the mass'. Second, they argued that there was no real danger of lay-off simply because while assembly had been laid off for long periods this supplier had still been producing; therefore, the convener argued, there must be a large stock of the components concerned and hence no real danger of lay-off (the situation at this plant was to become important a week later).

The other factor of interest was of a different kind, and suggested to us as observers that the long task of educating the membership had been successful. This was a number of brief disputes immediately before the day of the mass meeting. We have already discussed the machine-shop strike over an issue where they had in the past failed to develop a policy. Now they had not merely developed one, but also had taken concerted action in pursuit of it. A similar readiness to strike occurred in other departments; we observed it most clearly in assembly. There an 'atmosphere' had been developing over the last few days; the day before the mass meeting it was particularly acute. It is difficult to explain what is meant by atmosphere; but we found that stewards, men, and managers could also identify it. It is a certain tenseness, often indicated by an overall tone of animated, taut conversation rather than the normal desultory chatting. This had been building up since the men had learnt from their stewards that the mass meeting was to be held on Wednesday, and that the sole JSSC recommendation would be for strike action. A good deal of laughing and joking of the following kind occurred: 'Roll on the mass meeting! Cor! The sparks are going to fly; just hands up [in favour of the strike] and out in the sun.'

This building up of morale — the creation of a collectively oriented normative atmosphere, fostered not least by 'public' discussions of the kind noted above — meant that workers became less ready to accept any abnormal work or conditions. Hence, on the morning of the day before the mass meeting, there were two stoppages in assembly, the first for several months. Both lasted less than an hour, ending when management rectified the problems, one concerning safety, the other poor working conditions. This success could only serve to foster the readiness to strike. The mood of the members more generally was indicated by the increasing number of cartoons, jokes, and poems which had been circulating over the last few days. One example is the following, entitled 'An Exhortation':

> The government exhort you before a contract you make
> To read the small print for your very own sake.
> This company's no different to the salesman that lies —
> Their object's the same, to pull wool o'er your eyes.
>
> They give you a pamphlet and promise you this
> And sit back on their haunches with confident bliss,
> That you're gullible and easy, and equally naive
> If they offer a plum you will surely believe.
>
> That plum is a mirage as desert water I fear
> If you reach it, it will soon disappear.
> [Two key directors] like the Gods of finance
> Attempt simply to play on your ignorance.
>
> Piecework they say is the cause of all trouble
> Measured day work's the answer to burst the bubble,
> If [another car firm]'s the pattern you can be most sure,
> The company will be happy with five days in four.
>
> To you who think in a 'benevolent' way
> It won't affect you at the end of the day,
> I assure you my friends it's not only the tracks,
> The whip too will fall hard on your tender backs.
>
> Read then the small print, both hard and long,
> And one thing we must be is united and strong.
> Let the company know, without shadow of doubt,
> AT THIS POINT IN TIME THEIR PLANS ARE OUT.

Footnote

If you think I'm a militant, you could not be more wrong,
Tho' I've been a trade unionist for forty-two years long,
For what we have fought, AND NOW YOU ENJOY,
Don't throw it away like a broken toy.

Before the mass meeting the next day, the general view of the members appeared to be that they should strike. But the stewards were by no means certain; as one convener stated: 'I'm worried about the mass, about the lads who are saying nothing but get working in little corners.' Certainly a few isolated members still stated that the unions should negotiate MDW. It was also rumoured that a group of members were trying to persuade an opinion-leader to draw up a resolution to be put to the mass meeting in favour of MDW. At an assembly stewards' meeting that morning, one of the most militant stewards expressed the view that 'It could go either way.' It was therefore agreed that if things did 'go the wrong way' there would be an assembly shop meeting the next day. But other assembly stewards were more optimistic. Recently the track speeds had been reduced but it had proved impossible to reduce manning to any significant degree. One Q-E member therefore argued, 'The blokes have learnt a lot today, because they couldn't drop many men even with lower track speeds.' It suggested to the men that the company's proposals to reduce manning were impracticable. The conveners felt that the mass meeting would be a 'close thing'. They determined that to minimize the risk they would have to stick to the JSSC resolution and forbid any discussion of MDW.

The Mass Meeting

Three mass meetings were held; one for the day-shift, another for the night-shift, and one for a more isolated part of the plant. All of them, which we observed, took basically the same form and produced similar questions and majorities. We shall briefly outline the main day-shift meeting.

Several thousand men were crowded into the canteen, with the conveners on a platform at the front. One convener called the meeting to order and explained that it had beeen called to report on the annual negotiations and that the stewards had a recommendation to put to them. He called on another convener to report on the negotiations. The second convener said that five meetings with management at the plant led to a failure to agree and this was ratified at the NJC. He read out a letter from the union side of the NJC stressing executive committee support for any action. He went on to explain that the unions had claimed a substantial wage increase and a retirement pension; then came the Government's Stage Two and the company all along said 'No £1 plus 4 per cent unless it's part of a package.' He stressed that this was wrong; 'The union put in a claim and instead of answering it, management themselves put up a claim. All other companies, large and small, were getting £1 plus 4 per cent, and [their company] was the only firm refusing it.'

Then he turned to the retirement pension. 'This was not a flash in the pan' for a group of stewards had been seeing insurance companies about it since 1966. The company said they would administer a scheme but that was no good. The average age in the plant was 43 years; the pension was not for one group but for everyone: 'we're all going to be old age pensioners one day, and the [old age pensioners'] demonstration of 200,000 people got nowhere. If we're going to get reasonable pensions, we've got to get them through industry. But the company's offering nothing.'

The first convener then put the JSSC recommendation: 'Seven days' notice to management in support of our claim for £1 plus 4 per cent and a retirement pension'. He was about to move to the vote when an opinion-leader and griever objected, saying they wanted to discuss the question more — 'People feel they want a wage increase, but that we should negotiate, and some of us are ready to talk MDW.' The convener said they were not there to talk about MDW for it was not included in the terms of reference. He asked the mass if they wished to vote now and this was 'carried overwhelmingly'. A worker asked about the company saying it was not £2.50 but 95p. The convener explained that this figure was reached by including all the wage drift last year which the company claimed had to be done. But the unions said this was not so because the wage increase would be 'straight across the board'. Again he pushed for the vote but the question was raised about outstanding claims. The convener explained, 'It's been agreed that the increase will have to wait. I understood that everyone had been told these things in previous meetings.' Other questions followed: 'Would the strike be official?' 'Yes.' 'When would the seven days' notice start?' 'From 4.00 this evening.'

An opinion-leader, who had been 'set up' by the conveners and

Q-E to raise a number of questions, asked why they should not strike now. A convener explained that 'the platform has to say that because of the government legislation. But that doesn't mean we agree with it.' The opinion-leader said that in that case he would give warning of a motion. The convener again pushed the vote but there were objections from a griever and his mates. The convener again asked for all in favour of taking the vote and there was a majority. So he put it to the vote, after repeating the recommenda-tion, and declared it 'carried overwhelmingly'. (We, and others, estimated the vote to be about seven to one in favour. Accurate estimates, however, were extremely difficult to make.)

The opinion-leader then said he wanted to put a motion and the convener stopped people from leaving. If there had to be seven days' notice he wanted a resolution to ban overtime. The convener said this could mean the company would refuse to negotiate because they were under duress. The opinion-leader pointed out that otherwise 'This company would get lots of overtime and get the stuff out.' The convener said this was a good point. Someone else said if the machine shops stopped overtime this would lead to lay-offs in assembly and some would refuse to agree to everyone striking in support, 'and we don't want that'. The convener said that he thought individuals should decide whether or not to work overtime in view of the notice to strike. He put the resolution for an overtime ban and it was defeated.

This was the end of the meeting and the stewards were surprised at the result and the size of support. There was also admiration for the conveners since 'they really pushed it'. Several stewards said that the men were hoping that the company would now negotiate, and that many were already saying there should be another meeting before the strike because 'they're on the change already'. The conveners, however, were both surprised and elated. Chatting to a number of the Q-E members, one convener declared:

It was a great meeting . . . I'm chuffed. One problem up to now has been that there was no real trade unionism in the plant . . . This is the first issue . . . since I've been convener that I've had full support from the lads for a line I wanted to follow. Up to now it's just been a case of them sticking up their hands. Now we've got some real union feeling and strength.

We made a point of talking to a number of workers about their impressions and feelings on the decision. In all, we asked individually about fifty men: just over half were unconditionally in favour of the decision taken, the others thought it was 'probably right' but were critical or doubtful of the wisdom of the action. Scarcely any stated unconditional opposition to the mass decision. Similarly, our fieldnotes go on:

> There is an air of content in the assembly shop; several say the decision is a good one. [One member] says he's surprised and takes back all he said about his mates. [One steward] goes over to [another who had been very cynical] to chide him; he replies that 'We're not on strike yet; the men are on the change.' Then over to [another group of members]. All of them say it's a good decision, but they should have another meeting so that they can change; several stress that the company is bloody-minded and is trying to get MDW on the cheap. There are jokes about getting jobs lined up for the strike period.

Many members began to discuss the company and the state of industrial relations more generally. There appeared to be a consensus that the company was 'going downhill', and that management were being aggressive and bloody-minded. In other words, many were gaining support for their decision by reviewing the behaviour of management more generally.

The same had happened before the mass meeting. Several members pointed to the company 'trying to get MDW on the cheap' and repeated the arguments against the management's proposals. But also there was a more general discussion in many groups we observed about the class structure more generally — about burglary as a 'way of getting on . . . all top people are burglars.' It seems reasonable to suggest that both before and after the mass meeting many members were employing a wide range of vocabularies which served to legitimate and justify their decision to strike.

A Summary

The decision to strike had now been taken. It was five weeks after the confirmation of the FTA in the negotiations, and over three weeks since the JSSC had decided to recommend strike action. In that time, the stewards, led by the conveners and the Q-E, had attempted to educate the membership. They had succeeded, in the main, in altering the perspectives of their members and developing a trade-union-oriented collective consciousness. Despite a number of potential disruptions, they had been able to develop and maintain a high level of unity. For us, as observers, it was a remarkable and exciting feat.

At the same time, it would be wrong to suggest that either stewards or members unhesitatingly decided on strike action. Accounts of strikes often give the impression that the men concerned were totally committed to 'taking on' their employers. Certainly in this case they were not, and we would suggest that this is true more generally. Many of the members with whom we had a good deal of contact throughout this period changed their views from day to day, if not from hour to hour. In the same way, we have seen that for the stewards, and more particularly the conveners, there was a good deal of uncertainty. There were problems of how far the men could be led, and of what the result of strike action might be. But, with a clear resolution of opposition to MDW, the development of support for a 'fail-safe' strategy or for a more simple agreement to negotiate MDW was limited. The stewards, given the JSSC resolution, had no choice but to attempt to educate the members and they did this even though they themselves were often having second thoughts. Finally, when the mass meeting came, they had to push and lead, and they were encouraged in this not so much by signs of wholehearted support from their members but because the conveners in particular were convinced that the company was in a weak position. This meant that, in their view, one major problem disappeared. If they did manage to persuade the membership to strike, there were unlikely to be problems about 'how long the members can last'; indeed, they suspected that the strike might never happen.

The extreme difficulty of gauging membership feeling is also worthy of note. We as observers found it difficult, and so did the majority of the stewards and conveners. In part, the very development of a normative group atmosphere in favour of a strike made it more difficult to assess individuals' feelings because many members were aware of the informal verbal sanctions for going against the norm. But this atmosphere also existed at the mass meeting, and it was something developed by the stewards. Most importantly, it was led by the conveners and Q-E, who, through the JSSC and through various opinion-leaders, were able to persuade, inform, and lead. We see the importance, therefore, in one key issue of the networks which we have discussed in our previous volume. It is worthy of note that all of the half-dozen or so groups we knew who attempted to develop support for negotiating MDW came from sections where the stewards were not leaders.

Once the decision to strike was made, many new issues arose. Some members, as we have seen, hoped to be able to change their minds; some of the conveners and Q-E members suspected and hoped that management would concede their demands before the strike began. But at the same time they had to assume that there would be a strike and make preparations accordingly.

13
Preparation for Confrontation

The day after the mass meeting, members' views varied. As one steward argued, 'The blokes will start changing when the wives put the pressure on.' This appeared to be so, for some of the more isolated members began to argue that the decision to strike was wrong. One, for example, complained to his steward: 'It's stupid to strike because it's going to be a long one until the holidays, and then we'll lose . . . it's daft to strike now because of [the situation in a suppliers']. We'd get lay-off pay if we stayed in.' The steward replied: 'The company may give. Anyway, you should be willing to give up your holidays.'

The view that 'The company may give' became increasingly common. The conveners, and some members of the Q-E, had been chatting to management and attempted to assess the possibility of management 'giving' in the face of the mass decision to strike. Their conclusion was favourable. As one convener told a member of the Q-E: 'The company is saying they're not worried about the strike, which means they are . . . I don't think we'll have to strike.'

The members, however, merely hoped this was so since they would then not be faced with the costs of a strike. Rumours abounded, and stewards were bombarded with questions of this kind: 'Has anything happened about the strike?' 'Is it true the officials have been called in today?' 'What's this about a meeting in London on Sunday?' 'Is the company giving?' The leader stewards, particularly, rejected these rumours. They emphasized the need to prepare for the strike, in terms of picketing and ensuring that the company was unable to move vehicles either out of the factory or out of the country.

Many members were naturally concerned about the domestic

implications of strike action. Many asked about the organization of pickets — would it be compulsory? Would they get paid for picketing? In addition, several members discussed various sources of income. There were jokes that 'A lot of blokes will be going on the box' (registering as sick), and there was a good deal of discussion of other jobs; some had other part-time jobs on a regular basis, others had jobs available for lay-offs. Others were less fortunate and were thinking of seeking casual employment. One steward explained to a group of his members: 'It's a good time for a strike. You'll get your holiday money half-way through, and there's a good chance of casual employment.' Many stewards also explained to their members that they could claim social security benefits for their families, and that there would almost certainly be strike pay.

Other groups of members, particularly those whose networks involved them closely with leader stewards, were keen not only that the strike should go ahead but that the unions should not attempt 'to do a deal'. Certainly, these members and some stewards expressed views such as the following: 'I feel like blowing the bloody place up . . . We've never really tried the company on before;' 'We need to take the company on because these sorts of companies are bastards.' Consistent with this view, some members were joking at the foremen and telling them that they would get a rough ride when they tried to go through the picket line.

At the mass meeting the conveners had been able to explain that a formal overtime ban could not be instituted because it would be interpreted as duress by the company. At the same time they had pointed out that to work overtime would be to fall into company hands. In other words, the ideal was not to have an overtime ban but for no one to be available for overtime. Some sections did pass resolutions that sanctions would be placed upon any men who were found to be doing overtime; for example, treating them unfavourably in terms of their position on the lay-off and overtime rotas. The night after the mass meeting one or two men did work overtime, but the next day, when their workmates discovered this, they were strongly criticized and jeered; some members proposed blackballing them. Few, however, did work overtime. For example, at the weekend, when the company offered overtime, only 1 per cent of the assembly shop worked it.

Some stewards attempted to impose sanctions upon these people by publicly listing their names. Several of these men complained to a convener. He sympathized with them, and reprimanded the stewards concerned, pointing out that such behaviour was 'contrary to all union principles'; men could work overtime if they so wished for there was no ban, and, if a few men did work, it would prove to management that no ban existed.

The conveners and members of the Q-E were primarily concerned with preparing for the strike. They dispelled rumours and tried to prevent any panic. For example, on one occasion two populist stewards raced into the conveners' office to declare that the company were shifting incomplete vehicles to another location. The conveners told them not to panic: 'The company's only trying to upset the men.'

More importantly, the conveners wrote formally to their officials to inform them of the decision of the mass meeting and request that the officials set the procedure in motion for making the strike official. The conveners had, of course, been talking informally to the officials before this; the latters' reaction to the decision to strike was on the whole favourable, although at least one feared the consequences of the decision.

The conveners and Q-E members also discussed how picketing should be organized. The ideas which developed paid little attention to the niceties of the law; rather, they pursued the lessons of the miners' recent successes. In particular, they determined that, at least initially, there would be a mass picket at the plant, that they should picket other locations where vehicles were stocked, that through the unions, especially the TGWU, they would seek the co-operation of dockers and transport drivers, and that they would attempt to organize a squad of 'flying pickets' who would be able to move swiftly to any location where the plant's products were being moved. These issues were discussed at the next JSSC.

Management Reaction

Management were, of course, aware of the decision of the mass meeting to strike. They also prepared for confrontation. We have seen that in planning their counter-claim they also had undertaken long-term preparations to ensure that strike action did not have a major impact upon sales and, hence, their market situation. They had vehicles stored in a variety of places, unknown to the shop-floor. However, it should be added that these plans had almost certainly not been fully realized, because of frequent interruptions to production over the preceding months.

Management's strategy had also been somewhat confused

because the reaction of the shop-floor had not been what they expected. The membership had formally rejected any discussion of MDW in principle, whereas management had expected problems over the detailed content of their proposals and the cash rewards involved, rather than outright rejection. As we shall see, this, along with problems in other plants, later led to a major change in management's strategy.

Immediately after the mass meeting, however, management could do little (other than attempting to ensure maximum output) to improve their strategic position. In discussions with conveners and Q-E members, more senior managers sought to assess the real strength of the shop-floor and to give the impression that they, as managers, were unconcerned and confident. Management were not solely concerned with winning the strike, but also with minimizing problems in the resumption of production. In the past there had been an informal understanding between the conveners and management that they would always attempt to ensure that machinery and equipment did not suffer during strikes and that, when work resumed, all workers would be able to resume on a full working week. (The idea of all returning together was seen to be an important symbol of unity.) Accordingly, management formally called in the conveners and requested that certain groups should be allowed to work during the strike and that safety 'cover' should be provided in particular areas. The conveners stated that they thought this could be agreed but they would have to refer the matter to the JSSC. As we shall see, this 'cover' was in fact refused.

The Mobilization of the Union

At the JSSC meeting a few days after the mass meeting, there were therefore two main issues which the stewards had to discuss. The first concerned the management request for 'cover', the second picketing arrangements. A third item, which seemed of lesser importance to the stewards, was the situation of staff workers during the strike. The last of these was briefly discussed at the end of the meeting. There was no disagreement when the convener stated 'We should let the staff through because then they'll get paid — and that'll cost the company.'

The other two questions were not so easily dealt with. When one of the conveners reported the management request for 'cover', several of the more militant stewards rejected it: 'We've got to be ruthless.' And another added, 'The battle is not our choice; we've got to use everything we can.' In addition, one steward argued that if they refused 'cover' then pressure might be imposed upon management by their insurance company. The conveners stated, first, that: 'You should think before you leap. When we return, we will want it so that everyone is able to work . . . otherwise people will just moan to the conveners if they can't all start at the same time.' Second, they argued that 'It's a union principle to leave a certain number of men in to keep the place right.'

Certainly the conveners, as they made clear, did not see these as primary considerations. All that they were trying to do was to pursue the traditional limits to conflict (thereby limiting their members' long-term losses), and to ensure that the JSSC realized the implications of a literally all-out strike. However, after some discussion it was agreed that no 'cover' would be provided and all the elements of the management request would be rejected. Indeed one steward (a populist) went further and proposed that they 'should take over the plant because the company has been obstructive and it would be good for publicity'. One of the more militant members of the Q-E supported this idea: 'We would be saying this establishment is as much ours as theirs.' The conveners led the opposition to this idea and few other stewards supported the idea of a sit-in. The conveners pointed out that 'The men wouldn't agree . . . We'd look fools if we had a sit-in . . . Very few occupations are successful and we'd have to take it to the mass.'

The organization of picketing was rather more complex. There was a strong awareness expressed by many stewards that isolated picketing on their part would be of little use — there had to be 'outside support'. This was important to ensure no movement of vehicles, and to provide publicity and, later, funds with which to finance a hardship fund for those on strike. As one steward stated, 'We've given a lot to other plants — so we should do pretty well.' Such endeavours on their part would involve direct contact with other steward organizations. But, as one Q-E member argued, 'we've got to use the officials — it's their fight as well.'

Of equal importance was, of course, internal organization. The stewards had to ensure that picket lines were successful so that 'we seal the place up' and this meant that the various groups of pickets had to be co-ordinated. Finally, one of the conveners stressed the importance of the stewards being on the picket lines, for they were crucial for the success of the strike; others referred to 'the importance of enthusiasm'.

178

It was agreed, following proposals by one of the conveners, that particular gates should be picketed by particular sections, and the stewards in those areas would be responsible for arranging rotas of pickets twenty-four hours a day. It was also agreed that at least initially there would be mass picketing. On the first day of the strike all members would be expected to picket, and afterwards rotas would be prepared so that all men picketed and there would generally be about fifty men on each gate.

With such a number of men picketing, plans were developed to ensure supplies of hot drinks and the provision of portable toilets. A request would be made to the owners of caravans to put these at the disposal of the JSSC and the pickets. A number of stewards volunteered to provide their caravans.

One of the more 'hard-line' Q-E members, who had a good deal of experience of picketing, warned of the risks which the men faced from the police. He paid only scant attention to the law on picketing, and instead emphasized the more subtle ways in which the police had treated pickets elsewhere. So, for example, if strikers' cars were parked in the area there was a likelihood that the police would be over-vigilant as far as parking offences, car tax, and tyre regulations were concerned. He stressed the need to warn the men of these possibilities.

Two other points were discussed. The first of these was the financing of the strike, particularly the printing of leaflets and the expenses of men who acted as flying pickets. (Members who were ready to undertake the latter duties were to be asked to inform their stewards.) In order to cover these costs, it was agreed that a 10p collection would be taken from all members.

Finally, it was agreed that a Strike Committee representing all sections should be formed, with the conveners attending when they were able (for they envisaged that they would spend much of their time on the picket lines and elsewhere). Meetings would be held in one of the union's offices. Again at the suggestion of one of the hard-line Q-E members it was agreed that three ordinary members — one from each of the major areas — would also sit on the Strike Committee. This was based on the practice of other Strike Committees where it had been found that such members provided an important means of assessing members' feelings and overcoming problems of the Committee becoming distanced from the members. Further, it was agreed that one of the Strike Committee would be appointed Publicity Officer and that he alone would be allowed to comment to the press. The conveners, in particular, were concerned that journalists might begin to exploit off-hand comments made to them by members; they therefore emphasized the need for stewards to tell their members not to speak to journalists.

This meeting of the JSSC therefore sketched out the way in which the strike was to be conducted. The decisions reached are of interest for three reasons. First, there was a clear policy of near-total commitment: no 'cover' or skeleton manning would be permitted, and there would be mass picketing and flying pickets. Second, very few stewards had in fact experienced picket lines before, despite the number of years they had been trade unionists. (This largely reflects the brief, small, and unofficial nature of most strikes, for picket lines are rarely used on these occasions.) Indeed, the next day at a department stewards' meeting only two of the fifteen stewards said they had ever been on a picket line, and several stewards had to ask what they were meant to do as pickets. Not only is this of interest in its own right in a strong shop steward organization, but it also confirms the view that the stewards were adopting strategies which many of them had learnt from general discussions of collective action, and, more importantly we suspect, from considerable press coverage of the strategies employed by other groups on strike, most notably the miners. Third, and associated with this, some stewards assumed a new prominence. This was particularly true of one or two 'hard-line' members of the Q-E.

In this new situation of confrontation these stewards provided experiences and ideas which 'fitted'. Their aggressive postures, normally seen as excessive or 'too political', were now seen by many stewards and members as consistent with their situation and their needs. This is not to suggest that such stewards began to assume the conveners' role — far from it; but, whereas once such stewards seldom received much respect, they now did so and found themselves elected to such bodies as the Document Sub-Committee and the Strike Committee.

The actual method of going about organizing the picketing rotas varied from department to department and section to section. Where department stewards' committees existed these played a crucial role. Where they did not, many decisions were taken at section level. This led to problems in a number of cases: for example, one indirect section which had been somewhat hesitant over the JSSC policy (for they would receive a sizeable increase under the company proposals, as well as having their differential problem solved) had a populist steward who took the question of picketing to a section meeting. The members decided not to picket, much to the disgust of other stewards and members. As two Q-E members agreed: 'The steward was wrong to let [the question of picketing] go to the vote.' More generally, criticism was made of 'people who vote for strike action but then won't picket'. In the case of the section discussed above, several Q-E members agreed that, in view of this lack of solidarity with the rest of the plant, 'We'll man up their jobs next time they go out.'

Where members of the Q-E, and, to a lesser extent, leader stewards existed, such problems did not arise. Through the departmental stewards' committees these stewards were also able to help, support, and guide populist stewards. In one such committee which met the day after the JSSC, it was the Q-E members who stressed, 'We've got to avoid just the stewards and a hard-core picketing — we've got to shame the blokes, and tell them they'll be letting down their mates [if they don't picket].' At departmental level, the stewards worked out the details of how they would picket the gates for which they had been delegated responsibility. Rotas were worked out, allocating the various sections to particular days and shifts for picketing, and the length of picketing shifts was agreed. In one case, at least, there was also a good deal of discussion concerning when the strike-fund collections should be taken and whether there was a need for rapid organization of the pickets; in this instance, lay-offs of some of their members led to complications. The delay in this department was criticized by the conveners. (Such mass picketing, we believe, would have been important not only for sealing the plant up but also for the maintenance of morale.)

Once such arrangements had been worked out at departmental level, if only in general terms, the individual stewards developed the requisite rotas of their sections — who should be on picket duty when. We observed this process in detail on one section. The first problem for the steward was how to allocate men to the different groups required; the easiest way was merely to acquire a list of men and break it down into the required group sizes. This was the approach favoured by the steward; another steward argued that, despite the administrative complexity, the groups should be based on friendship cliques. This would ensure a better turnout, facilitate transport to and from the picket lines and probably ensure a better atmosphere — it would make non-attendance more obviously a case of 'letting down your mates'. In fact, the former method was chosen but members were told they could swap with each other so that they could go with friends. This organization of the picket rota was done with various members clustered around who joined in the debate. It was largely due to their pressure that friendship cliques — or at least the possibility of reorganization on these lines — were agreed.

More generally, rumours that management were 'giving' abounded among the membership. But in the main, discussion and joking concentrated upon the picket, and particularly upon the detailed arrangements and the sanctions they would impose upon those individuals who failed to picket. For example, in one case a member said he personally did not intend to picket; he was told by his colleagues: 'If everybody else has to picket, then so do you. If you don't we'll sort you out on the rota [for overtime and lay-offs].'

The exhilaration which had existed at times, particularly before the mass meeting, was now rather muted. The reality of strike action was looming closer, and the hope that the strike would not occur was dimming among the membership. The mood, was, therefore, increasingly one of grim determination. Jokes and comments reflected this; for example: 'I hear all the doctors [in the area] are being swamped by blokes trying to get sick notes;' And: 'I notice all the big-mouthed militants are quiet now.' In other words, the men were looking out for signs of 'cowardice' on the part of their colleagues. In part, such concern was over unity; but at the same time, as the quote on picketing above indicates, it was over fairness: in effect, 'If I have to suffer by picketing then so must everybody else; no one's going to get away with it.'

The members received a good deal of information concerning strike details from their own stewards in the course of casual conversation. But in the production areas shop meetings were also held. We observed one of these. A member of the Q-E explained the picketing arrangements, volunteers for the flying picket were sought, and the importance of this strategy was emphasized. In addition, a shop-floor worker was nominated and elected to the Strike Committee.

A number of questions and arguments were put forward by members. One asked why the stewards did not propose a sit-in; one or two were critical of the picket arrangements; a question was asked as to whether or not foremen should be allowed through the picket (the answer was yes). Another member asked about the legality of picketing, and a militant member of the Q-E explained the limits to picketing and stressed the various police strategies mentioned above. However, most questions concerned strike pay and whether the strike was official. Many members had been asking their stewards this earlier in the day. The latter explained that the strike was not yet official because of the length of the procedure involved, but it almost certainly would be made official, and hence strike pay would be paid: 'But it's possible that it won't be, so we can't definitely say "yes". If we were wrong, we'd get hung.'

Meanwhile, the conveners had been busy in a number of ways. First, they had been involved in co-ordinating the various picketing arrangements, advising stewards on particular problems, and where crises arose, or groups found they needed extra men for their picket areas, they attempted to resolve these. They were involved in a co-ordinating and 'fire-fighting' role. One of the conveners was also involved in receiving the money stewards had collected from their members for the Strike Fund. Such monies — like all union funds — had to be carefully recorded; in addition, the convener reminded the stewards to keep the lists of those who had contributed, primarily because, if the money was not used (i.e. if the strike did not occur), it could be handed back. Further, in collecting money from the stewards, the convener was in a key position to reassure them, keep a check on arrangements, and pick up cues regarding potential problems and difficulties.

One of the conveners was also actively concerned with the preparation of banners for the picket lines, and similar detailed arrangements. One interesting aspect of this was that one or two more junior managers, who sympathized with the men's case and were themselves privately opposed to MDW, provided certain items as an expression of their support. (The reasons for this have been discussed earlier. Basically, they needed to maintain good bargaining relationships, and also MDW would have implications for their power and position.)

Of greater importance was the organization of outside support for the strike. In particular, it was necessary to ensure that lorries did not cross the picket lines. Here the TGWU was particularly important since it was a major union in the plant and also organized the lorry drivers concerned. Not only was the TGWU official responsible for the plant involved, but also the official responsible for road transport. This task was facilitated by the informal relationship existing between the latter and the convener. Lists of the companies involved were drawn up, leaflets prepared to give to drivers, as well as more general advice and aid being provided. Indeed, in the week after the mass meeting, there was a very high level of contact between this convener in particular and his officials, as the administrative resources of the union were employed, detailed arrangements worked out, and the general situation discussed.

Early in the morning of the last day of work before the strike, the JSSC met again. The members of the Strike Committee were elected — four members of the Q-E, two leader stewards, and one populist. Final picketing arrangements were agreed and checked, and it was agreed that £200 should be drawn out of the JSSC Central Fund to cover the expenses which would be incurred in the strike. Other than a few last picket details, continuing to collect contributions to the Strike Fund, and checking on the progress of preparations relating to the transport drivers, the domestic organization was formally prepared and ready to wage a long strike.

Attitudes as Strike Action Approached

In the main, the stewards and members were tense and many were now eager for the experience of the strike. Except possibly among the conveners and a few of the Q-E, hopes that the company would 'give' had disappeared. We noted that in the preceding days, as hopes had waned, members and stewards alike had discussed the general course of events, basically attempting to assess where the company and the unions had 'gone wrong', and how the strike had come about. A few still felt that the unions had been wrong in failing to negotiate MDW. More common, however, was the view that the company had been wrong. The phrase, 'The company was trying to get MDW on the cheap; the bloody cheek!', was to be frequently heard. Others felt that management had made a number of strategic mistakes: questioning the efficiency of the union organization, discussing in detail the number of men to be made redundant, and having a low opinion of the shop-floor (that they would not strike).

The tone of such discussions was generally sad. As we have seen, despite the number of disputes in the plant, many stewards had good relations with management, and members and supervision generally had at least tolerable working relationships. There was a realization that a strike on such a basic question as MDW would change this situation. But, at the same time, the assessment of the reasons for the strike pointed the finger of blame towards management. It would be wrong to believe that most members saw themselves as causing the dispute; their assessment of the situation pointed to the conclusion that management, in attempting a 'try-on' of such proportions, caused the strike while they themselves had no choice.

On the day that the strike would begin (at 4.00 p.m.), self-questioning had generally ceased. The strike was inevitable and they were in the right. Excitement was building up. One of the major elements of this was the sense of unity which generally existed. As fieldworkers, we found it exciting; for the majority of workers it was equally so. This day was not one of the general routine and boredom of work but one when they would 'show the company'; as several pointed out, it was 'the first time for ten years that we've told this company where to get off'. A number of other quotations typify this situation. A Q-E member stressed that 'We're organized — the company has never had to face a united front before, with control by the JSSC'; and a member declared, 'This company's bloody awful — after the strike, we'll really hit them . . . We'll refuse to use bodgers [tools which, while formally impermissible, were essential to maintain production], that'll bugger them up . . . We've taken too much from this company, it's about time that we sorted them out.' These views met with general assent. The membership had been 'educated' and the domestic organization, with the support of the larger unions, was prepared for a strike. The stage was set.

14
The Eleventh Hour and the Resumption of Negotiations

At the final JSSC meeting the conveners had outlined the final preparations for the strike. At 11.30 a.m. they received a message that management wished to see them. They went to the manager concerned. After apologizing for the formality of the meeting — explained by its importance — the manager read out a statement that the company had contacted the chairman of the union side for plant bargaining seeking a renewal of negotiations, and he had agreed. The latter was getting in touch with the other officials to arrange a date for a meeting. The conveners replied that the strike would almost certainly be called off in view of this, and sought permission for an immediate meeting of the JSSC. A time and place was agreed, and the conveners began contacting stewards to inform them of the JSSC meeting. It was also agreed that a mass meeting would be held at 3.30 that afternoon. The manager then left to enable them to discuss the matter between themselves and phone their officials.

Why Did Management Avoid the Strike?

A crucial question is, of course, why the company offered to re-open negotiations. The first factor must be that their optimism was somewhat reduced when Stage Two of the incomes policy was introduced. Indeed, we have seen that initially the company thought they would be unable to go ahead in attempts to negotiate MDW. Second, they found their market position was not favourable and they had not expected such a strong reaction from the JSSC, and, more importantly, from the shop-floor. It would appear that they were surprised by the size of the majority in favour of strike action and, contrary to their expectations, 'could see no splits in the ranks'. They had thought that those who would gain most from the MDW proposals, maintenance and the indirects, would be ready to negotiate. Related to this was their conception of the way in which negotiations would go. We have seen that they distinguished two stages — first, over the principle of MDW, and then the detailed negotiations. They had expected agreement on the former, and a strike on the latter. Given this conceptual distinction, some managers feared a second strike over the details. In fact, such a distinction was incorrect. Third, and more importantly, it was feared that, if there were a strike and the company won, the unions might well pursue a policy of non-cooperation and a situation even worse than that experienced in another local company might ensue. The fourth factor — certainly in the eyes of more senior managers the most important — was the situation in another of their plants which was a major supplier to our plant. This was the establishment which worried many stewards when the mass meeting drew near and they feared a lay-off as the result of action there. A full-scale strike had developed at this plant since the mass meeting. It might be thought that this would have made the company more ready to 'take on' our domestic organization. But this was not so. As a senior manager explained, the company decided 'against fighting on two fronts at once, and we thought the [other plant's] situation was more important to us'.

Factors both internal and external to the plant were important; in addition, it would appear that it was not merely the brute facts of power but also a particular ethos and 'way of seeing things' which were crucial in management's decision.

Shop-Floor Reaction

One of the conveners said that he had expected they would be called in, for his local office had phoned him and, on the basis of the probable resumption of negotiations, had advised him to call a mass meeting. Another said that he had won a few bets because management had 'given', and, while happy, he was frustrated because of all the work he had done which now had no purpose. The first convener agreed, but added: 'It's done good, though — it's brought unity to the union organization for the first time.'

The chairman of the union side then phoned to explain the

course of events. He emphasized that he had told the company that negotiations had to be meaningful and 'There's to be no funny business — the credibility of the company, the officials, and the conveners rests on the outcome.' The company had agreed. The conveners told the official that they thought they should call the strike off, and that in their view the JSSC would agree. A happy banter between the officials and the conveners ensued.

The conveners then went off to ensure that all the stewards knew of the JSSC meeting. The stewards and the men standing around them immediately concluded that they had won. One of us was with a steward and a group of his members when he was told of the JSSC meeting. He told the group that there was to be a JSSC meeting. There were shouts of 'The company's cracked' and 'The bloody cowards'. They agreed that a section meeting which had been arranged to devise a means of penalizing non-pickets should be adjourned and that all members should be told why. There were cries of delight and jokes about management being cowards as the other members were told.

The steward, a member of the Q-E, went off to tell other stewards. A foreman was with a leader steward and then told them that management had called the foremen in and given them a statement about the resumption of negotiations. Then the Q-E member went over to another section where the view was expressed that: 'We should keep the strike on. The company's only conning . . . A week's time, after all the [vehicles] are out and the park is empty, they'll refuse to negotiate again . . . We want the money on the table.'

The reaction of the membership, was then, a mixture of delight and suspicion. On their way to the JSSC meeting many stewards still felt they should strike, for they were suspicious of the company and wanted some kind of guarantee that their claim would be met. At the JSSC meeting the conveners explained:

There's been a change in events in the last two hours. The company has approached the union with a view to talks. [The official concerned] made it clear that we were always available but that it would be no good having talks if they served no purpose. The company said they would be meaningful . . . We agreed to call a meeting of the JSSC to tell you, and the officials say officially that we should forget our action. We can always put it back on if we're dissatisfied.

Two views were expressed on this. The first is best seen in the following statement by a Q-E member: 'This is what we all expected;

that we'd have the piss taken out of us at this late hour. The company has had three months and seven days [to negotiate]. Let's have the meeting, but continue the action.' The other view was in favour of calling off the strike: the company would not negotiate under duress, negotiations would have to start sometime, and the stewards were merely proposing to delay the action. In addition:

It could be that most stewards feel [that the strike should continue], but it's got to go to the shop-floor, and I'm not sure they'd agree. The stewards have done a good job but we shouldn't ruin it by separating ourselves from the shop-floor. I think the feeling of the shop-floor will be one of relief. It's a question of the definition of 'meaningful'. The company know our position on MDW and that we want £1 plus 4 per cent. As I see it, we've won the battle without fighting it. We should not disaffiliate ourselves from the shop-floor.

The conveners favoured this latter view. No matter what the JSSC decided, they as conveners would have to call a mass meeting and the members would decide finally. In addition, they added:

We've been pleased by the reaction of the shop-floor and the stewards. But playing cat and mouse will get us nowhere . . . We'd do the same as the company and play it up to the brink . . . The thing is that unity has been restored to the plant [shouts of hear! hear!] . . . You've got to look at this objectively.

If we strike for one or two weeks and then [the company] got in touch with us for a meeting, we'd return for that meeting. I'm frustrated because we saw our organization work for once . . . we've given the officials strength, because the company thought the plant was weak — now they know that that's not so. So we have a dispute — about what?

But the conveners temporarily changed their minds when they learnt that the company had already informed some members that negotiations were to be resumed, for this endangered 'the sanctity of the position of the JSSC and the union'. One convener, on hearing of management's actions, therefore reacted: 'In that case, I feel we should still go out. The JSSC are the custodians of the union movement and the company is trying to undermine it.' However, while they were determined to stress the seriousness of management behaviour to them, they finally returned to the view that 'We won't lose while we're talking, but we will if we don't talk and then the shop-floor rise against us.' It was, therefore, finally agreed — with about 30 of the 120 or so stewards present voting

189

against: 'That we should accept the recommendation from the officials and we should suspend strike action until the conclusion of discussions . . .'

The assembly stewards in particular were unhappy with the decision and their members, like many others, were opposed to calling off the strike. For example, we heard the following comments: 'We should still go out — you can't trust this company . . . we've got the company on the run for the first time in years . . . we should go out and push them further.' Some feared 'a sell-out' by the officials and were opposed to their involvement: 'When it came to it before, the officials just left it to action by the shop-floor.' Hostility to the company grew: 'I'll blow this bloody place up . . . If this is a management con, then we'll occupy the place . . . this management is rubbish.'

Some stewards advised their members to vote against the JSSC resolution and in favour of continuing the strike. Many members agreed with this view, and the mass meeting was likely to be a 'rough ride' for the conveners in particular (as before, mass meetings were also held at one of the more isolated areas and for the night shift).

At the mass meeting one of the conveners explained the background — that one of the officials had received a call from the company who had promised meaningful negotiations; the officials had recommended ending the strike and negotiating, and the JSSC recommendation was to delay strike action. He emphasized the officials' recommendation, 'And after all, we pay them for advice.' Another convener repeated the arguments and stressed that even if there was a strike 'we'd still return for negotiations'. The delay in the resumption of negotiations (to start a week later) was due to the other commitments of the officials.

The meeting was, as our fieldnotes describe it, 'heated and noisy'. The conveners were interrupted on a number of occasions and accused of selling out; they retorted that it was up to the members to make the decision, and on one occasion one declared that 'I don't mind either way.' There was a demand, 'What about our money?', which was applauded. A convener said that the purpose of the meeting would be to negotiate £1 plus 4 per cent. 'What about it only being 95p?' A convener replied, 'We have never accepted that it's only 95p.' 'What about our pensions?' A convener explained, 'That is included in the claim . . . there will be no discussion of MDW.' A number of other questions and arguments followed. One member expressed the fear of a 'sell-out', to which a convener emphasized that they never had or would sell out. The results of the negotiations would be brought back to the mass, they would only negotiate £1 plus 4 per cent and the pension and there would be no discussion of MDW. One speaker favoured a return to work: 'We've got what we want, we'd gain nothing by staying out.' An ex-steward argued that they should stay out: 'The company's had three months to negotiate [applause] . . . we can't trust them.' One convener emphasized that it was up to the mass to decide whether or not to trust the company. Another convener made a powerful speech which was applauded. He stressed his own frustration, particularly since he had done so much work; he had expected the company to give in, and even though it was at the eleventh hour, they should agree to it for they would have to return for negotiations anyway. 'Would the company negotiate while we were out?' The conveners doubted it and added: 'We've got superb solidarity here now. The response to the picket was good, we've got unity in the plant for the first time for years. We're cemented together, and that cement won't break.' A member retorted that 'If we don't strike, then that cement has broken already.'

The meeting had lasted about half an hour when the conveners moved the vote. The resolution of the JSSC to call off the strike was carried; our estimate was that the vote was two to one in favour. Some aggrieved members doubted whether the majority was in support of the JSSC resolution, but the more general view of those favouring the continuation of the strike was summed up by one steward:

I disagree with the result, but the vote was clear . . . and it's true as [one of the conveners] said, even if we did strike we'd return for negotiations — that was good and logical . . . We've got the organization now so we can strike if we've got to.

After the mass meeting the members disappeared quickly for it was after the end of working hours, but the next day those in favour of continuing the strike were particularly vociferous. They were disappointed at the decision, suspicious of the company and somewhat suspicious and critical of the conveners, claiming that they had done a deal. As one of these argued, 'I'm fed up with this bloody company and the union.' Some wanted to remove the conveners. But the 'voice of reason' was not totally absent: 'Why strike? The company's given in — we've got to be reasonable.'

Stewards were bombarded with questions about the delay in the resumption of negotiations, whether £1 plus 4 per cent really would be £2.50, whether it would be backdated. But what appeared to be the single most important concern was maintaining unity; it was this which appeared to be behind the demand for the continuation of the strike; for example: 'We've got to preserve the unity of the plant. It's never existed before, and if we're not careful we'll lose it. We should strike, if only to use that unity.' It is far from mere romanticism to describe this as a high value being placed upon collective consciousness. There may be some truth in the cynical view that such grand statements could now be espoused because it seemed that the unions had won. But what cannot be denied is that men were happy and excited at the thought of unity and strength. The quotations throughout demonstrate the importance of these as values — now they had become much more of a reality. The uncertainties had now gone and the signs of success meant that collective unity was seen both as valuable in its own right and as something which could pay dividends.

The suspicion of the company was sufficiently strong to ensure that most stewards persuaded their sections with little difficulty to maintain the *de facto* overtime ban which had been in existence for the past week, on the grounds that 'We've got to make sure the company don't clear the park [of vehicles] and emphasize to them that we still feel strongly.'

The debate on the advisability of calling off the strike continued further at the next meeting of the JSSC; several argued that they should have continued with their action, and fears of 'the company playing tricks' were expressed. The conveners assured the stewards that 'The people who will be negotiating are quite capable of telling the company they're not on.' In addition, the conveners had two other points to make. The first was to criticize those stewards who had been 'putting the poison down against the JSSC resolution' and encouraging their members to vote against it; this was bad and contrary to all norms of steward behaviour. Second, they reported that they had complained to the company about their giving information direct to the shop-floor and 'trying to undermine the conveners'; the company had apologized and explained that it had been due to a misunderstanding. The convener concluded: 'We have to expect tricks — we do it, they do it. But I think the company attitude is pathetic.'

The unity of the plant, however, was significant but somewhat tenuous. Complete unity is probably impossible; in this case it was essentially issue-specific although it could be diverted to other issues. However, the disagreement over the continuation of the

192

strike weakened that unity. (At the same time, it is probable that a continuation of the strike would have weakened it even more.) Furthermore, as time passed and new sectional problems arose, some groups threatened isolated action. Within a week of the mass meeting, a group of Q-E members and the conveners agreed that 'The union organization is breaking up again after the strike.' Certainly the excitement of unity had declined, but, as we show later, it had far from disappeared.

The Resumption of Negotiations

Early in June — a week after the mass meeting — negotiations re-opened. Management began with a review of the situation up to the present, and then continued, referring to a number of press articles:

These lead to my conclusion that you are not as opposed [to MDW] as you suggested. The mass did not vote against it because it was not discussed. You are not opposed because you have negotiated MDW elsewhere and because of the comments recorded in the press. You are not opposed in principle. We never said we could negotiate it in a matter of weeks. We want to negotiate a time-table. We propose extending the present agreement for a period during which we would discuss an MDW system.

The union's reaction was strong; as one convener told a Q-E member afterwards, '[An official] really roasted [management]. He was good'. The official argued:

It's degrading to be brought here and told that we're here because of a few press statements. You know the decision of the mass. The credibility of this negotiating committee is at stake . . . You wish to impose MDW . . . the NJC objects to your documents. You tried to convince everybody, and you still got the answer you did; and now you still want to talk MDW. We have a mandate.

After complaining about the leak of information to the shop-floor on the resumption of negotiations, an official continued: 'We do not intend to spend the rest of the day here in discussions unless there is a definite statement from you that you will move in the direction required by the workers if they are not going to go into dispute.' A convener added, in a more conciliatory tone: 'I could say the company has made a lot of mistakes. There was a fear in everybody's hearts about MDW. But we've always been able to get over problems here, but at the present time things have turned sour.'

The unions stressed that they could not and would not discuss MDW and the company agreed to adjourn to consider their position. Management returned to state that they were:

prepared in view of the restrictions of legislation, to negotiate a conventional piecework agreement, having provision for an agreement in principle to discussions during the term of the agreement for the introduction of MDW, to discuss the allocation of money within the £1 plus 4 per cent formula, and to negotiate a retirement grant the cost of which to be included in the money available or to be separately financed by the employees.

The unions adjourned to consider this offer and immediately agreed that 'We won't put ourselves in pawn for twelve months.' The question was whether the reference to MDW was a face-saver on the part of the company or not. They experimented with ways of rephrasing the statement to provide such a 'face-saver' for the company without suggesting any commitment on their part, but agreed that they could not accept this because 'We would be accused of letting the shop-floor down. This conference is a good thing but we cannot be party to accepting MDW.' To management they explained: 'Four thousand five hundred blokes disapprove of MDW as the vote indicated; if we are party to any formula which hints at MDW the blokes won't accept it . . . The word MDW is poison; it'll only get people's backs up . . . There will be a revolt if you push MDW. If you want that, then OK.'

Management therefore agreed to drop any reference to MDW and agreed to pay £1 plus 4 per cent to all shop-floor workers, after some discussion of the norm for new piecework values and the question of drift. The union side argued that a lump-sum payment could be paid separately from the piecework base rate and that consequently 'you can't say that the drift is *not* due to effort'. The company were initially hesitant about this since they felt it was a 'retrograde' step; only a few years ago they had got rid of all pay supplements in order to simplify the payment system. However, they finally agreed, subject to the ruling of the Pay Board. The increase would be paid retrospectively to the end of the previous agreement. A number of minor adjustments to the piecework agreement was made.

Another problem was the retirement grant. Management insisted that they would not fund it. In adjournments the officials argued that the workers should fund the grant, if only because this would establish the principle and provide some control over the scheme. The conveners, who were hesitant because of their mandate, finally agreed that 'We could ask the lads if they would pay for the grant.' This formed the basis of agreement. The union side agreed to take the question of the retirement grant to the shop-floor. They also agreed to take the total offer back to the shop-floor but pointed out that they could not formally recommend it because of union opposition to the £1 plus 4 per cent legislation. The company also gave an assurance that communication of the offer would be left to the shop-floor.

Shop-Floor Acceptance

Inevitably over the next few days, members and stewards tried to discover what had happened in the negotiations, and rumours were rife. Only members of the Q-E, as trusted and influential stewards, were told of events by the conveners. More generally it was rumoured that £1 plus 4 per cent had been offered, but the retirement grant had not. Among the stewards, at least, discussion focused on whether they should strike over the latter — most of those whose opinions we learnt were opposed to a strike.

A few days later the JSSC was formally told of the negotiations and the company offer by the conveners, emphasizing, as one put it, 'We left no stone unturned. We got the best deal possible.' Discussion focused on the pension (as many were now calling it). The conveners argued that the members should finance it, emphasizing that this was the advice of the officials. One or two stewards pointed out that the conveners were 'changing your tune'. One convener retorted: 'The facts are clear: I don't want it that way. I'm frustrated. But if we pay, the officials say we will have some control. I would prefer that the company pay, but the advice of the officials and the law mean that it's not on.' In addition, it was argued that the shop-floor would not strike over the pension, that the principle would be established and company financing could be achieved in later years. In opposition, some stewards argued: 'We've got to push pensions because otherwise the company will have an ace for MDW next time. We've got to remove that weapon.' And 'The company is weak because of the feeling on the shop-floor. The JSSC has got to lead as they have done in history. If we don't ask the members for support, we won't

195

get it.' Nevertheless, the officials and conveners' advice was accepted. There was a large majority in favour of the resolution: 'That we accept the company offer of £1 plus 4 per cent which means that every employee gets £2.47 across the board, and we will leave it to the EC to select one of the five retirement schemes to put before the JSSC for their approval.' It was also agreed 'that we hold a plant mass meeting at 3.30 today'.

The stewards returned to their sections, informed their members of the mass meeting, and answered the many questions on the details of the offer; the majority appeared to be ready to pay for the pension.

Another element entered the discussion in the assembly shop, particularly among the stewards. This was the idea of reducing their manning and thereby further boosting their earnings. The company had of course proposed this and the stewards had realized that they could do better if they reduced labour themselves and hence achieved all the resulting 'savings'. Management had, then, acted to expand horizons. As one Q-E member put it, '[The offer] still only gives us £48.50. If we reduced our labour load we could get our money up over £50, and lay-off pay to £40.' In addition, this idea became more attractive because many were convinced that the company would again attempt to introduce MDW and it would make it more difficult and costly for the company if they were to boost their earnings. Several sections discussed this and within the next few months boosted their earnings in this way.

At the mass meeting that afternoon the conveners pointed out that 'We haven't got all that we wanted, but we have got some of the way.' They went on to explain that the company's agreement to £1 plus 4 per cent meant £2.47 and not £2.50 because, in accordance with the mass decision, everybody was included (the previous company proposals excluded canteen workers), and in addition they had the extra days' holiday negotiated nationally. A convener then raised another point: 'The first of these is the thing we had agreed not to discuss — we have not discussed it, and there has been no agreement to it whatsoever even in principle.' A number of questions followed — whether the offer was retrospective; what had happened to the sectional claims ('they were dropped because of the mass decision'). One member asked if they could continue to pursue their sectional claims; the conveners explained that such an attempt would have little chance because of 'the present legislation'. In answer to a further question, the conveners pointed out that the cash offer could not be boosted through piecework effort. Finally, a member asked what the JSSC recommended. It was explained that they could not recommend anything because of union opposition to the legislation. A vote was taken, and we estimated that only about twenty out of several thousand members voted against accepting the offer. A convener then outlined what had happened to their claim for a retirement grant: 'We failed to get the company to pay, so we have to fund it.' After giving details of the scheme, he went on: 'While it's not what we asked for, it does have certain advantages. We'd get our foot in the door . . . we can jack it up if everybody comes into it . . . if the other plants came in we can cut the cost or improve the benefits.' A variety of questions on details of the schemes were asked and answered. It was proposed that the conveners should be permitted to negotiate the details of a scheme. Only two voted against this; a convener joked: 'I trust you'll fall in line with the majority.'

The bulk of the members appeared perfectly happy with the result. A number had been so convinced that the company offer would be accepted that they did not bother to attend the mass meeting, preferring to leave for home early. These latter were to lose half an hour's money, and, when they complained, the conveners told them it served them right for failing to be proper trade unionists.

Detailed questions on the retirement grant and when back pay would be given were asked of the stewards for several weeks afterwards. In addition, as we have noted, in assembly the stewards became far more bonus-conscious. They had been disputing the payment of 'make-up' for some time, and the day after the mass meeting one steward rejected management's make-up offer as insufficient, led his members out for a meeting, and received support for a diplomatically phrased threat of sanctions if the offer was not improved. In our view the timing of this incident was not mere chance.

Postcript

The unions had achieved £1 plus 4 per cent which was generally accepted to be £2.47; they had achieved the principle of a retirement grant although they had failed to persuade the company to finance it. In addition, there were the significant organizational gains in terms of unity; several months later this was used in two all-out strikes against mobility — an issue where previously the mass meeting had rejected JSSC recommendations to strike.

In fact, the problems were not over. First, several months later, it became clear in discussions with the company and a number of insurance companies that the idea of a retirement grant was impracticable. This original idea did not, then, become a reality. However, the national level of the union had begun to investigate improvements in the company pension scheme after discussions at the NJC. This led to some criticism from the stewards since the officials had in the past been hesitant over the issue of pensions. They were now thought to be 'muscling in' on the stewards' success.

Second, after the local agreement had been ratified by the NJC, it was sent to the Pay Board. At the beginning of August the stewards learnt that, as the JSSC minutes state: '[the company] had been advised by the Pay Board that so-called piecework drift would have to be offset against the settlement.' After a lengthy discussion, the JSSC resolved: 'That we decline [a company] invitation to attend any more meetings, because as far as we are concerned the wage settlement has been concluded and we inform our national officials to come and meet us and give us a directive.'

A meeting was held about ten days later with the company. The Pay Board had stated that unless the company and unions could agree on the offsets, then it might be necessary for a Pay Board investigator to look at the situation. The unions had been suspicious of the way in which the Pay Board had been informed of the agreement, and thought that the company had in effect suggested that offsets should be subtracted from the £1 plus 4 per cent. At the meeting, the unions emphasized that they saw no purpose in the meeting — the only offset agreed had been the retirement grant, and there was no question of the unions becoming associated with the Pay Board. They expressed their suspicions of company behaviour.

The company explained that they had merely complied with legal requirements, and that the Pay Board had then requested further information: as the minutes state, 'The company pointed out that throughout the negotiations it had maintained that it would remain within the legislation, and at no point did it instigate the problem by the way in which it had submitted its answers to the Pay Board.' They went on to suggest that the unions, if unwilling to discuss the problem with the Pay Board, could at least 'indicate whether they considered the Company's figures to be correct'.

The unions referred to their previous views that no offsets had to be made, and repeated that the company must have raised the possibility of an offset with the Pay Board. But since new norms for piecework values had not been made, they argued, drift was unlikely, and added that day workers linked to pieceworkers also had to increase effort when the latter improved their performance. The discussion of detailed offsets continued and, finally, according to the minutes:

The Unions reiterated that they could not agree to any offset and were not prepared to make an approach to the Pay Board. Whatever the outcome of any further discussions between the Company and the Pay Board, the Unions wished to emphasize that they had reached agreement for the payment of an award of £2.47 per week from which an offset would be made for the provision of a retirement grant.

The union side also stated that they would be informing the stewards of the situation at the next JSSC.

At the JSSC, the report of events led to a lengthy discussion. It was finally resolved: 'That we instruct the Factory EC to look at the document that will be submitted to the Pay Board. If anything is wrong with the document, this will be reported to the JSSC next Monday.' In fact, the document sent to the Pay Board was acceptable to the conveners, and was accepted by the Pay Board. Over a year after the first discussions among the stewards, the members received their wage increase.

15
The Dispute in Retrospect

In this chapter we attempt to draw out from our detailed study of one near-strike a number of more general conclusions. In particular we are concerned with questions relating to the mobilization of consciousness and the role of steward leadership. Before we examine these, however, it is useful to summarize the main course of events and look a little more fully at the issues in dispute.

An Overview of the Near-Strike

In accordance with normal practice, the unions had prepared an annual claim. What changed the situation was management's introduction of proposals to change the payment system from piecework to MDW. More importantly, the union negotiators, realizing the significance of the question, chose to break with custom and seek a mandate from the JSSC. This mandate was one of opposition in principle, which the unions followed.

There were doubts as to the sense and representativeness of this mandate among stewards. Management doubted whether the resolution expressed members' wishes, and attempted to overcome it. This meant two things: they had to refuse resolutely to negotiate anything else, and, second, to attempt to shift the problem to what they believed was a more receptive membership.

They very nearly succeeded in the former. The union side were beginning to consider seriously a 'package deal' including a retirement grant; but, in our view, two apparently trivial factors, and a third of greater significance, prevented this. First, the move in the unions' position occurred in the late afternoon just before the meeting ended. Second, and more importantly, the unions had asked management to consider an issue separate from the annual negotiations but which was causing a great deal of debate on the

200

shop-floor, namely the interpretation of the lay-off pay agreement. Management's unsympathetic reply soon killed the conciliatory tone of the unions which had developed during the adjournment.

These two points can be related to a third which is more basic. This was the failure of management to react to the cues which were given by one or two of the union side that an offer of MDW plus a retirement grant might be acceptable. These were merely hints because of the constraints of the mandate upon the union officials. Moreover, for them openly to make such an offer would suggest weakness. It was also contrary to the policies of several of the unions concerned, and, in the view of some, contrary to union principles.

It was essential, therefore, that the company take the initiative. But they did so only to a limited degree because they felt a grant was a proper subject for national rather than local bargaining. They therefore merely offered to cost the retirement grant while the unions would consider their position on the company's proposals. But this meant that the conveners really had little to put before the JSSC. To talk openly of MDW would invite the charge of going against JSSC resolutions, and they had no offer from the company which would serve as an excuse. The offer of a package including the grant, however, would have made the JSSC more divided, and would have enabled a mass meeting to be called, so that the blame for acceptance of the company's proposals could be shifted to the members. Instead, the fail-safe strategy was voiced informally.

Events overtook this tentative move towards a possible compromise, for in the next negotiations the contrasting definitions of £1 plus 4 per cent — as a right and as a maximum — became clear. By then the unions had committed themselves to this figure at least as far as the maintenance workers were concerned. The failure to agree resulted from this and the realization that they had been acting upon the totally false assumption that management would be ready to pay the legal maximum even if MDW was rejected.

The room for compromise was now quite different. The major problem for the unions disappeared to a degree; it was not a fight *against* MDW but *for* £1 plus 4 per cent. The policy of management also forced the unions into a major move towards educating the shop-floor. For the company began to act upon its conviction that the membership were, or could become, favourable to MDW. This might well have been true at the start of the propaganda war, but it became less so. Management's '*overkill*' policy meant the unions were forced to counter this attack, particularly since management's actions were in effect a criticism of the union. The structural conflict between management and union meant that for many members, if management were challenging the union, then the union could well be right, so that the company's documents backfired.

This is not to decry in any way the mobilization efforts undertaken by the stewards. They were undoubtedly the most crucial factor and we consider this aspect more fully below. Nevertheless, there was still a certain hesitation on the part of some members and stewards, including some of the Q-E members. They were basically pursuing two strategies which formally had a coherence in the form of the fail-safe strategy, but for some populists it was certainly a means of entering upon negotiations over MDW.

The fail-safe policy reflected uncertainty as to the way members would vote and/or the success of strike action. But there was a limit to the delay which was possible. A great deal of effort had been put into education and there came a point when there was no reason for delay; influential stewards pushed for a mass meeting. Again, an extraneous factor was crucial for confirming the resolution of the conveners. The fact that management had 'given' in another dispute supported the view of company weakness derived from clues picked up from informal chats with management.

A mass meeting was held and the conveners pushed the JSSC recommendation of strike action very hard. They quickly squashed any move for discussion of MDW. Education and leadership achieved the desired result: a large majority in favour of strike action.

The conveners had been optimistic because the question of the probable outcome of a strike appeared to them to be answered. They could win if the strike was well organized, and management might give in with merely the threat of strike action. They were right. Management's forecasts had been incorrect, for the market had not dropped. The company had also interpreted the JSSC resolution at face value and hence as contradicting their predictions. They were surprised by the mass vote (although they could explain it by saying that their proposals were not discussed), and they were concerned about the costs of their own success in a strike if it led to non-cooperation. But, again, an extraneous factor was crucial. They were facing major industrial relations problems in another plant and felt this to be a more important issue on which to concentrate their efforts. They therefore offered a resumption of negotiations, and, on finding the unions even more resolutely opposed to MDW, agreed to a conventional piecework agreement and £1 plus 4 per cent.

The near-strike was carefully planned; it was not a wildcat. But one of the most impressive aspects — which we suspect is very often true in such strikes — is that the move towards it was so nearly checked on a number of occasions and in a number of ways. And, of course, management's withdrawal of their proposals for MDW meant the strike in fact never came about.

The 'Causes' of Strike Action and the Role of Legislation

In our brief overview of the near-strike we have suggested that there were critical occasions when the course of events could have been very different from what actually happened. To that extent, the failure of management to provide support for those negotiators who were seeking some sort of compromise can be seen as the cause of the near-strike. But in our view there is a more basic factor which relates to government legislation on wage increases. By imposing a maximum wage increase, the government of the day imposed a clear basis for the assessment of negotiators. In a situation of free collective bargaining, such bench-marks are less easily or generally available; in addition, the bench-mark, since it was part of a counter-inflation policy, was not a very high one. Consequently any self-respecting negotiator in effect had to achieve £1 plus 4 per cent.

The success generally achieved by negotiators meant that the £1 plus 4 per cent ceased to be a maximum but rather a norm for many negotiators. In our plant, the union negotiators expected the company to offer £1 and 4 per cent. The legal limit on wage increases led, therefore, to misunderstandings, for management believed it had to be negotiated while the unions initially saw it as an immediately available alternative. The question for the latter was whether the company would pay more. We suspect that this belief on the part of the unions made them more ready to reject in principle the company's proposals for MDW.

The pay limit, therefore, made the structural changes which management wanted far more difficult to achieve. It might be argued that it was this proposal of a basic change in the payment system which led to the near-strike. But, in our view, this is only partially true. The JSSC were opposed to MDW, but it is open to question whether, in a situation of free collective bargaining, opposition would have been so strong. We have seen that when they first heard the MDW proposals, many stewards rejected them less on principle than as a negotiating stance. The conveners, Q-E, and officials were generally opposed to MDW in principle, but all of them were very aware that, at least in the surrounding area, no domestic organization had successfully opposed changes of this kind. In a context of free collective bargaining, it would therefore have been an open question whether strike action over MDW would have been supported by the membership. However, given the existence of legislation, the FTA was recorded and a vote for strike action taken, *not* because of the proposed change in the payment system, but because this was a management condition for paying what many had come to see as a right. Comparisons with other firms, 'tin-pot little firms', who had received £1 and 4 per cent, and frequent comments about 'the cheek of the company', support this view.

The 'causes' of the near-strike, then, basically related to the problems which government legislation imposed upon a management seeking major changes. The irony of the situation is obvious. The counter-inflation policy of the company was thwarted by the counter-inflation policy of the government. However, this merely explains the existence of a problem, and ignores the possibility that the membership would have accepted the company's proposals. The reason for their rejection relates to the organizational pattern of the shop-floor and the nature of workers' consciousness.

The Changing Definitions Accepted by the Membership

In Part I we stressed that problem identification was not an automatic process. Rather, discussions among workers create definitions of situations. This can be seen clearly in the case of the near-strike over the annual negotiations. Many workers' views of the company proposals changed considerably because of the efforts of the stewards. Moreover, this change involved a different perspective upon the company more generally and was associated with the development of a strong collective consciousness.

The ability of the stewards to change the perspective of the majority of workers rested upon what can be described as the existence of a 'dual consciousness' (this term is in fact a simplification of a description of members' attitudes). In our previous volume we have noted the existence of ambivalence and the variety of perspectives which workers employed. The stewards were able to create a dominant perspective which was considerably different from that typically found in the plant.

We can trace this process to a degree. In the early stages of the negotiations, members showed little interest. However, many workers were attracted to management proposals because they promised improved earnings and fewer disputes. As management and union attempted to persuade them of their respective cases, uncertainty developed, leading to a belief on the part of the majority that ideally MDW should not be introduced, but at the same time they doubted their own strength and chances of success. The development of a 'normative atmosphere' removed at least the expression of these doubts.

There was also another element of importance: the refusal of the company to pay what workers were convinced was legitimately theirs — £1 and 4 per cent. This led to a dramatic change in attitudes: on individualistic and collective grounds it meant that they were forced to strike. It cannot be emphasized too strongly that in this case, as in most others, workers did not decide upon strike action as part of a sinister or cynical plot. They were convinced that their action was correct and necessary, for they saw themselves as given no option but to fight. So, rather unhappily at first, they committed themselves to strike action.

The development of consciousness, then, spread from a definition of self-interest. Workers who were far from radical in the normal course of events adopted more militant perspectives. The nature and the range of imagery available and employed by them meant that workers' perspectives were volatile and to a degree situationally specific.

We can see this in the informal discussions among workers. In the days leading up to the mass meetings there was a process of hardening attitudes, indicated, for example, by an increase in the number of small strikes. But we also noted a process of generalization. Hence, the £1 plus 4 per cent and the company proposals were not seen in isolation. They were related to a more general picture of what they defined as company exploitation in the past which made the immediate situation more meaningful. At the same time it made sense of particular aspects of their day-to-day experience which only rarely found expression — the alienating nature of their work (at other times the great majority of workers thought their employer was as good as, if not better than, most in the area). In talking of their work we found a double standard. The work was 'not really too bad', all things considered, but at the same time — compared with an ideal (rather than immediate alternatives) — it was 'soul-destroying'. The latter element of their work experience now became more central, and hostility was directed primarily towards the company.

It has sometimes been argued that in major strikes there is an explosion of class consciousness (Mann, 1973), and it is useful, therefore, to consider how far such a process can be said to have occurred in this near-strike. The first aspect we need to consider is the extent to which workers' attitudes can be said to constitute class consciousness. It is generally argued that this involves a number of crucial elements. The first is a strong and dominant identification with one's class, and, second, the identification of a major structural conflict between one's own and another class. Such conflict is seen to be all-pervasive. Finally, class consciousness involves a conception of an alternative structure of society (Mann, 1973:13; Touraine, 1971).

On these criteria, our workers did not demonstrate class consciousness. The focus of their opposition was the company, although certain themes did extend beyond the plant. First, there was some generalization encompassing other, similar companies. However, this did not apply to all companies. Second, we noted that there was discussion of society more generally, but this focused upon the existence of 'fiddles' which were not consistently seen as attributable to the larger structure of society. In addition, some workers expressed moral indignation at the distribution of wealth in society. But these themes can scarcely be said to be central to their opposition to the company's proposals. Such views played a subsidiary legitimatory role.

The same difficulties apply with the question of how workers perceived themselves. The experience of 'unity' and 'solidarity' was highly prized. Its strength can be seen in the reaction of many workers and stewards when it was proposed that the strike be called off. But that sense of unity, the basis of their identification, focused on the domestic organization itself.

Again, however, the nature of that factory consciousness links up with larger units of identification. The condition for plant unity was the reaffirmation of the values of trade unionism. To that extent, the larger trade union movement and its history were important points of reference which served to bolster what was essentially a parochial consciousness. Trade union mythology provided a set of arguments and norms which fostered plant unity and an awareness of their action as part of a larger 'working-class' struggle. But at no time did this larger perspective dominate the particular local experience of unity.

This factory consciousness also lacked any idea of an alternative structure, even for the plant. The idea of a more dramatic challenge in the form of a sit-in was swiftly dismissed. Workers' more enraged outbursts were essentially negative and unconstructive — 'I'll burn this bloody place down.'

One final point should be noted. The strong collective identity which developed in the plant was delicate for much of the time. Stewards were very often afraid that it would rapidly disappear. As the frequency of smaller strikes and near-strikes indicates, the opposition to management and heightened bargaining awareness associated with this consciousness frequently endangered its own existence. Thus sectional action could well break what were really somewhat brittle bonds holding workers together.

The sense of unity which developed cannot, then, be said to approximate to class consciousness. It might more accurately be described as a trade union factory consciousness. While it drew upon larger and more general types of legitimation, its focus was the plant. This was scarcely surprising, for their opposition concerned a particular set of proposals put forward by their own management. In this respect, our findings suggest that the idea of explosions of class consciousness in strike situations can be easily exaggerated. Nevertheless, it would also be wrong to underestimate the importance of this collective experience. A lesson had been learnt. Many workers realized the strength which derived from a united, plant-wide perspective. As a result, on two occasions within the next few months plant-wide strikes occurred over the question of mobility. In the previous few years, such strike proposals had been consistently rejected by mass meetings.

Such consciousness as developed cannot be described as an 'explosion'. It was very much the creation of the stewards and took many weeks to build up. The mobilization which they were able to undertake was possible because their members were more predisposed to the values and vocabularies which they employed than were, for example, the staff. Mobilization and members' models are mutually interdependent to a degree; each can facilitate or constrain the other. But, even though shop-floor members were more union-oriented, the stewards still had to create and maintain strategies of whose success they were by no means certain.

One reason for this uncertainty is important. In the build-up to the strike, members were fluctuating between individualistic and collective perspectives. In addition, given the development of a normative atmosphere, many stewards were afraid that members were not saying what they really thought. That is, they were afraid that the apparent dominance of the collective definition might well be broken when its full implications for individual interests were realized. This has more general significance: the assessment of members' feelings is complicated not merely by the mechanics of counting, but also by the variety of perspectives between which workers may, and often do, fluctuate and the social pressures to which they are subject. This is crucial in understanding the stewards' dilemmas.

Leadership and Mobilization

In the previous section we have indicated the conditions and processes of consciousness change among the membership. Members' commitment, partial though it was, to trade unionism was an important and crucial condition for their being persuaded to support strike action. They were versed in the mythology of trade unionism; they knew what it was 'all about' and accepted it, at least to a degree. Certainly they accepted it more readily than the clerical staff whose commitment to collectivism was constrained by, in many cases, a commitment to individualistic careerism. If there had been no possibility of members reacting to 'education' (as they perceived it), then the stewards would have been most unlikely to set themselves the task of mobilizing the membership.

As we have noted in earlier chapters, the stewards can be divided into a number of categories, each of these typified by differing definitions of their role. But, within the various types, stewards differed on what should be done in the face of management's proposals. It was among leader stewards, particularly members of the Q-E and the conveners, that the central dilemmas were seen clearly and carefully considered.

One initial problem was the choice of strategy, given, on the one hand, a set of union principles and policies, and, on the other, a membership which at least initially may have been ready to accept management's proposals. In part the policy of their unions but, more importantly, union principles themselves fostered opposition to the company proposals. As members of the Q-E and the conveners defined it, MDW had a number of unpleasant implications: a slower increase in earnings in the future; a reduction in the freedom of individual workers since they would be more exposed to managerial orders and supervision; the ending of such practices as the informal rotation of jobs; redundancy; increased effort, without commensurate financial reward; and a retreat from the existing 'frontier of control' as management reasserted their power.

Finally, the conveners and Q-E members were concerned with the implications for union organization. The section system would disappear and with it the institutional pressures towards collectivism. Moreover, the number of stewards was likely to fall, in part because of the reorganization of work, but also because there would be less for stewards to do. The status of the domestic organization would decline because the unions would lose important areas of autonomy and joint decision-making, and would not be able to bargain, particularly about money, on the shop-floor. More generally, it should also be. added that most stewards were committed to piecework and rejected the view that this system of payment was the cause of disputes in the plant. Opposition, then, rested upon union principles, and particularly upon the implications of the loss of piecework for union organization and the long-term earnings potentials. This analysis of the situation demanded that they fight the company's proposals.

However, there were clearly problems and dangers with such opposition. There were certain advantages to be gained from MDW, and some officials argued these. But two other aspects were of greater importance. First, would the membership be ready to accept the changes proposed by management? In many other plants they had been willing to do so, attracted by significant increases in earnings and unaware of, or not caring about, the wider implications of accepting management's offer. Many of the Q-E members thought that certain areas of the plant, notably those which were not on piecework or those on low earnings, would welcome management's plans. Second, would the stewards be able to persuade the membership otherwise, and, assuming success in this respect, would the membership be ready to incur the costs of what might be a long strike over the issue? The majority of the Q-E members feared that they would not.

In addition to the question of principle, then, there was also the question of members being ready to strike, and here the relative strength of men and management had to be taken into account. In other plants management had usually won, and there was a general acceptance in the plant that MDW was 'bound to come' sooner or later. A strike was likely to be lengthy (or so the Q-E members and conveners thought in the earlier period), and the members would possibly be loath to endure the costs involved. Management would therefore win.

The situation, as the conveners and Q-E members saw it, could be summarized in the following way. Their union principles demanded opposition. If they pursued this course of action and failed to persuade the membership then their standing as leaders and representatives would receive a nasty jolt both with members and with management. On the other hand, if they persuaded the membership to strike, and the strike failed, not only would management win but, more importantly, the membership was likely to turn against them for causing a loss of earnings for nothing. Their leadership would probably cease and union organization would be in total disarray. It might therefore be safer to allow the membership to accept the company proposals. But this would be contrary to union principles, and any leadership to this end would make them open to blame for the subsequent problems which they believed would be inevitable.

The situation was rather different among other stewards — leaders and populists — for a number of reasons. First, they were far less involved in informal discussions with powerful stewards about the development of a strategy, particularly in the early stages. This was particularly true of populists who generally assumed an inactive role for the bulk of the period. They tended to accept the advice of conveners and JSSC resolutions unless any countervailing pressures existed. On the other hand, leaders were rather more involved, discussing the issue with individual members of the Q-E and conveners, and playing a more active role at department level in the later period. This general contrast is not surprising, in view of the differing networks of leaders and populists.

Particularly as the situation became clarified, some stewards were subject to countervailing pressures. This was especially true of those stewards who felt estranged from the rest of the domestic organization and who either were not pieceworkers or represented low-earning pieceworkers. The propaganda war made it clear that some of these groups would achieve significant improvements to their position, as they had been demanding, under MDW, but would not do so under the modified proposals of the JSSC (that any increase should be across the board). Such groups therefore tended to pressurize their stewards and, since these stewards were usually populists, they were inclined to submit to this pressure. Some, therefore, voted against the recommendations of the JSSC, and others took other forms of action. But with the rising tide of collectivism, and the general mood of the plant fostered by documents and the efforts of other stewards, such opposition was generally muted — despite, as much as because of, their stewards. These stewards, then, tended not to create situations but to react to them and to be swept along by them to a far greater degree than leader stewards, particularly members of the Q-E.

We have so far argued that those who generally displayed a greater disposition and ability to lead tended to be more fully involved in the development of plant policy and to be opposed to any straightforward acceptance of management's proposals. That this should be so is scarcely surprising, for we have noted previously that such stewards demonstrated a greater commitment to union principles and were more aware of the dilemmas of the steward role. Having established this broad static pattern, we can now consider the organizational dynamics which led to the near-strike and the achievement of an acceptable agreement.

The 'formal' democratic bodies were undoubtedly of crucial importance in the course of events that led to the near-strike. It was inevitable that sooner or later any agreement would be taken to the JSSC and to the mass meeting. Unless this were done, the agreement could not be accepted. But once the conveners brought the matter back to the JSSC they were bound by its decision unless they went to a mass meeting or got the JSSC to change its mind. Another possibility was to negotiate an offer which would be accepted, and therefore legitimated, ignoring the JSSC instruction. But otherwise the conveners could not openly go against the JSSC resolution, so that doubts about its wisdom were stated only to close confidants. When the conveners went back to the JSSC to sound out the possibility of modifying their opposition to MDW, they did so in a very hesitant, indirect manner. Later acceptance of the funding of the retirement grant was legitimated by practicalities and the advice of the officials. In other words, going against formal resolutions of the JSSC and the mass meeting had to have strong legitimations. They were not always totally binding but the occasions when they were not were few and far between.

The democratic mechanisms, then, were crucial. Democracy was also important more generally: most obviously, great concern was shown about the attitudes of the stewards and members. On such important issues as the annual negotiations the negotiators could not ignore them. More effort was concentrated towards the members and stewards than towards management.

However, it is clear from the preceding pages that the formal democratic mechanisms do not operate automatically or within a social vacuum. While the JSSC agreed to the initial claim, it was developed by a wide variety of groups, and was built into a coherent set of demands by a sub-committee largely made up of members of the Q-E and the conveners. These also played an important role more informally; for example, the conveners advised certain modifications to the assembly claim.

The same is even more true when we consider how the company's proposals were handled. The propaganda war and informal discussions influenced opinions which were expressed at JSSC and mass meetings, and we shall consider this more fully below. In the same way, when and how these formal meetings were run was important. Most significantly, the conveners, despite some pressures from stewards, members, and management, were able to have a major influence on the timing of the first mass meeting. Indeed, it was approximately two months between the revelation of management's MDW proposals and the mass meeting.

The conveners were able to influence the course of meetings not only by a variety of techniques of style and prior organization but also by reference to a variety of rules, both standing orders and custom and practice, which they used selectively. Both formally and informally, rules provided them with some discretion which they were able to employ as and when they liked. Furthermore, because they played a key role as the link between the negotiations as such and the domestic organization — a role which they effectively monopolized — they had considerable power as gatekeepers.

The conveners also had a third source of influence. This was through the networks emanating from themselves directly, and indirectly through the Q-E, to most members via their stewards. By persuading key members of the domestic organization, they could influence large numbers of people. While, then, their influence upon formal institutional mechanisms was far from total, it was by no means insignificant.

In the same way that they were able to influence events through this network, so also could others. First, some individuals had sectional networks which they could employ. We have noted, particularly as the first mass meeting approached, one or two localized attempts at fostering opposition to the JSSC recommendation, and these could have thwarted the conveners' endeavours. But, because they were able to influence the operation of the key institutional mechanisms, other members of the Q-E were very important.

In the main, consensus between conveners and Q-E members was facilitated by their acceptance of broadly common goals. Given that consensus, they had a great deal of influence over other stewards, at least in the production areas and in most craft areas where the Q-E members were concentrated. Here they also had structured systems of influence in the form of department stewards' committees, as well as informal networks with many other stewards, both leaders and populists. This, along with their dominance at JSSC, meant that they could be reasonably confident of persuading the majority of the stewards.

The mobilization of such networks, both formal and informal, was a crucial part of educating the shop-floor. The Q-E members and conveners had to persuade stewards in order to gain the support of the membership. But the systems of influence were not automatic — they had to be mobilized by the Q-E members and, like all social processes, were not 100 per cent effective. They were least effective where countervailing pressures existed in the form of membership views.

In the same ways that conveners had influence upon stewards, leader stewards could influence their members. Formal occasions such as shop and section meetings meant that leader stewards were able to use their skills in the way the conveners had at mass meetings. The plant-wide issue of documents, the JSSC recommendation, and the mass meetings themselves facilitated the stewards' task. Many of the stewards had close contacts with opinion-leaders in their sections; by gaining their support they gained further means of influencing the membership. Leader stewards also formed the focus of informal groups themselves and could therefore disseminate facts, interpretations, and references to broader values. The strategies of public discussion, a continual emphasis upon the worsening of conditions proposed by management, and joking relationships and public criticism — all of these helped to develop collective consciousness. Such strategies, however, demanded the active co-operation of opinion-leaders and it was these who played an important supplementary role in the mobilization and education of the shop-floor.

Relations with the full-time officials were also important: these were largely co-operative, although the officials felt less constrained by the JSSC mandate. But on the whole they accepted the views of the conveners. The officials did provide resources and knowledge; for example, by providing legal and social definitions of the £1 plus 4 per cent legislation, and by acting as 'fall guys' for calling the second mass meeting and justifying the final agreement. The officials also provided informal advice and would have been key figures in achieving official recognition for the strike.

The situation of crisis, then, ultimately demanded resort to democratic mechanisms. But we have seen that in going to the mass meeting a great deal of preparatory work was done; mainly through the use of less primary democratic mechanisms, and through social networks. These did not constitute dictatorship. The conveners were constrained and influenced by the members of the Q-E. The Q-E members had similar relationships with other stewards; many stewards, particularly the Q-E members and leaders, had comparable relationships with opinion-leaders, and they with other members. There was, then, a system of informal checks and balances, a system of biased but nevertheless mutual influence.

The processes involved in the mobilization of the membership can be seen by looking at the contacts of members of the Q-E and the conveners and the systems of argument they employed. Table 15.1 shows that up to the JSSC decision to recommend strike

TABLE 15.1

CONVENER AND Q-E CONTACTS (EXCLUDING NEGOTIATIONS) RELATING TO THE ANNUAL NEGOTIATIONS

	From rejection of company proposals to JSSC decision to strike	From JSSC to mass decision to strike
Contacts with:	%	%
Other conveners/Q-E	82	31
Leader stewards	7	17
Populist stewards	–	11
Opinion-leaders	3	13
Members	3	23
Management	5	5
Total	100%	100%
No. of contacts observed	139	776

SOURCE: Observation.

action, discussion of the negotiations was primarily confined to the conveners and Q-E. In this period, they were basically working out strategy and trying to reach some interpretation of the course of events. Between the JSSC and mass decisions to strike the pattern of Q-E and convener contacts changed dramatically. Not only did they have much more contact with stewards, but also with the membership generally. It will be noted, however, that such contacts were disproportionately focused upon those most capable of influencing others, namely, leader stewards and opinion-leaders. In this period, the conveners and Q-E were concerned not only with strategy but also with the process of educating stewards and members.

The contrasting nature of these tasks can be seen by looking at the systems of argument employed by conveners, Q-E, and other leader stewards (Table 15.2). Up to the JSSC decision to recommend strike action, discussion focused upon the problems of ensuring plant-wide opposition and the difficulties of educating the

TABLE 15.2

LEADERS' ARGUMENTS CONCERNING THE ANNUAL NEGOTIATIONS

	Up to JSSC decision to strike — arguments to leader stewards	From JSSC to mass decision to strike	
		To leader stewards	To others
	%	%	%
Importance of unity	17	5	3
Shop steward awareness of implications of company proposals	4	8	–
Members' attitudes	15	18	–
Shop-floor strength	11	16	3
Need to lead, educate members	17	33	3
Modesty of worker demands, and the legal context	9	1	7
Management 'hard line' and behaviour	9	4	14
Dangers of MDW	8	7	65
Inevitability of mass final decision	3	–	–
Job of shop stewards to oppose company proposals	7	8	5
Total	100%	100%	100%
No. of arguments observed	532	772	464

SOURCE: Observation.

membership. Hence, we find that the dominant arguments concerned unity and shop-floor strength, what exactly members' attitudes were, and the need to educate the membership. The actual nature of management's proposals received relatively less attention. After the JSSC had agreed to strike action, the pattern of arguments changed. In discussions among leader stewards, concern with the education process and its success was dominant. Over two-thirds of arguments to leader stewards were of this kind. At the same time, the actual education process is clear. To members and populist stewards (who make up the 'others' category), the leaders concentrated their arguments primarily upon the dangers of MDW in terms of the likely changes in work, management control, and union strength. Through these networks and systems of argument the opposition to management's proposals was strengthened and the mass decision to strike achieved. The course of events shows, then, the crucial role of the conveners and Q-E members, and the manner in which they were able to mobilize the membership through their networks of influence and their fostering of particular perspectives.

16
Mobilization and the Management of Discontent

Strikes are a form of collective action and therefore involve some degree of organization. Much of this book has been concerned with how the requisite degree of organization is achieved. It is clear that it is often a complex and uncertain process, particularly where large numbers of workers are involved. For example, the achievement of the requisite support for strike action against the company's offer in the annual negotiations took many weeks.

One of the interesting aspects of the movement towards strike action concerns the resort to particular vocabularies. Many of the arguments put forward in considering strike action relate to the details of the issue concerned. But in all the near-strikes we observed, detailed events were placed in a larger context which provided a means of explaining managerial actions and often involved reference to larger principles. This is all the more interesting since at a general level the shop-floor workers studied can be seen as quite instrumental, or economistically oriented. And yet cash figured relatively little in the arguments for and against strike action.

In our previous volume we noted that the general priorities of workers need not be accurately reflected or dominant in their day-to-day concerns. This appears to be equally true in strike situations. For, in the act of work, even a concern with financial reward involves taking account of the costs involved in getting the wage packet at the end of the week. In other words, the worker is inevitably involved in the wage–effort, or as we prefer to call it, the reward–deprivation bargain. This bargain is central to the relationship between employer and employee (Baldamus, 1961). When disputes arise, therefore, they may often relate less to financial reward than to the effort (or deprivation) side of the equation. Moreover, it is quite likely that discussion of financial rewards will involve debate over 'effort'. Once this occurs, the definition of the work situation changes. It ceases to be simply a source of income and instead becomes a political arena. Negotiation of the wage-effort bargain involves awareness of the differing priorities of employer and employee and some challenge to the prevailing situation.

When seen in this context, the day-to-day concerns of workers with political notions such as fairness and justice are quite understandable. It is equally clear why the vocabularies employed in strike mobilization should be equally dominated by essentially political ideas. It is only in this way that workers can easily justify challenging the *status quo*. However, the fact that work is still defined at times in less political terms, or terms which accept the *status quo*, indicates the basic ambivalence which is both the source of, and constraint upon, collective action.

The day-to-day awareness of the political context of work which we have seen in our previous volume also reinforces a further point. Strike action is a continuous possibility in our system of industrial relations and merges into other forms of collective action and work behaviour. This is true not only at the level of ideas but also in the nature of action. The limitation of effort can be seen as a common day-to-day endeavour on the part of workers; its collective organization — for example during the negotiation of new piece-work values — is merely a limited extension of this common individual practice. Once such collective opposition to management has developed, the strike is simply a further tactical extension. From this perspective the normality of strikes lies in the common practices whereby workers attempt to improve the wage-effort, or reward-deprivation, bargain by negotiation with management, and by individual and collective 'making out' strategies (Goffmann, 1968). Strikes therefore constitute simply one means by which the 'frontier of control', the relative power of management and workers over the work situation, is changed or maintained.

However, it is as part of this conflict over the frontier of control that strikes may constitute an aspect of class relations. In other words, strikes may have a class significance in that they constitute one means whereby class relations are modified. We would argue that the strikes typical of the plant we studied and, indeed, of British industry more generally can be seen to play only a marginal role in terms of developing class consciousness. We have shown

that in many near-strikes even the degree of collective consciousness in support of work stoppages is rather limited, and
that collectively defined interests are often part of a vocabulary
opposing strikes. In the larger strikes or near-strikes we observed,
collective consciousness did assume greater significance. But, as we
have argued in previous chapters, such consciousness was limited in
scope, and in some cases was oriented almost as much against other
groups of workers as against the employer. Even these limited
forms of consciousness do gain strength from the more general
rhetoric of industrial and class conflict. (Nor does it follow that
consciousness can never assume a greater breadth.)

In the strikes or near-strikes we observed, however, the elasticity
of concepts of collective interest and union principles was worthy
of note. By their very nature, these grand conceptions are very
general and it is not immediately obvious how they should be
applied to particular situations. For example, where a small group
have what is generally accepted to be a valid claim, do union
principles indicate that the group should not strike because this
would harm other workers or do they indicate the need for other
workers to strike in their support? No simple answer can be given
because what is 'right' depends upon the importance of other
priorities and questions of practicality.

In view of these 'practical problems', it might be suggested that
reference to more general vocabularies in support of strike action is
in fact a relatively meaningless exercise. But nothing could be
further from the truth. From a sociological perspective, a number
of points are of particular significance. First, the range of vocabularies is not unlimited, and there are some groups of workers
for whom reference to notions of conflict or union principles
would be of limited significance. If these general vocabularies
are to have any impact, they must be related to the experiences and
perceptions of the workers concerned. Second, our data suggest
that the ability to employ these general vocabularies is differentially
distributed. In particular, we have noted that leader stewards, and
especially the conveners and Q-E, make most use of notions of
unity and union principles.

These general vocabularies constitute an important element of
the management of discontent. Such management concerns the
ability to influence the perspectives and actions of other workers. It
depends upon the networks of influence which we have discussed at
some length in this and our previous volume. It also involves
decisions concerning what vocabularies to employ and how to

make use of them. As Becker states,

> Values . . . are poor guides to action . . . Since values can furnish only a general guide to action and are not useful in deciding on courses of action in concrete situations, people develop specific rules more closely tied to the realities of everyday life . . . If general values are made the basis for specific rules deduced from them, we must look for the person who made it his business to see that the rules were deduced. And if specific rules are applied to specific people in specific circumstances, we must look to see who it is that has made it his business to see that application and enforcement of the rules takes place. (1966: 130-34)

Networks and vocabularies intermingle; without the possession of a network of relationships it would be difficult to mobilize others by the specific application of a general value. At the same time, acceptance of those values is often an important basis of the network of relationships.

To ask what leaders are *really* trying to do is, to a degree, a rather meaningless question. They are subject to a variety of pressures and each will often hold conflicting values himself. Their chosen courses of action, and hence their use of general vocabularies, may in part be influenced by personal considerations of an easy life, the security of their positions and so on. But it is clear that these are often not their primary considerations, for they do on occasion initiate strike action and in other cases it would be easier for them to play a passive role rather than try to prevent groups of workers from engaging in strike action.

A number of factors appear to be particularly salient for leaders. First, while they may to a degree manipulate notions of union principles, they are at the same time constrained by them. To the extent that their position is legitimated by those principles, their leadership is limited. Second, a continuation of their leadership requires a continual compromise between maintaining those principles and practical success. To lead members on the basis of union principle into a continual series of defeats would probably be to weaken the power of both principles and leadership. Accordingly, the use of general values has to be selective and often instrumental. They have generally to be employed for specific substantive ends, and then 'cooled' or reinterpreted to prevent their exhaustion through failure. Principles are therefore often both a source of action and a tactical weapon.

Nevertheless, such strategic usage of vocabularies can lead to its own problems. On occasion, leaders may be criticized for their application of union principles. Disaffected groups may argue, for example, that the conveners should show solidarity with them and call other workers out on strike in support of their own sectional demands. Moreover, the management of discontent can create other problems for leaders. Such management, it should be remembered, involves not merely the 'cooling' of righteous indication, but also its creation in the first place. In the plant we studied there were occasions where conveners, by resort to union principles and other values, had created discontent among certain workers but were then unable to control it either in terms of courses of action initiated by these workers or in terms of the demands which it fostered among other groups.

These 'problems' of leadership can be seen in a number of the strike or near-strike situations discussed in previous chapters. We have noted that many strikes occur over long-standing issues, such as piecework negotiations. Often the conveners and Q-E have been instrumental in raising members' bargaining awareness over these issues and, in stressing the possibilities of improving piecework prices, have fostered coercive comparisons. Having done so, they occasionally lose control when the course of negotiations with management fails to match the members' expectations. Moreover, major successes for some groups can lead to greater dissatisfactions on the part of others; this was an important factor in the strike-proneness of the indirect workers in the plant over the last few years.

The build-up to the strike over the annual negotiations also demonstrated the limits of the management of discontent in two ways. First, around the periods of the mass meetings, collective consciousness had been built up to such a pitch that workers became far more ready to strike over other issues. The generalization of the specific issue involved in the educating of the membership led to actions which the conveners and Q-E could not totally control. Second, when they attempted to persuade the membership to suspend strike action, a significant proportion of the membership wanted to continue the strike.

These examples not only suggest the limits and problems of managing discontent but also indicate why the amount of negotiation of strike action may vary considerably. A number of the strikes we observed involved relatively little negotiation and, to an outsider, might well have appeared to be spontaneous strikes, if not 'explosions' of discontent. Because of the history of an issue, or because of other events in the plant, much of the negotiation leading up to strike action has already occurred. A problem has been identified as important, the workers' claim defined as legitimate, and management as unfair. It may need relatively little additional negotiation to spur workers to stop work. Similarly, the heightening of the awareness of conflict as occurred around the annual negotiations may serve to break down the normal hesitancies concerning strike action. If these points are true more generally, then many apparently spontaneous strikes are really nothing of the kind.

The analysis of the mobilization of strike action indicates the importance of understanding the patterns of power and influence among workers. It has largely supported our arguments concerning the importance of opinion-leaders, leader stewards, Q-E members, and conveners. These have all been seen to play a major role in the 'management of discontent' and strike action. At the same time, as the preceding paragraphs have stressed, leadership is both conditional and delicate. Workers do on occasion go against the advice of the conveners and Q-E in striking. More generally, changes in patterns of influence may occur before, during, or after strikes. In the threatened strike over the annual negotiations, the 'hard-line' stewards assumed a greater degree of influence and, after our fieldwork was completed, it appears that they achieved a great deal of power during one strike. Earlier in the history of the shop-floor organization it seems that the nature of the domestic organization changed considerably, in part as the result of defeat in a major strike. More generally, strikes have often led to major changes in the nature of union organization — this was so in the case of the Pilkington strike (Lane and Roberts, 1971) and in many other cases where unofficial strikes have occurred both in Britain and elsewhere in Europe.

The role of organization in strike action is complex. On the one hand, certain kinds of worker and union organization may increase the probability of strike action, but, on the other, it is still difficult to predict the actual pattern of strikes within a firm simply because the nature of organization is continually negotiated and therefore subject to change. So, for example, the strength of shop-floor organization in the plant we studied meant that strikes were quite likely. The union played a central role in the work experiences of its members, while these institutional factors and the continual reaffirmation of union principles by leader stewards kept alive notions of unity and the collective interest. Collective action was therefore easier to create than, for example, among the non-manufacturing staff. In this respect, we could agree with many of those theories which have argued that strike-proneness reflects a variety of institutional and organizational factors.

At a general level such theories point to the conditions under which strikes are likely to occur. But strikes involve groups of workers making common decisions to stop work, and the dynamics of this process are too frequently given little attention. In this volume we have looked at how workers negotiate together over the strategies they should employ. In any one situation it seems that the decision can so easily be in favour of or against strike action. For this reason we looked at strikes and near-strikes. When union organization is strong there tends to be a greater variety of means whereby problems can be overcome. There are other forms of collective and individual sanction or accommodation, procedures for the resolution of grievances exist, and there are often strong bargaining relationships between various stewards and managers. Accordingly, the groups of workers most able to strike (in terms of bargaining awareness and collective strength) may rarely in fact have to resort to strike action.

Larger structural factors influence patterns of strike activity. But, equally, pressures by workers, including strikes, influence the larger structural factors. Strikes and the threat of collective action have played their role in the establishment of collective-bargaining procedures. They have also had an impact upon wages, working conditions, and job control. These, after all, are what strikes are generally about. The experience of strike action may also serve to encourage its use so that it becomes part of the common stock of strategies, or to discourage its use; similarly, management may change its behaviour in relation to strike action. Structural factors may foster conditions which make strikes easier, but at the same time strikes and other forms of collective bargaining, along with many other factors, may change those factors. Moreover, the nature of worker organization may change quite rapidly while the process of mobilization for strike action is by no means a certain one. In addition to debate among workers themselves, management may adjust its own behaviour to avoid strikes. An understanding of the phenomenon of strikes may start from an awareness of the subordination of the worker, but it has to go further and recognize the complex historical interplay between structure and consciousness as mediated by organizational processes. A study of the mobilization of strike action therefore constitutes an important aspect of any overall theory of strikes and industrial conflict.

Bibliography

Bailey, F. G. 1969. *Stratagems and Spoils*. Oxford: Blackwell.
Bain, G. S., D. Coates, and V. Ellis. 1973. *Social Stratification and Trade Unionism*. London: Heinemann.
Baldamus, W. 1961. *Efficiency and Effort*. London: Tavistock.
Barratt-Brown, M. 1972. *From Labourism to Socialism*. Nottingham: Spokesman.
Batstone, E. 1974. 'Strikes and Sociologists'. *Bulletin of the Society for the Study of Labour History*, XXVIII. 86-90.
——, I. Boraston, and S. Frenkel. 1977. *Shop Stewards in Action*. Oxford: Blackwell.
Becker, H. S. 1966. *Outsiders: Studies in the Sociology of Deviance*. New York: Free Press.
Berger, P. L., B. Berger, and H. Kellner. 1974. *The Homeless Mind*. Harmondsworth: Penguin.
Berger, P. L., and T. Luckman. 1967. *The Social Construction of Reality*. London: Allen Lane.
Beynon, H. 1973. *Working for Ford*. Harmondsworth: Penguin.
Boissevain, J. 1974. *Friends of Friends*. Oxford: Blackwell.
Brannen, P., E. Batstone, D. Fatchett, and P. White. 1976. *The Worker Directors*. London: Hutchinson.
Braverman, H. 1974. *Labor and Monopoly Capital*. New York: Monthly Review Press.
Brown, W. 1973. *Piecework Bargaining*. London: Heinemann.
Castles, F. G., D. J. Murray, and D. C. Potter (eds.). 1971. *Decisions, Organizations and Society*. Harmondsworth: Penguin.
Chaumont, M. 1962. 'Grèves, syndicalisme et attitudes ouvrières'. *Sociologie du Travail*, IV. 142-58.
Child, J. 1973. 'Organization: A Choice for Man'. *Man and Organization*. Ed. J. Child. London: Allen & Unwin, 234-57.
Clack, G. 1966. *Industrial Relations in a British Car Factory*. London: Cambridge University Press.
Clegg, H. A. 1954. *General Union*. Oxford: Blackwell.
—— 1970. *The System of Industrial Relations in Great Britain*.

Oxford: Blackwell.

Clegg, S. 1975. *Power, Rule and Domination*. London: Routledge & Kegan Paul.

Cole, G. D. H. 1939. *British Trade Unionism Today*. London: Gollancz.

Crozier, M. 1964. *The Bureaucratic Phenomenon*. London: Tavistock.

Department of Employment Gazette. 1976. LXXXIV, No. 2 (February).

Donovan. 1968. Royal Commission on Trade Unions and Employers' Associations 1965–1968. *Report*. Cmnd 3623. London: HMSO.

Dubois, P., R. Dulong, C. Durand, S. Erbès-Seguin, and D. Vidal. 1971. *Grèves revendicatives ou grèves politiques*. Paris: Éditions Anthropos.

Durcan, J. W., and W. E. J. McCarthy. 1974. 'The State Subsidy Theory of Strikes'. *British Journal of Industrial Relations*. XII. 26–47.

Eldridge, J. E. T. 1968. *Industrial Disputes*. London: Routledge & Kegan Paul.

—— and G. C. Cameron. 1968. 'Unofficial Strikes: Some Objections Considered'. *Industrial Disputes*. J. E. T. Eldridge. London: Routledge & Kegan Paul, 68–90.

Fox, A. 1971. *A Sociology of Work in Industry*. London: Collier-Macmillan.

Gamson, W. A. 1971. 'Influence in Use'. *Decisions, Organizations and Society*. Eds. F. G. Castles, D. J. Murray, and D. C. Potter. Harmondsworth: Penguin.

Gennard, J., and R. Lasko. 1974. 'Supplementary Benefit and Strikers'. *British Journal of Industrial Relations*. XII. 1–25.

Goffmann, E. 1968. *Asylums*. Harmondsworth: Penguin.

Goldthorpe, J. H. 1974. 'Social Inequality and Social Integration in Modern Britain'. *Poverty, Inequality and Class Structure*. Ed. D. Wedderburn. London: Cambridge University Press.

Goodrich, C. 1975. *The Frontier of Control*. London: Pluto Press.

Gouldner, A. W. 1955. *Wildcat Strike*. London: Routledge & Kegan Paul.

Gramsci, A. 1971. *Selections from the Prison Notebooks of Antonio Gramsci*. Ed. and trans. Q. Hoare and G. Nowell-Smith. London: Lawrence & Wishart.

Hickson, D. J., C. R. Hinings, C. A. Lee, R. E. Schneck, and J. M. Pennings. 1973. 'A Strategic Contingencies Theory of

Intraorganizational Power'. *People and Organizations*. Eds. G. Salaman and K. Thompson. London: Longman.

Hill, S. 1974. 'Norms, Groups and Power: The Sociology of Workplace Industrial Relations'. *British Journal of Industrial Relations*. XII. 213-35.

Hiller, A. T. 1969. *The Strike*. New York: Arno.

Hillery, B., A. Kelly, and A. Marsh. 1975. *Trade Union Organization in Ireland*. Dublin: Irish Productivity Centre.

Hyman, R. 1972. *Strikes*. London: Fontana.

Industrial Court Report. 1974. 35-53.

Ingham, G. K. 1974. *Strikes and Industrial Conflict*. London: Macmillan.

Institute for Industrial Education. 1974. *The Durban Strikes 1973*. Durban: Institute for Industrial Education.

Israel, J. 1974. 'The Welfare State — a Manifestation of Late Capitalism'. *Acta Sociologica*. XVII. 310-29.

Jay, A. 1967. *Management and Machiavelli*. London: Hodder & Stoughton.

Johnston, E. 1975. *Industrial Action*. London: Arrow.

Kahn, R. L., D. M. Wolfe, R. P. Quinn, and J. D. Snoek. 1964. *Organizational Stress*. New York: Wiley.

Kapferer, B. 1972. *Strategy and Transaction in an African Factory*. Manchester: Manchester University Press.

Karsh, B. 1958. *Diary of a Strike*. Urbana: University of Illinois Press.

Knowles, K. G. J. C. 1952. *Strikes: A Study in Industrial Conflict*. Oxford: Blackwell.

Kuhn, J. W. 1961. *Bargaining in Grievance Settlement*. New York: Columbia University Press.

Lane, T. 1974. *The Union Makes Us Strong*. London: Arrow.

—— and K. Roberts. 1971. *Strike at Pilkingtons*. London: Fontana.

Lester, R. A. 1958. *As Unions Mature*. Princeton: Princeton University Press.

Mann, M. 1970. 'The Social Cohesion of Liberal Democracy'. *American Sociological Review*. XXXV. 423-39.

—— 1973. *Consciousness and Action Among the Western Working Class*. London: Macmillan.

Marchington, M. P. 1975a. 'A Path Model of Power Generation'. University of Aston Management Centre Working Paper Series no. 36.

—— 1975b. 'Sources of Work Group Power Capacity'. University of Aston Management Centre Working Paper Series no. 41.

Miliband, R. 1969. *The State in Capitalist Society.* London: Weidenfeld & Nicolson.

Mills, C. Wright. 1948. *The New Men of Power.* New York: Harcourt Brace.

National Board for Prices and Incomes. 1968. *Payment by Results Systems.* Report no. 65. Cmnd 3627. London: HMSO.

Office of Manpower Economics. 1973. *Measured Daywork.* London: HMSO.

Paterson, T. T., and F. J. Willett. 1951. 'Unofficial Strike'. *Sociological Review*, XLIII. 57-94.

Peach, D. A., and E. Livernash. 1974. *Grievance Initiation and Resolution.* Cambridge, Mass.: Harvard University Press.

Pettigrew, A. 1973. *The Politics of Organizational Decision-Making.* London: Tavistock.

Pope, L. 1942. *Millhands and Preachers.* Yale: Yale University Press.

Ross, A. M., and P. T. Hartman. 1960. *Changing Patterns of Industrial Conflict.* New York: Wiley.

Sayles, L. R. 1958. *The Behaviour of Industrial Work Groups.* New York: Wiley.

Shorter, E., and C. Tilly. 1974. *Strikes in France, 1830-1968.* London: Cambridge University Press.

Silverman, D. 1970. *The Theory of Organizations.* London: Heinemann.

Taylor, L., and P. Walton. 1971. 'Industrial Sabotage'. *Images of Deviance.* Ed. S. Cohen. Harmondsworth: Penguin.

Touraine, A. 1971. *The Post-Industrial Society.* New York: Random House.

Toynbee, P. 1967. 'The Language of Inequality'. *The Incompatibles.* Eds. R. Blackburn and A. Cockburn. Harmondsworth: Penguin.

Turner, H. A. 1969. *Is Britain Really Strike-Prone?* Cambridge: Cambridge University Press.

——, G. Clack, and G. Roberts. 1967. *Labour Relations in the Motor Industry.* London: Allen & Unwin.

Walton, R. E., and R. McKersie. 1965. *A Behavioral Theory of Labor Negotiations.* New York: McGraw-Hill

Westergaard, J. 1975. 'The Power of Property'. *New Society,* 11 September, 574-7.

Index